# From Borroloola to
# Mangerton Mountain

# From Borroloola to Mangerton Mountain

*Travels and stories from Ireland's most
beloved broadcaster*

MICHEÁL Ó MUIRCHEARTAIGH

PENGUIN
IRELAND

PENGUIN IRELAND

Published by the Penguin Group
Penguin Books Ltd, 80 Strand, London WC2R ORL, England
Penguin Group (USA) Inc., 375 Hudson Street, New York, New York 10014, USA
Penguin Group (Canada), 90 Eglinton Avenue East, Suite 700, Toronto, Ontario, Canada M4P 2Y3
(a division of Pearson Penguin Canada Inc.)
Penguin Ireland, 25 St Stephen's Green, Dublin 2, Ireland
(a division of Penguin Books Ltd)
Penguin Group (Australia), 250 Camberwell Road, Camberwell, Victoria 3124, Australia
(a division of Pearson Australia Group Pty Ltd)
Penguin Books India Pvt Ltd, 11 Community Centre, Panchsheel Park, New Delhi – 110 017, India
Penguin Group (NZ), 67 Apollo Drive, Mairangi Bay, Auckland 1310, New Zealand
(a division of Pearson New Zealand Ltd)
Penguin Books (South Africa) (Pty) Ltd, 24 Sturdee Avenue, Rosebank, Johannesburg 2196, South Africa

Penguin Books Ltd, Registered Offices: 80 Strand, London WC2R ORL, England

www.penguin.com

First published 2006
1

Set in 12/14.75 pt PostScript Monotype Bembo
Typeset by Rowland Phototypesetting Ltd, Bury St Edmunds, Suffolk
Printed in Great Britain by Clays Ltd, St Ives plc

A CIP catalogue record for this book is available from the British Library

ISBN-13: 978-1-844-88121-5
ISBN-10: 1-844-88121-0

To the countless people at home and abroad who have contributed to the moulding of a better Ireland.

Micheál Ó Muircheartaigh
Samhradh 2006

# Rambles Long and Short

Long before Lee Marvin sang of the wandering star, I had come to the conclusion that I must have been born with an inclination to move about this country and well beyond its bounds whenever an occasion calls. I am fortunate that I am familiar with all parts of Ireland, and more blessed still in that I can say I know people in most of those places. For that I thank my links with several movements, especially the GAA and the doughty institution called RTÉ, now a venerable eighty-year-old. My mind is constantly revisiting the many places of interest I've seen and travelled through, and now I invite you to come along with me in the hope that you too will find both place and person worthy of a few minutes of your time.

My Ireland is not confined to the area bounded by the waters that surround the island. Ireland, or being Irish, is as much a state of mind as anything else, and I have encountered it in many parts of the globe, sometimes in the unlikeliest of places. When one meets with people of Irish descent in other countries, matters like accent or mode of dress might suggest initially that there remain no traces of Irishness in them. But very often one finds the opposite to be true: there are legions of 'Irish' people in the world who have rarely, and in many cases never, visited the Emerald Isle. They have nonetheless contributed much to the status Ireland enjoys today, a fact to which our Government should pay more heed. While retaining a strong interest in their Irish connections, no matter how far back these stretch, most are loyal citizens of the countries where they reside.

This is something we should all bear in mind when forming opinions about and meeting with the many immigrants who share modern Ireland with us. Our emigrants were made welcome in their adopted homelands, their strong work ethic allowing them to survive and prosper. When abroad, I always like to hear the stories of the escapades of former Irish emigrants, even if they happen to be of the calibre of the notorious Ned Kelly of Australia, or that alleged North Kerry man in America, Jesse James.

This anthology of memories and moments is a journey through Ireland and to Irish people, wherever they might be. Indeed, we shall commence our perusal on distant shores. Like the Sioux Indian, I am pitching my eyes at the start of the voyage, beyond the extremity of the island horizon, and beginning on the other side of the world, where in my travels I have met some very interesting people and become acquainted with many aspects of the lives of others. From there, I hope to bring you all the way back to my native Kerry with random stops and musings, mostly in Ireland, to ponder on events of the past or to meet a small selection of interesting people.

Micheál Ó Muircheartaigh<br>Samhradh 2006

# John Moriarty, the Aborigine from Borroloola

*Is fánach an áit in a bhfaighfeá breac*

These are the words of an Irish proverb I have often heard invoked down in the Kerry Gaeltacht. Volumes of wisdom are snared within the words of proverbs, regardless of the language in which they are cast. The one quoted above simply warns us not to be surprised by what we might find in any quarter or, put literally, 'you could find a trout in a strange environment'.

The story of one Moriarty I met in a far-flung land is in perfect harmony with that sentiment. His name rang a little bell in my mind when I first heard tell of him a few years ago, when he was interviewed by Marian Finucane on RET radio. He was Australian, but the fact that we bore the same surname – even though his was the Anglicized version – forged some tenuous bond between us, even at that stage. I often wished I could meet up with him, but like many another idea no real effort was made to realize it. Then, in October 2005, I found myself in Aussie land thanks to a series of International Test matches between Ireland's Gaelic footballers and Australian teams. Moriarty's name drifted into my mind once more, and thus began the search to locate him.

The first step was a phone call back to Radio Sport in RTÉ, in the hope that some detail could be gleaned from the Marian Finucane interview with Moriarty. I was surprised by how quickly I received information from Bernadette Kelly in the Sports Department after she consulted with some of her colleagues there. The man's full name was John Moriarty, he had given the interview from a London studio and his domicile in Australia at that time was Sydney.

Once the Test matches were over and the Cormac McAnallen Trophy in the possession of the host nation, I set about making a real attempt to meet up with John. It might seem overly optimistic to have imagined a link between us, but all Moriartys the world over have Kerry origins and I did not doubt his connections with the Kingdom.

Eventually, after some work on the Internet and in Melbourne offices that deal with indigenous people's rights, a useful phone number was added to the file. As too often happens, however, it was the dreaded answering machine that took my call, informing me that 'John Moriarty is away and will not return for some days'. With a little patience and perseverance, finally it was his voice that answered from Sydney one bright morning. After an introductory conversation, I arranged to fly up from Melbourne to meet him at his office.

I must say, it was my privilege to meet one of the most extraordinary people I have ever encountered in any part of the world. Physically he was smaller than I imagined and bore the looks of an Aboriginal. I quickly learned that he was also extremely interested in his Irish ancestry. Before we parted, and not for the last time I hope, we exchanged autobiographies – *Saltwater Fella* and *From Dún Síon to Croke Park* – half a world apart and yet joined by our Irish roots.

The title of his book suggests he was born close to the sea and indeed his birthplace has a sort of Irish ring to it – Borroloola, in a tribal area of Australia's Northern Territory, close to the Gulf of Carpentaria. He was born 'around 1938'. His mother saw herself primarily as a Yanyuwa, although also connected with other tribes. She gave him his father's name, John Moriarty, a wandering Kerryman, like many of his Irish neighbours for generations. John states in his autobiography:

. . . being half-caste meant that I would eventually be taken away, as I was paler in colour than my mum. It was a policy of government when I was young to take away half-caste children and send them to missions or settlements. The policy was intended to breed out the Aboriginal culture and identity. This was the identity and culture that I was born into, and it was what the assimilation policy of the government set out to destroy. It was an insidious, arrogant policy that amounted to cultural genocide.

Those words sum up his opinion of the Australian government's policy, which had such a profound effect on his life from a very young age. As a member of Australia's Stolen Generation, John's curiosity about his father's history increased with the passing years as he sought to piece together his own background. It would be more than forty years before he was able to patch up his father's side of the family tree, which led him to relatives in Kerry and London. At first, all he had known about his father was that he had come to Australia in 1928 and worked as a cook in the Borroloola Hotel, in which his cousins had an interest. His inquiries and contacts eventually yielded the information that he had Irish cousins by the names of O'Shea and Kirby, which ultimately led to a meeting with a May Ulyatt in Alice Springs.

May Ulyatt had been May O'Shea, from Kerry, before she married and settled in Alice Springs. She produced a photograph of a group of young emigrants, herself and John's father among them, taken in Castlegregory, Co. Kerry, prior to his departure to Australia in 1928. This was a very useful lead. May was also able to tell John that his father was 'a beautiful dancer and a good person to be with'. By a curious coincidence, I have a book in my possession that my daughter Nuala picked up a few years ago in Victoria Market, Melbourne, and it carries a reference to 'Jack Moriarty, host of the inn, with never a guest in years'. The book was written by Ernestine Hill and published in 1940 and describes the author's roamings through Australia in the 1930s. The Moriarty mentioned is almost certainly John's father because the reference is part of the account of Hill's visit to Borroloola.

It is understandable that John was anxious to travel to Castlegregory when work and other commitments allowed it. Through the help of many people, including another John Moriarty, an undertaker who was not a relation, the visitor was directed to the home of Pat O'Shea in Castlegregory. This particular Pat would be very well known in Gaelic football circles as the famous Aeroplane O'Shea, the noted high-fielding midfielder on Kerry's All-Ireland winning teams of 1913 and 1914. He was in his nineties on that day in 1980 when John Moriarty arrived at his home. Standing outside, John did most of the talking, explaining who he was and the purpose of his visit. Of course, the moment 'Aeroplane' realized he knew his visitor and his father, he was invited inside for further conversation.

I gather that John then became the listener, and a rapt one at that, once inside the door of Aeroplane's house. John learned that he had a connection with Kerry football because Pat O'Shea's sister was married to a brother of John's father, which made the midfielder his uncle-in-law, if my expertise in genealogy amounts to anything. He heard how his father had spent three days in that house in 1928 and went fishing with the footballer/teacher. Aeroplane was able to recount their adventure in great detail, and John was amazed as to how anybody, moreover a nonagenarian, could remember the actual number of trout caught fifty-two years earlier. At this point Pat O'Shea took a little stool and stood on it to reach into a cupboard close to the front door. He produced a fishing rod – three pieces tied together complete with brass reel – and, after apologizing profusely for the state of the line, he handed it over to John uttering the words, 'he left this here for you'.

John was now in the right place, and before long he had addresses for cousins in Tralee and Blennerville, where his father was born. There he encountered more John Moriartys and an Uncle Eugene in Blennerville. He was treated royally on his visit to his father's birthplace. John had no memories at all of his father, but did learn that he had spent time in the British Navy, serving on the Russian front, and was fluent in Irish, English, Russian and the aboriginal dialect of Yanyuwa. Eugene was able to tell him that his father had died in Brisbane in 1961, probably of an alcohol-related illness. Thinking back, John recalled that he had played soccer for South Australia against Queensland in Brisbane around about that time. Strange, he thought, that the father he never knew was in the same city at the same time and they never chanced to meet. *Is ait an mac an saol.*

There were other clan meetings, of course, before John left Kerry. He has fond memories of talking late into the night with his cousin, John, in Tralee and his wife, Morna, and their children, Maeve and Darragh. He found the Kerry episode to be a source of immense relief and satisfaction in an extremely active and varied life. He described some of that extraordinary life to me.

In 1942, at the age of four or thereabouts, he was taken away from his home and brought to a mission 300km away under the guise of attending school. Years later, when he again found his mother, he asked her why she had let him go. Her answer was brief and simple: 'I was taking you to school for a while and then I went to pick you up this day and you were gone.' As it turned out, his stay at the mission was only a stage on a massive journey, by lorry and train, that shunted John and his mission group through Alice Springs and Adelaide and onwards to Sydney, a journey exceeding 2,000km on my reckoning. From the late nineteenth century until relatively recent times, successive Australian governments promoted policies that involved the forcible removal of Aboriginal children from their families and transferral to institutions in white communities. The theory behind their removal was that it would bring about the cultural assimilation that John grew to despise. The unfortunate children thus affected would become known as the Stolen Generation. So John was taken from his mother without warning or explanation and found himself bereft and heading for God knows where: 'When you're young you try to be a man. But a lot of the times when I was trying to be a man I remember crying and crying.'

Life at the mission was not easy, apart altogether from being separated from his family. He was allowed to keep the name Moriarty, but most were given new names because all traces of their own heritage had to be abandoned in this Anglican settlement. His identity paper 'gave' him 1 April as his birthday. His clearest memories of the place are the hunger, the religion and the discipline. There were times when the children were left free to roam the farmlands, to fish and to hunt, which was great fun and more natural to their previous way of life. I could relate to his memories of roaming the fields because that was not unlike my own young days in Dún Síon, not a million miles from where his father grew up.

By the age of eleven John was on the move again, this time to St Francis House in Adelaide to complete his primary education before moving on to a technical school and second level, and going on to qualify as a fitter. He was thirteen years of age by the time he was convinced to write a letter to his mother, but he found it difficult because he knew she could neither read nor write. It was obviously not an ideal situation for correspondence, but it worked because he received replies from friends and neighbours telling him his mother was fine. Then, at the age of fifteen, he was brought on holiday to Alice Springs and it was arranged that his mother would be brought down from Borroloola to meet him. It happened on the street: he and a friend saw a woman watching them from a little distance, they approached her and for the first time in eleven years John and his mother were together once more. He met her frequently during the rest of that holiday but then returned to Sydney to serve an apprenticeship and, incredibly, almost another twenty years elapsed before he met her again. Throughout that time, however, they kept in touch by letter.

John qualified as a fitter and was soon working with the Electricity Trust of South Australia and generally getting on very well. He was also gaining a reputation as a soccer player, and by the age of twenty he was a member of the South Australia Youth team. Two years later he made an appearance on the senior side for interstate action in Perth. He got good coverage from the media for his exploits there and later for the Australian championships in Melbourne. This earned him selection on the national team for a tour of South-East Asia, but other circumstances led to Australia being banned from international competition for eighteen months, thereby ending John's dream of playing for his country.

It was while in Melbourne that he learned that the State Soccer Association had to seek permission from the Protector of Aborigines every time a member of that community wished to travel outside the state. He regarded this as an indignity no Australian should suffer, and it was one of the reasons why he began to get more and more involved in righting some of the wrongs he and others had had to endure. To this end he founded the Aborigines Progress Association, which worked on the sporting and legal fronts, promoting Aboriginal land rights and general equality. John was deeply involved and the fight for Aboriginal rights in South Australia came to be seen as the model for campaigns in other states.

In 1966, at the age of twenty-eight, John enrolled in Flinders University, becoming the first Aborigine to enter university in South Australia. He read for a Bachelor of Arts Degree and his subjects were Australian, English and Colonial History, together with Geography and Politics. It took him five years to complete the three-year course, principally because he was ever more involved in national issues on rights. His contribution to progress in that field is best exemplified by the honours and positions awarded him in the following years, including Chairman of the National Aboriginal Sports Corporation of Australia, Vice-Chairman of the Commercial Development Corporation and Doctor of the University of Southern Australia; he also undertook important assignments for the Department of Labour. All the hard work and campaigning eventually paid off when a referendum on rights was passed by a 91 per cent majority.

There is another, and totally different, side to the character of this man, John Moriarty. His contact with academics who were interested in the entire Aborigine culture led him to appreciate the value of Aboriginal song, dance and language, and in particular their visual art traditions. In 1971 he spent nine months travelling overseas on a Winston Churchill Fellowship, studying the cultures of indigenous people from Alaska to India. He returned bursting with ideas on culture retention, integration, education and much more.

In the 1980s he began to deal in Aboriginal art as a commercial venture. He and his wife, Ros, set up a company called Jumbana, his own Aboriginal name, and a design label called Balarinji, which was their son's skin name. They produced fabrics and products carrying Aboriginal designs and, after the usual beginner's setbacks, the business turned good, as was very evident on the day of my visit to his Sydney office. The breakthrough came in the 1990s when they had the idea to approach Qantas Airlines with an aircraft motif in Aboriginal style. The presentation was so stunning that it was accepted immediately and work on the real 747–400 began quickly thereafter. The *Wunula Dreaming* plane was an immediate hit and gave a much-needed boost to Aboriginal art, to Qantas, to Australia – and the Moriarty designers. That plane is used for ceremonial functions and before long another was commissioned, *Nalanji Dreaming*, which flies regularly to Japan and all across Asia – the largest moving artwork in the world. Full marks all round for enterprise and pride in native heritage!

What an extraordinary man is this Borroloola John Moriarty. I would like to see him at an All-Ireland football final in Croke Park sometime, when he could think again of his father's fishing rod and Aeroplane O'Shea, visualizing in an art form that man's great leaps into the air in the All-Ireland finals of 1913 and 1914. It is quite possible, too, that his own father was present at those finals because the Ghost Train from Kerry to Croke Park was a phenomenon in transport at the time and many youths frequently made the journey. The Aborigines believe the Earth is criss-crossed with the memories of many journeys. Certainly, this seems to hold true for John Moriarty and the web of connections he has traced from Australia to Ireland and back again.

# Meeting an All-Ireland medal in Adelaide

So we bid farewell to the eastern coast of the friendly continent and cross its vast interior towards the pleasant west coast. The city of Adelaide is situated in South Australia and is the last stop before the Nullarbor Plain, which links the south with the west. Adelaide gives the impression of being an English-type settlement, but there is plenty of Irishness for the intrepid traveller to encounter. During my first visit to the city, in 1986, I called into the local GAA centre and it was there I read accounts of Irish activities that took place in the developing town in the spring of 1843. The news was gleaned from an advertisement in the contemporary local newspaper and was in the form of a challenge thrown down by the footballers of Westmeath, who offered to take on a team from any other county in Ireland, or a combination from a few counties, in a game of football on St Patrick's Day, 17 March. Details were given of proposed celebrations in the aftermath of the game, and it promised to be a lively affair. Back in Ireland, the founding of the GAA was still over forty years down the road, so this unusual advertisement bears testimony to the fact that the Irish emigrants of those days, forced or otherwise, carried with them a strong footballing tradition. It also lends credence to the theory that Australian Rules football is a derivative of the old, pre-GAA Irish football.

I was back in Adelaide during subsequent trips down under and it was in the same GAA environment that I saw an All-Ireland medal displayed next to a National League medal on the lapel of a coat worn by a proud Irishman. He was Johnny Boyle, a Carlowman who had played with Dublin in the All-Ireland finals of 1955 and 1958 and in the League finals of both years, winning all but the All-Ireland final of 1955. Actually, he also won a Railway Cup medal with Leinster in 1959, but it was not on display that night. Perhaps that one had been given away at some stage!

I spent a long time in Johnny Boyle's company during my visit to the club, and he certainly was proud of those medals and the game that had given him some great times. He rattled off the names of his colleagues with an air of friendship: Kevin Heffernan, Ollie Freaney, Jim Crowley, Cathal O'Leary, Norman Allen, the Timmons brothers Joe and Big John, and many more notables. At the time of our meeting he was in Australia recovering from a hip operation; up until then he had spent most of his time in New Zealand. Johnny and his likes really appreciate a visit from Irish football teams and they follow the fortunes of all teams back home – an easier task than it used to be thanks to the plethora of information sources that now churn out news twenty-four hours a day. So far from home, it was a joy to see those medals and meet their entertaining and engaging owner.

# Western Australia:
## Charles Yelverton O'Connor

Anyone lucky enough to be acquainted with Ireland's west coast, that lovely stretch of territory from the Bloody Foreland in Donegal to Dún Chaoin at the extremity of West Kerry, will tell you that the west of Ireland carries a charm all of its own. I sometimes wonder if my familiarity with it induces a bias towards the western sides of all countries and continents: for me, there is no place like the west of Scotland, the west coast of the United States and certainly Western Australia. I have been to Australia several times, and while it is difficult to find fault with Sydney, Melbourne, Adelaide and Brisbane, there is no magic in those places to compare with that of Perth, Fremantle, Kalgoorlie and the thousands of acres of wide and wild open spaces within easy reach of those frontier towns. I prefer the countryside to the city at any time because, to an extent, cities are the same the world over, often varying only in size. There is one exception though, and in my opinion that is Perth, the capital of Western Australia.

It is not an easy matter to explain why this is so, but for a start it is a clean city and I find there is always a fantastic atmosphere of relaxation permeating the place and the people. The climate is pleasant and there is no shortage of picturesque walking trails or sporting facilities within easy reach of all areas. Like most places in Australia, the west coast has evidence of many Irish connections and these hold a particular appeal for me.

The custom of raising monuments to people who have passed on is as ancient in Ireland as it is elsewhere. In time, structures like Newgrange gave way to less elaborate reminders of the past and we have any number of monuments commemorating the deeds and achievements of people in the various pursuits of life. They honour contributions in politics, sport, the arts, sciences, the economy and otherwise, but I have often felt that as a nation we have

13

too few to recall the great deeds of Irish people who spent part of their lives living outside the country. Their stories are often fascinating and edifying, and we would do well to remember them.

Whenever I find myself in a foreign land, I am always curious to learn about the contributions made by Irish people to the life of that country, or places that remain forever associated with their adopted Irish sons and daughters. I seek out such places whenever I get the opportunity, which is how I came to head eastwards from Perth to the once famous goldfield areas of Kalgoorlie and Coolgardie. There is a compelling romanticism about goldfields, even though we in Ireland might not have heard as much about the Australian fields as we did about the Klondike, Yukon, Montana and other gold rushes of North America. It was in Kalgoorlie that I first heard tell of an Irishman called Charles Yelverton O'Connor, whose story enthralled me and whose name will forever be associated with the 'Golden Days' of Kalgoorlie.

On a recent visit to that part of the world I journeyed again to the lovely seaside city of Fremantle because it is there that a magnificent monument to Meathman O'Connor stands. The life-size bronze statue is impressive and enjoys a commanding view of historic Fremantle Harbour. Countless Irish people sailed into that harbour in the nineteenth century, on their way to penal settlements or prisons. It was in the same harbour that I did a commentary on the Americas Cup in 1986 when *Stars and Stripes*, under the guidance of Denis Connor, ensured that the famous Cup was returned home to the United States. It was a huge event that claimed worldwide attention, especially as it was the first time it had taken place outside of American waters. The Gages Road district of Fremantle offered an excellent offshore venue and some of us touring with the Irish football team, which was due to play against the Aussies in the WACA (Western Australia Cricket Association) around about that time, had a special interest in that particular Americas Cup contest. The connection was Jim O'Sullivan, a journalist with the *Irish Examiner*, whose brother Tom happened to be a brother-in-law of Harold Cudmore, a crew member of the British entrant. We spent a most exciting day in the bay on board a yacht hired for the purpose by the Bank of Ireland, the sponsors of the Irish team, which was managed by Kevin Heffernan and captained by Jack O'Shea.

The bearded, Moses-like figure of Bank of Ireland's Jim Whitty was our host, but those among our number who hailed from inland counties in Ireland succumbed to seasickness and, unfortunately, GAA Ard Stiúrthóir Liam Mulvihill was among them. They were thus denied the excitement of a world-class final. We were all cheering for the British 'runner' on account of loyalty to colleague Jim O'Sullivan, but *White Crusader* and Harold Cudmore failed to make the final. We were then equally divided beween *Stars and Stripes* and Australia's *Kookaburra* – of course, with a field of two my commentary for Raidio na Gaeltachta was not too demanding. Third-man tackles were impossible, but I did have to be on the lookout for incidents like the dropping of the brightly coloured spinnakers. There was very little between them, but the *Stars and Stripes* got to the line first. I must say it was a different sporting experience for me, and I felt lucky to get the opportunity to commentate on an event of the magnitude of the Americas Cup.

In any event, Fremantle Harbour was Charles Yelverton O'Connor's point of entry to Australia when he had arrived in that part of the world almost 100 years earlier. An engineer by profession, O'Connor was born in *Gravelmount* in 1843, a large estate house at Castletown in Co. Meath. He studied engineering at Trinity College, Dublin, and gained experience in building railways and waterworks before he emigrated to New Zealand in 1864. He had connections in Ireland's developing railway network as his father was secretary of the Waterford–Limerick line.

It is said that the discovery of gold in New Zealand led to O'Connor's decision to go there, and so with the same hope carried by many an emigrant before and since he set sail from London on board the *Pegasus* on Christmas Eve 1864, destined for a new world. The ship carried fare-paying settlers and he shared his cabin with a doctor and a parson, so he probably felt extremely secure and safe during the three-month voyage. He would spend over twenty-five years in New Zealand, achieving promotion to two of the top positions in that British colony. He was responsible for the overall supervision of marine and public works with the titles of Under-Secretary for Public Works and Marine Engineer for New Zealand.

In 1891, O'Connor's life would take a new turn. Back in Ireland, political life was dominated by the Land War, Kitty O'Shea and the fall of Parnell and the rise of nationalism, while in sports there was the stuttering growth of the GAA, Kerry winning a hurling All-Ireland and Dublin claiming the football title. In New Zealand, meanwhile, the famous engineer from Meath caused a sensation when he resigned from his position as Marine Engineer.

His next move took him and his family on the long journey to Western Australia, a massive sprawling territory with a meagre population of less than 100,000 souls. The area was under-developed primarily due to lack of infrastructure. Before long, Charles Yelverton O'Connor had been appointed Engineer-in-Chief of Public Works and Manager of Railways and there are historians who aver that his appointment was among the most significant decisions ever made in that part of the world. The decade that followed saw enormous development in the western territories, all spearheaded by the redoubtable O'Connor, and I was delighted to learn that his role is almost universally acknowledged throughout Western Australia to the present day.

Not a man for dallying, O'Connor set about his projects immediately. The first task he attended to was the building of a suitable harbour for Perth. The location chosen was Fremantle, a short distance down the coast. In November 1892 Lady Robinson, wife of the Governor, pulled the handle to release the first load of stones on Rous Head, which marked the commencement of the building of a breakwater. Less than five years later the magnificent harbour was finished and became the primary port for large vessels, which docked at Victoria Pier. They were exciting times: railways were being built and transforming the face of the territories, there was breathless talk of goldfinds and more and more people were being drawn to settle there. It was fortuitous that the Castletown genius was there to play a leading role in the developments necessary for the expansion and maintenance of the burgeoning economy.

The most pressing problem was to supply water to the goldfields, which lay 557km away from source. In 1896 O'Connor submitted a plan to both Houses of Parliament proposing that water be pumped from a reservoir in the west to the goldfields. By then the population of Coolgardie had grown to 20,000 and the water shortage posed grave problems both for humans and the essential working horses. O'Connor's solution involved damming the water on the Darling Range before raising it 1,000ft over the hills and pumping it to Coolgardie via a series of overland pumps that would work independently of each other. There was no precedent for pumping water across such a huge distance and mostly through desert, where temperatures ranged from below zero to fifty degrees Centigrade. It was a brave proposal of staggering proportions and its estimated cost was AUS$5 million. It is to the credit of Parliament that they had the foresight to approve it, even though the estimated cost was twice the state's annual budget and there was no proof that it would work.

The parliamentary announcement of the building project stated that a pipeline was to be built capable of carrying 22 million litres of water daily, and that a loan would be raised in London to cover the costs. It was open season for stinging criticism and the plan was denounced as 'outrageous nonsense, a scheme of madness'.

Naturally, in the circumstances it was not easy to raise the loan, but funds eventually materialized and, to the delight of O'Connor, the Goldfields Water Supply Construction Bill was finally passed. The construction of the dam was soon underway in the Helena River Valley. The wisdom of the Fremantle Harbour venture was quickly appreciated as thousands of tons of steel had to be imported and unloaded for the massive pipeline, which would comprise 60,000 lengths of pipe, each 8.4m long and 76.2cm in diameter.

By 1899 the dam work was proceeding as planned, with all the back-breaking work it required being carried out manually: lines of men pushed barrows of concrete along steep embankments as railway works were undertaken simultaneously along the route. The criticism of O'Connor's 'folly' was still to be heard, but all the while the men worked and the Mundaring Weir was completed and the pipe crept eastwards. In spite of the progress, the critics were intent on causing mischief, and O'Connor was accused of corruption, gross blundering and robbing taxpayers of millions of dollars. The old adage about mud sticking held true, and early in 1902 the government announced a Royal Commission into the conduct and completion of the water scheme. It was heartbreaking news for the driven, hard-working O'Connor. While he remained utterly confident that his scheme would work, he was dogged by stress and exhaustion in the face of ongoing criticism and questioning.

On 10 March of that year O'Connor took his pistol out, placed it in his pocket, then mounted his steed and set off slowly through Fremantle. It was a sight common enough to the inhabitants in those days, so nobody sensed anything unusual as he rode along the busy Cantonment Street. The horse was cantering as he left that street, heading for the jetty and his beloved harbour before turning for the beach and the water. Man and horse cantered straight into the sea and as the waves lapped at the flanks of the horse, O'Connor drew his pistol and shot himself. His despair was not deserved: he left behind a splendid harbour, a major rail system which he had designed and expanded, and had planned the world's longest pipeline, all within just eleven years of arriving in Western Australia. The great man left a final note, which stated, among other things, that he had lost control of his thoughts: 'I could finish it if I got a chance and protection from misrepresentation – better that it should be given to some entirely new man.' Typical of the perfectionism of the man, he added a postscript: 'Put the wing walls to Helena Weir at once'. Charles Yelverton O'Connor was buried in a grave overlooking Fremantle Harbour.

Ten months later there was unprecedented rejoicing in Kalgoorlie and Coolgardie: every possible inch of the towns was decorated, and there were bands and parades and celebrations in anticipation of the arrival of Sir John and Lady Forrest, by train, for the switching-on ceremony of the Great Water Scheme. Members of the Boys' Brigade were on hand to pull the float that carried Sir John and his lady along the streets before the official business of the day was conducted. In due course, and amid great cheering, the valves were opened and the dream of the Meathman became a reality as the water released from the dam two days earlier gushed forth, 557km inland. There were speeches, of course, but the most telling words of all carry a resonance to this day in Western Australia: 'two men and two men only were responsible for the Coolgardie Water Scheme, Sir John Forrest and Mr C. Y. O'Connor, the man who gave his life for it.' To the amazement of his critics, the whole scheme had come in almost on budget, at a cost of AUS$5.2 million.

The Great Water Scheme proved to be a catalyst for massive development throughout Western Australia, on a scale that even O'Connor himself might not have envisaged. The pipeline was expanded and extended thereafter, enabling huge tracts of land to be made suitable for farming. Towns and settlements sprang up in response, as people came to earn their livelihoods on the land. Even though it is now over 100 years since water flowed eastwards for the first time, that pipeline is still one of the Aussies' proudest achievements. The part played by a hero who is largely unknown in his homeland is one reason why I think there is something special, unique even, about that part of the world. It gives me a thrill to touch that pipeline and to stand once more beside the monument to the man from Co. Meath that overlooks Fremantle Harbour.

# Mundy Prendiville:
# The footballing Archbishop of Perth

There is another reason why I have a special *grá* for Perth and its environs and that is the fact that former Kerry footballer, Mundy Prendiville, spent a long number of years there ministering as a priest and later as Archbishop of that beautiful city. I recall a comical incident that occurred during one of my earliest trips to Perth, when I went to see its most famous sporting venue, the WACA, or the Western Australia Cricket Association grounds. It is undoubtedly a beautiful venue, but I was taught a lesson on economics during my ramble through it. I noted with a certain amount of satisfaction that one of the stands was named the Prendiville Stand. In my naivety, or ignorance, I presumed it had been named in honour of the famous Archbishop/Kerry footballer. When speaking with Danny Lynch's equivalent in the Cricket Ground office later, I casually mentioned my liking for the name on the stand. He was obviously pleased and volunteered to go upstairs immediately and bring 'him' down to meet me, if I so wished. Knowing that the Archbishop had died almost twenty years earlier, I had no expectation of meeting him and did my best to restrain the PRO from leaving the room. My efforts proved futile, and in no time I was being introduced to Mr Prendiville, the man in whose honour the *ardán* was christened.

It was obvious I had supposed wrong about the late Archbishop Prendiville, but nevertheless I told the current Mr Prendiville a reasonable amount about his namesake, the former Kerry All-Ireland medal winner. I also made the point that the sporting association I represented in Ireland had a policy of naming grounds and stands in honour of noted people who had passed on. He listened in amazement and thought the whole philosophy was hilarious. Even though he had a notion that there may have been some drop of Irish blood in him, he had never heard of Kerry nor the fact that the county had won so many All-Irelands. Then came the economics lesson:

I made a contribution of $2 million to the development of this place and that is why my name is out there – in this country dead men pay no dollars.

I have often thought of the Australian approach to naming since then and wonder at times if it will eventually catch on here in Ireland. There was a time when any type of talk on sponsorship was anathema to the GAA, but witness the erosion of this principle that has taken place in relatively recent times: isn't Cavan's hallowed Breffni Park now known as Kingspan Breffni Park, for example? Are Croke and a host of other illustrious names in danger of being sunk without trace in the development of a future Ireland? Will living men and women bearing strange-sounding names be willing to pay fistfuls of dollars or euro for the honour of having their names aloft in the neon of the future?

It might sound far-fetched, but supposing the GAA was made an offer of, say, €200 million for the branding of Croke Park with a commercial name. I wonder what the reply would be? It is inevitable that such an offer will come one day, be it imminent or distant. I hope to attend the Special Congress that will be called to discuss the proposal, where democracy will, of course, prevail, but not, I imagine, before some orators have forecast mass resurrections from the graveyards of Ireland if the proposal is accepted.

During my first ever visit to Perth, a trip to the Catholic Cathedral was a priority because I wanted to see where the late Archbishop Prendiville had spent so much of his time. My initial reaction to the building was one of disappointment because I expected a massive ornamental edifice, but instead found a rather plain, red-bricked place of worship. Nonetheless, its connection with Kerry and Kerry football imbued it with a special aura and I wandered around, sitting on the Archbishop's *cathedra*, reading notices and generally getting a feel for the place.

I was surprised to discover the Archbishop had not been buried within the grounds, as is customary with Church dignitaries in Ireland, and there was nobody in the office who could enlighten me further. I was anxious to locate his grave, but a lack of time meant it had to wait for another visit. The opportunity arose in October 2005 when I was in Perth for the International Football Test between a team of Gaelic footballers from Ireland and Australia's Footie, or Rules, selection. I was far luckier in my search this time, being fortunate to meet Sr Frances Stibi, archivist in the Diocesan Office. She was most helpful and very knowledgeable on every aspect of the late Archbishop's life – I am convinced she knew far more about the Kerry All-Ireland player of 1924 than most people in Ireland – and she gave me details of where he was buried and much more.

My next stop was Karrakkatta Cemetery, on the outskirts of the city, armed with a map and a grave number. The Archbishop's final resting place was set in what one could describe as an Irish enclave, judging by the names and inscriptions on the surrounding headstones. The Archbishop's was easy to find because it stood out – it was large rather than elaborate and comprised a coffin-like concrete structure set atop the tomb flagstone. He had been laid to rest in 1968.

I stood there in silence, pondering the story of his All-Ireland football win, when the thought struck me that it was likely no Kerry footballer had attended his funeral due to the distance involved. It was likely, too, that no Kerry flag was flown over his grave at the time. I decided there and then that it would be easy and appropriate to do so, retrospectively. I had brought a Kerry flag as part of my luggage; GAA President Seán Kelly was in town as leader of the Irish party; and three Kerry players, Colm Gooch Cooper, Tomás Ó Sé and Eoin Brosnan, were members of the Irish team. I spoke to the four that evening and all agreed to help me pay homage to the illustrious former Kerry player from Castleisland.

The following day, in the company of my wife Helena, daughter Doireann and ubiquitous ace photographer Ray McManus of Sportsfile, we set off for Karrakkatta. This time I was able to lead them directly to the tomb. It was Seán Kelly's task to place the

Kerry flag over the grave. He found a little trough on top of the stone, which he filled with clay before planting the Green and Gold in a prominent position. We spoke for a while about Mundy, remembering him, said a few silent prayers and then retired to the adjoining cemetery café for refreshments. I felt pleased with our excursion – the presence of the GAA President and the Kerry footballers had put the appropriate finishing touches to the funeral of an All-Ireland man, even if it came thirty-seven years after his death.

Photographer Ray McManus was half-expecting a resurrection before he left, but perhaps we all left too soon because something unusual did happen between then and the following morning, when I returned to the grave once more. My reason for making a third trip was to check whether the Kerry flag had survived the night in the looseness of the clay in the flower trough. To my amazement, it had not only survived but was no longer where the President had placed it. Instead, the stick part was wedged firmly under the heavy flagstone, which had been raised slightly from its previous setting on top of the grave. How it got there is a mystery; Ray McManus later remarked jokingly that the Archbishop must have made an attempt to reach out to try and wave the flag during the night!

I have another theory to explain this mystery. While we were conducting our ceremony on the previous day, work was going on nearby to replace the large upright headstones with smaller commemorative tablets that lay flat on the ground, to facilitate grass-cutting. The workmen were using a tractor fitted with lifting equipment, and I believe the operator appreciated our little homage to the Archbishop and used the 'powers' available to him to lift the lid a little and secure the flag-stick, at least, for posterity. I had noticed the workman in question taking a rest while we stood and prayed. He must have decided to do the job properly himself. Good luck to you, *fear an tractor i gKarrakkatta, nár lige Dia thú. Le cúnamh Dé*, I will be back again to check the state of that Kerry flag! I wonder where the Archbishop's All-Ireland medal is taking its final rest?

Incidentally, I gathered more information about the late Archbishop from Sr Stibi in the Diocesan Office. I already knew that he was forced to leave All Hallows College in Dublin prior to ordination on account of absenting himself without permission in order to play for Kerry in the All-Ireland final of 1924 against Dublin. My understanding of his plight following this expulsion was that he was ordained in Carlow College before emigrating and gaining prominence in the Australian Church. Sr Stibi – who was a late vocation, joining the convent after the death of her husband and proving to be a Godsend to the church in Perth – set me right, however. According to her research, and she had the documentation to prove it, the expelled student footballer attended St Peter's College in Wexford, but for some reason he was once again not ordained. His next stop was St Kieran's College in Kilkenny; he was obviously determined in his ambition to be ordained a priest. However, the poor man suffered his Purgatory in Ireland because when ordination time came in St Kieran's, his name was again not put on the list. Instead he was told to take himself to the convent, and that the Bishop carrying out the ordinations might visit there later and ordain him alone. This came about and he was soon off on the missions with his All-Ireland medal, which had almost, but not quite, precluded him from the priesthood.

In the words of Sr Stibi, 'he was a wonderful and interesting man and a gift to Western Australia'. She was the only nun I ever met who had photographs of her daughters displayed prominently on her office desk. From my meetings with her, I believe she would make a wonderful priest, or even an Archbishop. An era accommodating such changes will undoubtedly come one day and some say, the sooner the better.

# John Boyle O'Reilly of Ireland, Australia and the United States of America

The vast tract of water that separates Australia from America was an escape route that proved a solace to many Irish people transported to Australia for various misdemeanours. One such person takes us across the Pacific Ocean and all the way to the shores of America, that is John Boyle O'Reilly. His name always struck a chord with me, for what reason I do not know. Unlike Charles Yelverton O'Connor, O'Reilly's departure from Ireland was not voluntary, but both men were destined to have connections with Fremantle thanks to the various turnings their lives took.

I remember spending a night in the John Boyle O'Reilly Club in Springfield, Massachusetts, a long time ago and meeting lots of Irish people there. That area, with its many towns and cities, was a favourite destination for emigrants from the Dingle area in bygone generations, and if I am not mistaken a few of the Lynchs from Dingle town were playing music in the club that night. I do know that Colm Lynch, who went to school to the Monks (our name for the Christian Brothers School in Dingle) around the same time as my late brother Paddy, was among them. I also remember that, as a visitor, I was forbidden to pay for anything while in the club that night. A first cousin of mine, Jim Quinn, spent most of his working life in Springfield and while I was there he showed me that part of America in great detail.

Ever since that visit I retained an interest in O'Reilly, and he and his ilk are definitely included in what I call 'my Ireland'. Oddly enough, he was a contemporary of Charles Yelverton O'Connor, being born in Dowth, near Drogheda, in 1844, a little less than eighteen months after the engineer's birth not too far away in Castletown. John was the son of the local schoolmaster, William O'Reilly, and his wife, Eliza Boyle, and by the standards of the time the young John received a good education. The *Drogheda*

*Argus* newspaper is still going strong, and it was there that the young lad first went to work as an apprentice at the age of thirteen. He stayed in the newspaper business until the age of seventeen, when he went to Preston in England and joined the 11th Lancashire Rifles. On his return to Dublin in 1863 he joined the 10th Hussars, but by 1865 he was on the other side as a member of the Irish Republican Brotherhood (IRB), or Fenians, fighting against the English for Irish independence.

His activities eventually led to his arrest. He was tried for treason and sentenced to death. He spent time in Mountjoy Prison before being transferred to England, where he spent two years in custody in various institutions, including Dartmoor. His death sentence was commuted to twenty years' penal servitude in Australia and he was off again into another unknown. Upon arrival in Fremantle, in January 1869, he was transferred to the local convict establishment and his incarceration continued.

Workers were scarce in that part of the world at the time and within a month O'Reilly was transferred to Bunbury as a member of a party of convicts engaged in building a road. He must have been effective in the PR business because he was soon appointed probationary convict constable, with responsibility for records, accounts-keeping and other administrative chores. It is even said that he began a romantic liaison with the warder's daughter, so perhaps convict life was not always as severe as people expected.

It was fortunate for him that he became friendly with the local parish priest, Fr McCabe. Before the year was out Fr McCabe had arranged O'Reilly's escape from the prisoner colony. On the appointed day, O'Reilly absconded from work and with that act of defiance the first stage of a dramatic escape was underway. Travelling with a group of Irish settlers who were familiar with the countryside, the escapees rode to the Collie River and then rowed out into the coastal waters of the Indian Ocean, and on to the safety of dune land where they laid low for a while.

The elaborate plan went without a hitch and soon O'Reilly was aboard the American whaling ship *Gazelle*, and on his way to freedom.

In America, with that comforting expanse of ocean between him and his past, he settled in Boston and got employment with *The Pilot* newspaper, an organ of the Irish Roman Catholic community. It did not take long for the Meathman to ascend to the post of editor. He must have appreciated his early assignments, covering the Fenian convention in New York and the subsequent invasion of Canada. They proved to be his road to Damascus, however, because thereafter he rejected armed struggle as a means of advancement and became a disciple of the peaceful methods of men like Daniel O'Connell and Thomas Davis. It was Davis who first preached that the pen was mightier than the sword, and John Boyle O'Reilly put that philosophy into practice in *The Pilot*, in his lecture tours and in his other writings. His views were widely accepted in Boston and he gained great popularity among the people. Even though he was editor, and eventually part-owner, of a Catholic newspaper, he was to the forefront in helping his community to assimilate with the Protestant/Yankee population.

I think it is true to say that he is remembered in Ireland primarily for his connection with the Fenians, his imprisonment, his escape and maybe his poetry, which was oft quoted by the late US President John F. Kennedy. The American perception of the man is very different, which in itself illustrates his versatility, ecumenism and political opinion. He had a great mind and it was to him John Devoy – another great Irishman who spent most of his life in America – turned in 1875 when plans were being hatched to rescue six military Fenians imprisoned in Western Australia. The plan first submitted to O'Reilly envisaged the storming of Fremantle Prison, with escape ensured through the use of arms. This did not appeal to him in any way, so he proposed a prearranged escape plan with a whaling ship, the *Catalpa*, which would be purchased for the purpose and would therefore be able to be in Fremantle at a certain hour on, as it would appear, legitimate business. It worked. In 1876 the six Fenians were picked up near Rockinham, and their escape is now part of the lore of Western Australia.

The prison is no longer used as such and is now a successful tourist attraction. I made a point of visiting it during my stay in

Perth for the International Football Test between Ireland and Australia in late autumn 2005. Our guide was excellent and brought us on a very informative tour of the prison, and I had little to say until he mentioned that there had been few successful escapes during its long years of service. He was made aware of an 'unusual one' before I left!

The attraction former prisons hold for tourists and natives alike never ceases to amaze me. The world over, these dreary institutions more than make up for years of no economic return by becoming profit-earning business entities. Ned Kelly has earned millions for Melbourne since his involuntary retirement! Given this fact, it might not be the best idea in the world to bulldoze Mountjoy Prison out of existence once the promised new centre is built somewhere in north Co. Dublin. The possibilities are endless. Consider that the church within the precinct walls of O'Reilly's prison, which was a most interesting building, is now in great demand for weddings. That surely is something we could emulate: Fáilte Ireland could retain part of Mountjoy and offer a good package – midday marriage in Mountjoy, with an afternoon reception in Croke Park!

The redoubtable John Boyle O'Reilly was the author of several books of poetry, including *Songs of the Southern Seas*, *In Bohemia*, *Songs, Legends and Ballads*, and of a novel, *Moondyne*, based on his Australian experiences. He remained editor of *The Pilot* until his death in Boston in 1890 at the age of forty-six. He is buried in Hollyhood cemetery in Brookline, Massachusetts, a place I have yet to visit, but will certainly get to. The Americans have a strong tradition of honouring people of great achievement by erecting memorials in their honour. It is a tribute to John Boyle O'Reilly that such a memorial has been erected in his name and stands proudly in Boston today. It took me a while to locate it on my way home from Australia last November, but once I put GAA President Seán Kelly on the trail we soon tracked it down. It was erected in 1896, in the Charles River area, and captures several aspects of O'Reilly's life. Under a heading of 'Erin, Patriotism and Poetry' there is a bronze plate with a message that reads as follows:

'Poetry and Patriotism give of their laurel and oak from which Erin weaves a wreath for her heroes.' There is an artistic interpretation of all three on one side of the memorial and a bust of John Boyle O'Reilly on the other.

It is a marvellous tribute and it is good to stand beside it for a while as the world goes by. Here was a worthy man who left Ireland involuntarily at the age of twenty-three destined, like many more of that dark era, never to set foot in his homeland again.

# Thomas Addis Emmet

Another man whose name is not as well known in Ireland as it should be is Thomas Addis Emmet, although his younger brother, Robert, is immortalized in song and story. I had to travel to far-away New York to discover details of the extraordinary life and legacy of Thomas Addis Emmet.

He was born in 1764 in Cork, before the Emmet family moved to St Stephen's Green in Dublin, where Robert was born. A brilliant scholar, Thomas studied medicine in Edinburgh, excelled in his studies at Trinity College and was called to the Irish bar in 1790. He had a reputation for intellectual ingenuity and was a passionate advocate for equal rights, both in and out of the courtroom.

He and Robert joined the Society of the United Irishmen and, among many other celebrated cases, he defended Napper Tandy. He was imprisoned in 1798 along with his close friend Theobald Wolfe Tone and other leaders of the United Irishmen movement. Finally, after four years' imprisonment, Emmet was exiled from Ireland under the Banishment Act. In 1803 he was in Europe, seeking French assistance for a new rebellion, when word came that Robert's uprising against the British had been brutally put down and Robert had been hanged in one of Dublin's public streets.

For me, what is most fascinating and impressive about Thomas Addis Emmet is his life from that point onwards. In 1804, at the age of forty, he set sail for America. Amid controversy he was admitted to the American bar, even though he was a foreigner, and he quickly established himself as one of the most notable lawyers of the day. He argued complex constitutional cases before the US Supreme Court, cases which are still spoken of today, and he even served as Attorney-General for the State of New York for a time. Meanwhile, his passion for social justice remained undimmed: he was active in anti-slavery cases and in supporting poor immigrants.

After only twenty-three years in America, Thomas Addis Emmet died in New York in 1827. Business was suspended throughout the city for his funeral and flags were flown at half-mast. His coffin was carried in procession through the streets by dignitaries, including a future president of the United States, Martin Van Buren. Emmet was buried at the New York City Marble Cemetery, a non-denominational cemetery he had helped to establish.

As well as his grave, there is also a monument in his honour that stands to this day in downtown Manhattan. It can be seen at St Paul's Chapel, the oldest public building in continuous use in Manhattan and located directly opposite the site of the World Trade Centre. This is the chapel where George Washington wor-shipped on his Inauguration Day as President of the United States in 1789. In the aftermath of the 11 September attacks in 2001, the chapel served as a place of rest and refuge for recovery workers at Ground Zero and became known to some in those dark days as 'the little chapel that stood'. It was also the location chosen by Mayor Rudolph Giuliani for his farewell oration when leaving office, during which he referred to it as 'thrice hallowed ground'. This is the location of the obelisk erected in memory of Thomas Addis Emmet by his adopted city. It is a marble obelisk standing 30ft high, weighing twenty-eight tons and carved with an American eagle and an Irish harp.

I worry sometimes that we in Ireland today are forgetting the part he and his like played in creating the freedoms we enjoy. I am more than ever convinced it would be appropriate to have some commemorative spot in Ireland to honour Irishmen like Charles Yelverton O'Connor, John Boyle O'Reilly, Thomas Addis Emmet and others who have added lustre to the name of Ireland with their achievements in exile. Would some philanthropist, like Chuck Feeney, be interested?

# Brendan O'Regan

It was home again for me from New York, after a journey that began by heading eastward from Dublin Airport some weeks earlier with destination Australia very much in mind. It is always nice to return home after a sojourn, and there is no better welcome to Ireland than the sight of truly green fields and the Shannon estuary glittering below as the aeroplane eases downwards for a gentle landing. For me, Shannon Airport has always had a major significance. As the plane touched down, I began to think of a man named Brendan O'Regan, long associated with the development of the Shannon area. So it is with him that I begin the Irish leg of my journey, where we shall meet some more interesting people, all very much 'part of what we are'.

Selecting teams from the best of the past is a favourite mental exercise of sports lovers up and down the country, and elsewhere too, no doubt. In the case of the celebrated Allstars in the world of the GAA, the past simply means the last twelve months. However, the allure of what has passed into history is too strong to allow the principle to be confined to one year, thus we get 'team of the 1990s', 'team of the Century' and even 'team of the Millennium' and so on, providing great fodder for debate, argument, controversy and a goodly amount of nostalgia.

These are great times for sport in Ireland as all codes are benefiting from the buoyancy of the economy. Sponsorship has increased substantially in real terms, aggregate attendances at matches are setting new records and there is a new emphasis on the value of sport as part of a healthy lifestyle. Most of the credit for these positive aspects of modern Irish life must go to the organizations facilitating and promoting the various sports, but in assessing the current state of play, one must not forget the parts played by those who guided the country through the twentieth and into the twenty-first century. Wouldn't it be interesting to nominate an Allstar team within that category of people, those who have shaped the country? Now here is a topic worthy of serious debate! So I offer you now a candidate for consideration on the team I shall call 'Architects of Modern Ireland': I am not quite sure whether I would place him at midfield or centre-forward, but Brendan O'Regan is definitely a member of this very special team.

O'Regan's name will forever be associated with Shannon Airport, but those two words have a far wider significance than terminal buildings, runways, arrivals and departures. In their infancy those words fostered an attitude of looking outward beyond the shores and hills of Ireland, and from that progressive frame of mind developed the hotel regeneration and building that led in turn to a burgeoning tourist industry, one now firmly established.

Dr Brendan O'Regan was central to the evolution of that essential industry. I had heard of, read about and observed his many roles over the years and had long been an admirer of his philosophy and achievements. I met him for the first time quite recently and found him to be most interesting in conversation. He spoke of development, entrepreneurship, courage, faith, co-operation, peace and idealism as if he were only starting out in life, such was his passion and enthusiasm.

O'Regan describes himself as one 'born after the Rising of 1916 and lucky enough to be part of the first generation that grew up in a free country where a government independent of outside influences operated'. He was born in Sixmilebridge, Co. Clare, in 1917 and by the time he reached his teenage years Ireland had experienced a War of Independence, a civil war and the initial steps towards a different, more industrial economy and nation. The Shannon Scheme was the start of the programme to bring electricity to the whole country; people from Clare and Limerick would be very familiar with its progress from the moment the ESB was set up in 1927.

Brendan received his secondary education at Blackrock College in Dublin, enrolling there for the first time in 1930. He has memories of playing both rugby and hurling as a student and of successfully making a case to the College President and future Archbishop of Dublin, John Charles McQuaid, for the college to re-enter the Leinster hurling championships. It had participated in the past, playing in the Leinster final of 1925. The Clareman remembers great excitement around the college whenever they won hurling matches. (In fact, Blackrock College won the Leinster title of 1935.)

The O'Regan family was in the motor car trade at the time, a fact that led, indirectly and accidentally, to his later interest in activities that were totally different: 'We were on holidays in Italy and my father met some people who suggested that he should become an agent for Fiat cars on his return; they also mentioned that the "capital" would be a better location than where he was then operating.' It would appear that the Italians knew nothing of the wonders of the 'Bridge at the time!

The Fiat deal was made, and soon after arriving back in Sixmile-bridge James O'Regan headed for Ennis, the 'capital' of Clare, in search of a suitable garage or place where he could set up his business.

My father found a garage all right, but there was a problem because it was part of a hotel that was then closed down; the only way to get possession of the garage was to buy the hotel as well – it was called the Old Ground Hotel.

And so it turned out that the hotel was reopened and, indeed, still stands today as firm as the Rock of Gibraltar, clad in ivy and now in the ownership of the sporting Flynns of Dungarvan. The move meant an unexpected turn in the life of the young Brendan O'Regan because he was sent abroad to study hotel management. He experienced life and learning in London, Switzerland, Germany and France before returning home to work for a while in the Old Ground. In 1938 he moved to the famous Falls Hotel in Ennistymon, an establishment rented by his father from the McNamara family for five years and of which Brendan became manager. Before long he was off yet again, this time for the real capital, Dublin, where he was appointed manager of the St Stephen's Green Club.

The club had a long history as a place where people of power, influence, wealth and enterprise met to socialize and exchange opinions and theories on diverse matters. It was there that the young manager first met Seán Lemass, then Minister for Industry and Commerce. 'I was very impressed by his attitude from the moment I met him,' O'Regan says of the former Taoiseach. It was he who later approached O'Regan with a request that he manage the restaurant set up in Foynes, Co. Limerick, to cater for the business generated by the Flying Boat terminus.

Flying Boats were the phenomenon of the time and the Foynes restaurant had great potential; the idea of managing it appealed to Brendan. Apparently it was initially run by English people, and Brendan told me a little story that highlights the attitude of that era. Taoiseach Éamonn de Valera had become aware of the arrangement while on a visit to Foynes and, according to Brendan, remarked that 'surely we should be able to manage this ourselves'. The story made me wonder: did 'Dev' actually ask Lemass to keep an eye out for a potential Irish manager?

Regardless of whose idea it was, O'Regan accepted the offer. His appointment was not universally applauded, however. One day the 'Bridge man dropped in to the Glenworth Hotel in Limerick, where some Flying Boat crew members were relaxing and chatting. Brendan happened to overhear them discussing the proposed changes at the Foynes restaurant, and their tone suggested they believed the result would be a drop in standards. O'Regan did not interject audibly, but simply mused to himself: 'just wait and see what we can do, we will show the world.' It was a telling reaction, one that showed the confidence he had in the people of Ireland. As Brendan celebrates his ninetieth year that same idealistic confidence is still there and as strong as ever.

The Foynes catering venture was a success, but before long Flying Boats went into rapid obsolescence with the regular arrival of land planes in Shannon. This precipitated another career change for Brendan. In 1945 he was appointed Catering Comptroller in Shannon, having spent two years down the road in Foynes, and with that move another era of great wonder and accomplishment was underway.

It was there, in Shannon, that the famous 'tonic' known as Irish Coffee was first launched and savoured as a speciality by the multitudes passing through the airport. The Comptroller does not claim full responsibility for the creation, however: 'I might have marketed the product, but the credit must go to Joe Sheridan, the chef at Foynes, who was familiar with the ingredients.'

Indeed, Joe Sheridan is still fondly remembered at Shannon, and Margaret O'Shaughnessy of the Foynes Museum has many a tale to tell about the man from Castlederg, in Co. Tyrone. He had previously worked in The Dolphin restaurant in Dublin, but applied to the Foynes restaurant in response to Brendan O'Regan's advertisement. His forthright approach caught Brendan's eye with its simplicity. His job application read as follows:

> Dear Brendan,
> I am the man for the job.
> Joe Sheridan.

He was correct in his own assessment: he actually was the right man for the position, as he had so succinctly put it. His 'discovery' of Irish Coffee was, like so many other inventions, accidental, born from necessity. Sea boats depended very much on the weather and it was not unusual for a pilot to make a decision to turn back to Shannon due to worsening weather conditions out over the Atlantic. It was while entertaining crew members who had returned on one of those occasions that Joe added a drop of whiskey to the coffee before presenting the mix. The guests liked the 'coffee' and one of them inquired if it was Brazilian, to which the chef replied innocently, 'No, it's Irish.'

Thus was the term coined. The heart-warming coffee got Brendan's imprimatur soon afterwards. It followed from a comment the Comptroller made regarding a duck dish that was being prepared by the chef. When asked what he thought of it, Brendan stated that it lacked 'eye appeal' and proceeded to garnish it with something that was on hand. Sometime later, Brendan answered a knock on his office door, admitting Joe Sheridan, who was holding a well-presented Irish Coffee. He inquired whether it had 'eye appeal'. The response was briefer than his own job application – just two words from the observant 'Bridge man: 'Genius, chef.'

The coffee quickly became a favourite for those in transit and its appeal spread beyond the airport's outlet. As whiskey was one of the main ingredients, Brendan O'Regan saw the fine opportunity it presented to market Irish *Uisce Beatha* to the Americans. This was one of the reasons that led him to develop the unique concept of a duty free shop at Shannon Airport, an idea that was a reality by 1950. It was the first duty free shop in the world and paved the way for a global industry of duty free retail. This 'industry' was worth millions to the Irish economy, also benefiting those Irish manufacturers who had their goods displayed in Shannon and other airports in the country.

There was one casualty, however, and that was chef Joe Sheridan. His Irish Coffees had become legendary and much sought after, and nobody could be found in the western United States who could make 'real Irish Coffee', so a journalist called Stan Delaplane suggested Joe Sheridan be brought over from Shannon Airport. The Yanks succeeded in luring him away in 1952 and he spent the remainder of his life in the Buena Vista restaurant on Fisherman Wharf in San Francisco, where his 'coffees' gave a further boost to Irish exports.

Back home, Brendan O'Regan continued in his efforts to prove that 'we could be the best' and in 1951 he established the Shannon Airport College of Hotel Management. He believed good hotel management was an essential component if a vibrant tourist trade in Ireland were to be developed. The Shannon College is now one of the leading institutions in its field in Europe. Three years later, in 1954, O'Regan promoted the notion of mail order sales from Shannon and before long the store at the airport was a fantastic success. It was inevitable that he would be called upon to serve on Bord Fáilte (now Fáilte Ireland), and in 1955 he was appointed a member, becoming Chairman just two years later. His fifteen years in that position constitutes a record.

During his time with Bord Fáilte he pushed for tourist amenities to be improved so Irish holidays offered variety and value for money, and he encouraged sustained development. His idea of establishing the Shannon Castles Tours was adopted and became the top tourist attraction in the south-west. Bunratty Castle was restored and the medieval banquets held there and at Knappogue and Dunguire were sell-out events. It was O'Regan, too, who pioneered the Rent-an-Irish Cottage scheme and the Bunratty Folk Park, among other popular and profitable ventures.

Always conscious of the possibilities of change, O'Regan was chairman of the Shannon Free Airport Development Company, which was set up in 1959 with the aim of establishing an Industrial Zone:

Seán Lemass was supportive and when I mentioned the desirability of a new town for Shannon he was a bit surprised, but approved nevertheless; it is Ireland's only new town since the foundation of the State and is Clare's third largest [town].

In his many different roles he has had a huge influence on the development of Ireland. He looked to the future at all times, planning and strategizing for future success and the next generation. For example, he had the future very much in mind when he arranged the first industrial training workshop at Shannon Airport in 1972. He appreciates the hard work undertaken by bodies like the Industrial Development Authority (IDA) since its foundation in 1986 and the ability of Irish society to change with the times and capitalize on its resources.

My conversation with Brendan O'Regan was carried out bilingually; he is most anxious to retain his fluency in Irish. Somehow he found time to serve on Comhairle na Gaeilge for many years and was responsible for a report on Gaeltacht development. He believes that all aspects of Irishness are important to the nation, although he has no difficulty in appreciating other cultures and customs: 'My own wife, Rita Barrow, who has unfortunately passed away, was English and I have a lot of friends outside of Ireland.'

He is the type of man who has been busy all his life, but never regarded work as a burden. He prefers to speak about the projects he is working on now than revisiting events of the past. His current mission is the promotion of peace on this island, a vision he has been involved in over a good number of years. In 1979 he launched Co-operation North, now called Co-operation Ireland, and its relevance is now greater than ever in promoting peace and understanding in practical ways between the communities of the North and the South. The organization is highly regarded at home and abroad, and the joint patrons are Her Majesty Queen Elizabeth and Her Excellency Mary McAleese, President of Ireland. Millions of dollars, and other currencies, are contributed annually to the movement's funds and are spent on a wide variety of projects that promote peace and co-operation between Ireland's communities.

Dr O'Regan is also Founder and President of the Irish Peace Institute (IPI), which is based in the University of Limerick. I was not long in his home before he handed me a booklet published recently by the IPI. The title spelled out his philosophy on peace: *Mankind Must Manage a World Without War*. It is one of a series of booklets devoted to the theme of peace and contains lectures given by the following personalities: Mary McAleese; Bertie Ahern, Taoiseach; Pat Cox, former President of the European Parliament; John Hume and David Trimble, Nobel Laureates; and George Mitchell, United States Senator and peace negotiator. O'Regan is passionate in his devotion to the cause of world peace and allied it to Shannon as far back as 1986 when he founded the Shannon Centre for International Co-operation. He is confident that the goal of peace can be attained, but as he points out: 'people must speak out and the Irish voice must be heard again and again as an Anti-War Voice.'

Since reaching the age when people would normally retire, he has worked consistently and has been showered with honours.

Retirement is simply not a word in his lexicon: he is as enthusiastic about his current projects as he was many moons ago, listening to those people in the Glenworth Hotel in Limerick and thinking defiantly, 'We will show the world' – it could well have been his motto. Here are just some of the numerous distinctions that have been awarded to the Sixmilebridge entrepreneur:

Honorary Doctorates of Law from University College, Dublin (1978), Queen's University, Belfast (1999) and University of Limerick (2002).
CBE (Commander of the British Empire), 1993.
Hall of Fame recipient from American Society of Travel Agents, 1977.
Freedom of the City of Limerick, 1995.

Although a self-effacing man and not a limelight-seeker, he was delighted to be honoured by the people of Foynes in 2002 in recognition of his long-serving friendship and support over sixty years.

At the outset, I said I wasn't sure where to place Brendan O'Regan on the 'Architects of Ireland' side, but having reviewed his extraordinary career and life, I have decided to place him at midfield on my team of alternative Allstars of the twentieth century. He is a fulcrum point, an essential link between past and present, so he will fit a midfield role perfectly. Shortly, we shall make acquaintance with the man I would place beside him at midfield: Ken Whitaker. Together, they present a formidable front for modern Irish society.

# The Hurling Bishop of Killaloe, Willie Walsh

It is not far from either Foynes or Shannon to Co. Clare, and it is there you are most likely to meet Willie Walsh, the hurling Bishop of Killaloe. In the past, bishops were treated as special persons and shown great respect and decorum on all occasions. My first sighting of a senior member of the hierarchy was on the day of my confirmation, when I was ten years of age. Pupils from schools within a radius of five or six miles of Dingle convened in St Mary's Church for the visit of Bishop O'Brien, who was coming all the way from his residence in far-away Killarney to bestow his presence upon us. The preparations during the weeks leading up to the ceremony were frantic: we had to memorize the catechism, we were questioned by our Christian Brother teacher and finally we were examined by Fr Beasley, who had the power to decide who was ready for the sacrament – and who was not. We were in fear of the Bishop before we ever saw him because we were aware that he would conduct a further examination before we were allowed to take part in the actual confirmation ceremony.

The waiting was an ordeal. The Bishop moved slowly along the lines of boys and girls, stopping in front of each pupil in turn to deliver a question and await the correct answer. When he finally stopped in front of me he seemed the biggest man in the world, clad in the most wonderful robes I ever saw and wearing an extraordinary, funny-looking hat that added almost another foot to his towering height. He was a mild and gentle man when he spoke, however. The question he gave me was easy and I rattled off an answer I had learned by rote. By the way, the question was posed and answered in English because religion was taught through that medium, even though all other subjects were taught *as Gaeilge*. There must have been doubts about God's knowledge of Irish at the time! At any rate, everything went smoothly from then on and nobody failed. Before we left the church we were, in the words of the catechism, 'strong and perfect Christians'.

I did not see a bishop again until an All-Ireland final day when a member of the hierarchy threw in the ball to get the match underway. There were no robes this time, but plenty of pomp and respect as he walked onto the field prior to a hearty rendition of 'Faith of our Fathers' by a choir of over 70,000. The custom of a bishop throwing in the ball at the start of a major GAA game is now but a memory of the past, nonetheless the attendance of many members of the hierarchy at All-Ireland and Provincial finals is still as regular as the seasons. Generally they are keen followers of sport and traditionally the Archbishop of Cashel and Emly is the Patron of the GAA.

Long before he was appointed Bishop of Killaloe, Fr Willie Walsh was a well-known figure at hurling matches where he was to be found in one of several capacities, ranging from coach, selector and mentor to spectator. It was as such that he first came to my notice and he was as good for the GAA as any other within the legions of the Association's unsung heroes. For that reason I followed his career, both as a hurling enthusiast and as a Church-man, and I regard him as an important figure in the strange and wonderful Ireland of today. I doubt if his interest in the sport has diminished much since his appointment as Bishop in the mid-1990s, but he has now emerged as a respected figure in the modern Church, a quiet man who is not afraid of hard work or embracing new approaches to problems. Although the role of bishops is a difficult one nowadays, Bishop Walsh's counsel is valued in many quarters. He comes across as a person with a good practical under-standing of social problems and a strong desire to find workable solutions. It is good to meet him at any time and it is not long ago since I last spent some time in his company in Limerick, a little beyond the bounds of his own diocese.

Most people associate him with Clare, but he was actually born in North Tipperary, close to Roscrea. He freely admits that 'neither of my parents had any interest in hurling, they were very much committed to the job of farming, which was a seven-day-a-week job at the time.' I am sure there were plenty of others like the Walsh family who were not very taken by sport, but young Willie took an interest from an early age:

Tipp were good at the time, but I suppose what heightened my interest was going to St Flannan's College in Ennis as a boarder in 1947; the college had a great hurling tradition and I was extraordinarily impressed by being in the same seat in the chapel with Jimmy Smyth during my first year; he was physically big and strong and even then was looked upon in the hurling world as a gifted player – didn't he play for the Clare minors for five years.

The same Jimmy Smyth was destined for a long inter-county career with Clare and played regularly on Munster teams, with whom he won six Railway Cup medals between 1955 and 1963. The Ruan man was not the only star player Willie recalled, he listed the Ryan brothers, Séamus and Liam, and Nicky Stokes from Limerick as being as good as the best.

I played a lot of hurling myself in Flannan's, but I would never consider myself a good hurler. I had an extraordinary experience in my last year in the college. I was a sub on the Harty Cup team the first day out, but I was replaced by my older brother for the second round. I was dropped in fact.

How did he react to the selectors' decision?

I could do nothing there and then, but it had a huge influence on my involvement with teams later on. I resolved that I would never drop a sub from a panel and rather than do it, I would simply add the new name instead. The feeling of being dropped from the subs stayed with me for a while because Flannan's went on to win the Harty Cup that year.

As was common among a good many students from diocesan colleges, the Tipperary-born student with leanings towards Clare proceeded to Maynooth College on completion of his Leaving

Certificate in 1952. After three years in Maynooth he was sent to the Irish College in Rome to complete his studies for the priesthood:

There was not much discussion about it. The bishop sent word through the parish priest that I was to go to Rome and that was it. I was very sad leaving Maynooth, I had enjoyed my time there and had many friends among the student colleagues.

Before long, though, he realized that studying in Rome presented a wonderful opportunity and he settled down to life outside of Ireland fairly quickly:

I loved Rome and the Italians and soon regarded it as a second home. There was much more freedom than was the case in Maynooth; we were allowed out about the city and further afield during holiday time. I will be grateful for ever for the opportunity given to me to spend time in that wonderful country.

After four years of study he was ordained in Rome in 1959, followed by a further three years of post-graduate study before the young priest returned to Ireland and straight into the world of hurling once more. He completed the Higher Diploma in Education in University College, Galway, then in 1963 commenced a twenty-five-year teaching career at his old *alma mater*, St Flannan's College in Ennis.

Hurling had always been part of St Flannan's culture and the returned 'Roman' was soon training and coaching the college teams. When Fr Gardiner was no longer available for coaching, Fr Hugh O'Dowd stepped into his shoes and the cherished Harty Cup made five visits to the college during that twenty-five-year span. Fr Walsh got to know Ger Loughnane as a student and college hurler, and remembers him as a very determined player on a team beaten by St Finbarr's, Farranferris, in the Harty final of 1971. The two would meet again in the mid-1980s when Fr Walsh was involved in coaching Clare Minor and under-21 players:

I became directly involved with him in 1990 when I was with the county under-21 side, that was the first time I saw Ger coaching and I recognized immediately he was the finest coach I had ever seen in action. I had gone to see other coaches over the years in order to improve my own style, but I have no hesitation in saying that Ger was absolutely brilliant in imparting and improving skills. He also kept insisting that Clare hurlers needed to speed up their game if they were to have a chance to compete with the best.

Fr Walsh also worked with Len Gaynor when he was manager of the Clare senior team and he admired him as the best man-manager he had come across: 'he had a wonderful relationship with players and his coaching methods were the traditional ones up to that time.'

When Fr Walsh was ordained Bishop Walsh for the Diocese of Killaloe in October 1994 he was no longer acting as a Clare selector, but he was as ardent a supporter as ever and enjoyed the reign of Ger Loughnane. The Bishop saw the new team of selectors – Ger Loughnane, Tony Considine and Mike McNamara – as three very different characters who succeeded in working extremely well together:

Under Len Gaynor, Clare had begun to beat some good teams and victory over Tipperary in the 1994 championship was an important milestone. Some of the groundwork for the successes that followed had been done, but it needed an expert coach with an ability to convince and steer the team the extra steps forward, and Ger was the man at that critical time.

I was surprised to learn that the new Bishop was not at the 1995 Munster final when the sixty-three-year gap without a provincial title was bridged in Semple Stadium with the defeat of the reigning champions, Limerick. JJ 'Goggles' Doyle was Clare captain in 1932, the last time they'd claimed the cup, and in 1995 it was Anthony Daly, a player who had been coached by the new Bishop, who stepped up to lift and hoist the Munster Cup for a jubilant

Clare team. So, if the Bishop wasn't in the park, where was he and how did he get the news of the historic win?

The Munster final clashed with the Diocesan Pilgrimage to Knock and I had the experience of coming down off the altar in Knock when a man whispered in my ear, 'We're two points up, Bishop.' The services were over and I knew it must have been close to the finish, and I responded by dashing into the sacristy, taking off the vestments and running across to the parish priest's house in time for the last few minutes. It was almost unbelievable and I did not delay in setting out for home. I was just about getting out of the town when I heard Anthony Daly's speech on the radio and when I heard him mention my own name the tears came rolling down my face; above all else, that is the moment I will remember the longest. I was back in Ennis in time for the fantastic home-coming of the Cup at long last, and for me and every Clare person it was magical and exceptional. Prayers may well have been said for Biddy Early, who obviously had refrained, for once, from casting her curse on the poor Clare hurlers.

What effect did the breakthrough have on the people of the county? 'It acted as an enormous tonic that gave new confidence to everybody. They felt they were now up there with the best and it made them walk tall through the sporting world. The feeling is there to this day and will endure for a generation at least; long may it last.'

The Bishop has long been involved with the game of hurling, but it has never been the most important interest in his life, devoted, as he is, to his life in the Church. He was equally anxious to speak to me about his vocation and the massive changes he has witnessed within a relatively short space of time. It does not take long in his company to realize his sincerity about and concern for the problems facing the Church and society:

When I set out to become a priest I was idealistic and felt that the Church of the time was nearly perfect and I was very confident that when I and my contemporaries got at it that we would make it perfect.

46

Certainly, it was an extraordinary time: fifty of us did the Leaving Certificate in Flannan's in 1952 and twenty from that fifty began studying for the priesthood in the autumn; everything around me was telling me that the best thing I could do with my life was to become a priest. When I returned to Ireland ten years later, there was 95 per cent attendance at mass on Sundays and the Church was a very powerful influence on society; I was very content to be on the team and, of course, the Vatican Council gave an added hope with the changes that were about to come.

It was a time of hope in other aspects of Irish life also – Taoiseach Seán Lemass and Northern Ireland Premier Terence O'Neill brought a new phrase – 'hands across the border' – into politics, and beyond the Irish Sea Prime Minister Harold Macmillan was talking about the winds of change, and we as young priests were excited about the changes expected from the deliberations of Vatican II. We were enthusiastic and the younger priests in the diocese held a meeting once a month for the purpose of having discussions and debate. We were looked upon with slight suspicion by the older priests and referred to as 'The Cell'. We were often critical of the status quo. We discussed matters like changes in liturgy, relations between parish priests and curates, how we were reaching young people and all that sort of thing.

Bishop Walsh was frank in discussing his views on bishops when he was a young priest: 'I would have seen bishops as very old men whom we saw in Maynooth three or four times a year during our student days. As a young priest I would have seen them as a fairly conservative group and I feel that some young priests today see me as a very conservative old man.' Nonetheless, he regards himself as one who always tried to work with members of the community as equals and he believes that his work with the GAA and with the Catholic Marriage Advisory Council (now Accord) helped him to remain rooted in the general community: 'I did a lot of training with Accord, dealing with laypeople always on a basis of equality and understanding, and regard myself as lucky to have got the useful training. I have learned a lot from the group and people like Barry Smyth in Ennis or Jack Heaslip would not be long in calling you to order once they thought you were straying.' The

Bishop's down-to-earth personality means there are no traces of pomp about his ministry; people find him approachable and always willing to help in a constructive way.

We also talked about the scandals that have rocked the Church over the past decade, and again he was characteristically outspoken on this difficult subject. He told me that it came as a huge shock to him to learn that the Church, which was apparently near-perfect when he entered the priesthood, was not really that perfect at all:

The revelations and scandals that were unveiled came as a huge jolt to me and a source of immense sadness. I had no idea until the late 1980s when, on account of my training in Canon Law and Church Law, I was asked by Church authorities in Dublin to act on a tribunal looking at a few cases of sexual abuse. I read up on what had happened by way of scandals in America and it was then I first became aware of the problems that were unfolding here, and I must say I was not prepared for it. It brought great pain and still brings it when I sit down to talk to victims of abuse and see the sufferings they have gone through, or indeed to sit down and talk to a colleague that you may have to ask to stand down from ministry. I don't hesitate in saying that it has been the single most painful experience of my life.

Of course, the scandals have contributed to the enormous fall-off in church attendance, but there are other factors, like the comforts of greater economic independence, that seem to push the need for spiritual matters to the side. I would not for a moment decry the economic growth that has taken place, it is wonderful, but it does not answer all the needs of people. I detect a hunger for the spiritual, even in people that are no longer church frequenters and a lot of them are very good people.

It is easy to listen to people like Bishop Willie Walsh, regardless of one's own opinions, although of course the fact that we share the common interests of Gaelic sports and the Irish language increases my enjoyment of our conversations. He could talk for ever about hurling and he uses Gaeilge any time he is addressed in that medium. Like most of us, he spends more time looking

48

backwards than forwards into the unknown, yet when I wondered how he saw the future of the Church in Ireland, he was quite willing to paint it as he sees it. Before long, I could sense that strong vein of hope that runs through his thinking:

Of course the future is important and we must prepare for it. It is not my Church but the Church of Christ and there is hope in believing that. We have tried to respond as best we can to the current environment. I and the other priests spent two years observing the new situation and listening across the county before we put out a pastoral plan for the future of the Church in the Diocese of Killaloe – more involvement by the laity is at the heart of it, and I am amazed at the number of things that are happening already. I reckon that in the parish of Ennis alone there are now about 1,500 people actively involved in one or more of the following roles – Ministers of the Eucharist, St Vincent de Paul, Readers, Pastoral Councils, Finance Committees, choirs and other activities – that gives me great hope as well. I would like to see more involvement by the youth, but I accept that their lives are so much on the move that it is not easy for them to feel tied to given times and responsibilities. I have to recognize the goodness that is in them and I admire their genuine commitment to the principles of justice, truth and integrity of life and to me those virtues rate high in the moral order.

I was amazed to discover that the Bishop with the common touch was in no way despondent about the dramatic fall in vocations to the priesthood and to the religious orders of Brothers and nuns. He agrees that it is a serious issue, but suggests we are a long way from the stage when communities will not have Mass on Sunday:

There are sixty parishes in the Diocese of Killaloe and of the priests serving, only fifty are under the age of fifty. Three parishes are already without a resident priest, but strangely that has not led to despair in those communities. In fact, the Church is more active than ever in one of them simply because the people have reacted and taken ownership of the church. I am overjoyed at that response to a situation that nobody could have envisaged twenty years ago. A priest comes from another parish for what needs a priest, but otherwise the people look after the religious needs of the community. The Pastoral Council meets regularly, groups are detailed to carry out specific duties, such as looking after the physical plant, taking communion to the sick, visiting people who live alone, providing means to raise the necessary finances and seeing to the other, usual activities that go on in most parishes. I was particularly delighted when informed that they themselves had organized a retreat for the parishioners: it was they who chose and invited the priests that officiated at the retreat and it worked wonderfully well. It made me think again of the hope I hold – not a foolish or superficial optimism, but a hope based on the belief that people still have a deeper meaning of life and values in spite of all the brokenness we have witnessed in recent times.

When I suggested to him that the influence once wielded by the Church had waned considerably, he was quick to interrupt with the words 'good riddance' before equating the old influence with a power that made people fearful of going against the Church. He then spoke of influence and defined a type of influence that all Churches could adopt and promulgate:

The best way to exercise influence is to lead by example, reminding ourselves first of all and then those in authority in the State of the need for justice, the need to care for people who find it difficult to cope, the need to include the marginalized and those with special needs. There is an enormous call for justice in the world today and we in the Church should be making that call strongly and not be afraid to do so repeatedly.

Does he see an increasing role for women in the Church into the future?

I certainly can. I think that, to some degree, we have been impoverished by the lack of meaningful roles for women, especially roles in decision-making. The question of admission to ordination is another matter and a very difficult one, but I think it is a topic for discussion some other time.

I often find myself asking the question: would we have done so poorly in relation to the management of the child sexual abuse issue if women were more involved? I just feel they have a deeper sensitivity to these problems than men and I find myself turning to women when I have a difficult problem, either personal or dealing with the Church. I think they bring a different dimension to a discussion on problems. I am fortunate that I have a small number of close women friends and I value their advice and support greatly. We try in our Diocese to have a proper gender balance and we now have an enormous number of committees operating. I find the balance healthy and something we lacked down the years, which made communities all the poorer.

Before I said *slán* to Bishop Willie Walsh in Limerick that afternoon, I felt I had to ask him about the circumstances that once saw members of the Travelling community park their caravans on the grounds of his residence in Ennis for a period of nine months, or thereabouts. He had not forgotten and, as usual, had a logical explanation for the unusual happening:

There was a particular problem in Ennis at the time and I suppose I always had a sort of a soft spot for the Travellers from knowing some of them when growing up in Tipperary; and then years later, when there was not enough space for them on halting sites, they were being moved from place to place in the town of Ennis and the surrounding area. So as I had a sizeable lawn I responded by allowing them to come in and park there for a period of six to nine months. They were grateful and made an effort to keep the place in reasonable shape; over the winter it got very mucky, but they did their best.

I asked him if his decision to allow these families to use his ground was in fact a ploy to highlight the plight of Travellers in general. He assured me this was not the case:

The original intention was to supply a temporary solution to a serious problem, but I think it had the effect all right of drawing attention on a wide scale to the issue. In fairness to the Clare County Council, they have worked very hard and it was not due to my intervention. I believe there was a genuine desire on the part of the Council to improve the situation and they have done so very considerably in the meantime. I admit I was taken aback by the reaction to my solution at the time, but I did not object to it because it was an issue that deserved attention. It is still a difficult problem and all of us are to blame to some degree – the Travellers, the settled people, the local authority – and I accept that so-called do-gooders, like myself, can be unreasonable as well. Really, we all share the blame and must share the responsibility also before a real solution is found.

# The dramatic change in the role of the Church

In the following days I mulled over the things of which Bishop Walsh had spoken. Speaking of change: can anything compare with the monumental change that has taken place in the role of the Church in this country over the past quarter-century? When I was growing up in Dingle in the 1930s and 1940s all churches were full for every Mass on Sundays and Holy Days, while on Saturday nights there were queues for confession – that was very much the norm and was taken for granted. The annual mission would also be well attended, which ensured that the fear of God was in no danger for at least another year.

Canon Lyne was the parish priest, a Killarney man and uncle of the Lyne brothers, Dinny, Jackie and Fr Michael – all three of them All-Ireland medal winners with Kerry. He was a dapper man who looked the part, especially when he donned the biretta for special occasions. I have a very clear image from my first communion of him sitting among the recipients for the traditional photograph. He was a friendly man and accepted being late for Mass or eating meat on a Friday as things that needed confessing. An elderly lady once confided in him that her sight was failing in the hope that he would offer counsel. I don't know if the response could be regarded as such: 'Ma'am,' he said to her, 'haven't you seen enough?'

Towards the end of his days, Canon Lyne's hearing had disimproved a little, which caused him to lose some of his regular clients for confession because it became necessary to shout one's transgressions a little louder so the confessor could hear them. The danger, of course, was that the waiting 'audience' could hear as well.

Fr Beasley was another curate who served during my time, and he was very involved in the development of the local sportsfield, Páirc an Águasaigh. Another curate, Fr O'Driscoll, had the reputation of being able to say Mass quicker than most, especially on mornings when people (including himself) planned to travel to a Munster final, or something of the sort.

At the time, and to my young mind, all priests seemed popular and respected. Mass was said in Latin, with the sermons and notices in English and the congregation packed tighter close to the back of the church. It was the custom for the canon to read out, in order of magnitude, the amounts given by each household in the collections for the seasonal dues of Christmas and Easter. It must surely be the power of repetition that allows my memory to inform me that the name of John J. O'Connor, General Merchant, was usually at the top of the list. The canon once dispensed with the traditional list, I would say for the sake of variety, and instead gave the increases per household since the last collection: he was right, it made for more interesting listening by far.

Throughout my primary education, first with the Presentation nuns and then with the Christian Brothers, all staff members at the school were members of the religious. This was a time when vocations were at a high level, so there was no need for the orders to employ lay teachers. There was a slight change when I went to secondary school, where laymen Tom Lundon and Seán Gillen taught with a bigger contingent of Brothers. They were all over-seen by An Bráthair Ó Dochartaigh, the Superior. He had a tremendous enthusiasm for the Irish language and almost daily sent us home with a request to our fathers about this word or that. He often got me to read poems aloud in class and although praise in school was not part of the philosophy of the time, he once stated in front of the entire class that I was a fine reader. I am not sure whether or not this singling out had anything to do with my drifting into broadcasting in later life.

Like everyone else, I took it for granted that religion and the religious were very much part of life. It was the same when I was a student with the De La Salle Brothers in Baile Bhúirne, in the Cork Gaeltacht, and again in the Teachers' Training College in Drumcondra, Dublin, where the Vincentian Fathers had control, headed by Fr Killian Keogh with Fr O'Neill, Fr Johnson and a few lay Brothers of that order. Nor did the situation change once I began my teaching career because, with the exception of a few weeks 'subbing' in St Finbarr's of Cabra West in Dublin, I never taught other than in Christian Brothers schools, namely St Laurence O'Toole's and O'Connell's.

In all my dealings with the Brothers and other clergy I encountered, I must say that I never heard of, or suspected, anything remotely connected with the scandals that later engulfed the Church. Those I met and worked with, and the many priests I got to know personally, were all honourable men according to my judgement and, like many more, they too suffered later on account of the deviations of a minority. The news of those scandals came as a jolting shock to most people, and I include myself in that category. The fact that there was unnecessary delay in taking action in some cases, even when there was clear evidence of sexual abuse, made a bad situation far, far worse. It was inevitable that the power and prestige of the Church would be considerably damaged, at least on a temporary basis.

Long before those evils were exposed, however, I had noticed, and I assume others had noticed too, a change in the attitude of some students towards religion, which in my environment meant the Catholic Church. It was sometime in the seventies, when I was teaching in the secondary school, that I first became aware of this shift in attitude. A movement known as the Maoists, or the Internationals, was occasionally featured in the news and was popular with some third-level students in Dublin, as radicals always are with the young and inquisitive. The movement, which seemed to offer an alternative to organized religion, gained a bit of support among students at second level. We on the teaching staff assumed it was just a passing phase, but I received a sharp reminder that things were no longer quite the same when the day of the annual Diocesan Religious Examination came round. This was an examination of long standing that was compulsory for all students in second-level Catholic schools. The papers were corrected in Archbishop's House and the results were solemnly returned in due course to each school.

The students took their places for the exam and I proceeded to distribute the question paper for the first test in the normal manner. I had not gone too far down the line before one of the pupils, already in possession of the paper, nonchalantly informed the rest that 'God is dead'. Before I could issue a rebuke, an answer came quickly from another who had not yet seen the paper: 'I didn't even know he was sick.' What provoked the original remark was a question on the paper that read somewhat like the following: 'God is dead; Comment'. It was in fact based on a famous quote from a book written by the German philosopher Friedrich Nietzsche. The examination proceeded normally thereafter, except that perhaps the traditional enthusiasm was no longer evident in the students' answers. It may be just a coincidence, but that year turned out to be the last of written Diocesan Examinations and I sometimes wondered if an unusual trend had developed in the answering of questions that year which led to a revision of the curriculum.

Since then, the changes in attitude towards the Church and religion have occurred at a rapid pace; the trend of decreasing vocations started even earlier. There are now no Brothers teaching in either the primary or secondary sections of O'Connell's Schools; during my tenure on the staff, the Brothers outnumbered the lay teachers. It is the same story in order schools throughout the country, and for the first time in the history of the State, it is now the case that teaching is almost totally dependent on lay personnel.

Some people lament the passing of Brothers, nuns and priests from the schools, but I don't think it is necessarily a bad thing. The religious orders filled a void at a time when there was no alternative and for that they are owed an enormous debt of gratitude, which should not be clouded by the recent, regrettable revelations. Their contribution stretches well back into the nineteenth century when few children had the benefit of a good education. They stepped in and provided it and, by degrees, it reached the point where society has ample numbers of qualified lay teachers to take the places of the order members. I think that is as good a commendation of their work as anything else.

I came across some statistics once upon a time in relation to the numbers attending university around the year 1900. As far as I can remember, UCD had less than 100 students on the roll, while UCG had less than two score! Those same honourable institutions now muster an aggregate close on 40,000, and it must not be forgotten that it was the service of the religious orders in the sphere of education that was largely responsible for the transformation on which the success of modern Ireland is built.

Over the past few years there has been much talk about the future of the Church, and arriving at an answer seems to be extremely difficult. There are people of great and concerned minds acting as Church leaders at the moment and the question is sometimes put by outsiders: would it be easier for them to solve the problems of falling numbers and indifference among the laity if the Irish Church were autonomous? We are told that, when taking the Universal Church as the standard of measurement, there has been no fall-off in the number of vocations, and I am willing to accept that. However, it does not solve our immediate problem and we should all be focused on finding a way out of the impasse.

The situation is a contradiction in many ways. I have had a fair amount of contact with young people going back over the years and, in my opinion, we have as fine a generation of young people today as at any time in our history, if not the best. These boys and girls are well educated, proud of their heritage, independent-minded, confident, conscientious, spiritual to a degree and willing to help. I have every confidence in them for the future, and I was glad to hear some Church leaders state lately that the future of the Church in Ireland rests with the laity, in other words with the people I am talking about.

I am not a theologian and I do not understand how the Vatican operates, so I would not know how to get these young people involved in the transition. If I were given the task of offering a suggestion that might work, however, I would immediately opt for the radical approach. Radicalism in the present tense is often seen in retrospect as conservatism, as something not to be feared, so why not be brave enough to take a chance and make a place for married clergy? Go a step further and make a place for women priests. Finally, allow certain people to view the priesthood as a job suitable for those with skills in caring and counselling and the other admirable qualities of the clergy of the past. If these things could be achieved, the end result might be the best 'Church' the country has ever had. This 'radicalism' is based on a simple fact: society needs people with the appropriate skills to be given responsibility and trust to take us forward.

# Bertie Coleman of Dunmore and Galway

Time now to cease musing for a while and meet more people. Galway is quite close to Clare and mention of Galway immediately brings to mind the Galway Races – *na Currachaí* – and other forms of sport. Sport and Galway are synonymous and the people of that region are passionate about their sports. Above all are the county's footballers and hurlers, who have brought honours and glory to the west and are revered and their names often recalled. A few footballers must have retired from the game in Paradise recently because some famous players, and good friends of mine, were called to fill the vacancies: Seán Purcell, Jack Mahon, Enda Colleran and Mattie McDonagh. These great men may have left us, but their deeds on the field have ensured the game will live on for ever.

A few months ago I dropped into the Mater Hospital in Dublin to see Bertie Coleman of Dunmore, Galway – a great behind-the-scenes man, the kind that are just as important as the battling men on the field. The GAA is blessed to have many people like Bertie in its ranks and it can truly be said that they are the soul of the Association, as well as the pillars that keep it in place. While talking to Bertie that day in the Mater, a memory flashed back to my mind of an occasion in Trim, Co. Meath, almost forty years ago when a man was introduced to me as 'a Galway man and Bertie Coleman's brother'. It was not that Bertie had won All-Irelands or anything like that, but as an activist and enthusiast in GAA matters he was widely known and respected throughout his native county. I had met him on numerous occasions over the years and the same old enthusiasm was there this time, so much so that no more than a minute was spent on the cause of his short detention in hospital.

Bertie Coleman is now eighty-three years of age and is President of the Dunmore McHale Club in Galway. He is proud of the honour and says: 'I have been associated with the club for as long as I can remember and, you know, it is the oldest in the county, dating back to 1887.' He had a good innings as a player: 'we won the minor championship in 1940 and again the following year, but that one was taken away from us.' He considered the decision to deny the team the Cup was fair enough because 'we played Seán Kitt from the college on our team and he was illegal'. I would say the college in question was St Jarlath's of Tuam.

In fact, I knew Seán Kitt later on, when he was a priest in Dublin. He married my brother, Donal, and Eileen O'Shea in Rathmines Church and was a popular parish priest in Crumlin for a long time. He was a great follower of Gaelic games, an avid Galway fan and a good card player, but I never heard even a whisper of his 'achievement' with the Dunmore minors in 1941 until Bertie told me about it in the Mater Hospital. Fr Seán has passed on now, so I will never get his version of how he was 'signed up' in the first place. Producing illegal players was a cult that was widespread within the GAA for a few decades. There are known cases of players winning county titles in different counties using different names. How Seán Kitt ended up on the field that day shall remain a mystery, unfortunately.

By 1946 Bertie had won a Galway Junior title, but 'one at senior level was always the dream as Dunmore's last win was in 1911. I was lucky enough to be on the team that got there in 1953'. He played with the Galway Juniors round about that time, but as soon as his playing days were over he became involved with other aspects of the club's affairs. He served as secretary and treasurer for twenty-eight years, and between that and acting as selector in the different grades of county teams he had an involvement in football that covered the best part of five decades.

The sixties were the most enjoyable of all. The club was doing well and I was a selector with the Galway senior team that won the three-in-a-row of All-Ireland titles between 1964 and 1966. We had several players on the team: John Donnellan who was captain in 1964, his brother Pat, John Keenan, Bosco McDermott and Séamus Leydon.

Is it any wonder that Dunmore were doing well at the time given that, from the outset, Bertie had advocated that the GAA should pay more attention to club football and hurling. The late Jack Mahon, a fellow Dunmore man, had the same vision and it was these two who sowed the seed that has since sprouted to become the very successful AIB All-Ireland Club Championships. They arranged games between Dunmore and club teams from other counties, and indeed provinces, and by degrees the dogma of the Dunmore gospels took hold.

The likes of Bertie Coleman mean an awful lot to a club and hard-working men like him are the true shareholders in the GAA. I remember talking to Bertie shortly after Galway's long famine had ended with the winning of the 1998 All-Ireland football title – the first such win since his own days as a selector with the three-in-a-row gods of the 1960s. Naturally he was 'over the moon' to see the Sam Maguire Cup returned to Connacht, and he wanted to know what I thought of the Dunmore representative on the team, Michael Donnellan. Those who saw that final will have no difficulty recalling the starring role played by the dashing Dunmore youth that day. The phrase 'poetry in motion' must have been composed to commemorate a display like that given by Michael in Croke Park in that All-Ireland final against a good Kildare team.

I spoke to Bertie about one particular Galway point that I labelled 'Donnellan's point', even though he was not the scorer at all. The point in question had come about as a result of a fabulous move that began with Donnellan soloing out of defence at a furious pace, from a position deep in the canal side of Croke Park. At a certain stage, still behind midfield, he delivered a long, accurate forward pass to midfielder Kevin Walsh on the wing before accelerating faster than I had ever seen anybody do before, or have seen anybody do since. In an instant he was within forty yards of the Railway goal, where he took the return and almost instantaneously sent a slick pass to Derek Savage that bought a point from defender Seán Óg de Paor.

The mini-opera took far less than a minute and for me it

was the score of the match and could justifiably be attributed to Donnellan's double-acts and ground-devouring strides. Bertie agreed with me and then asked if I would contribute a few words to a little booklet 'they' intended to produce covering magic moments from the final. It was yet another example of the fact that his club was his primary focus and of his willingness to honour a fellow club man who had brought glory to town and county.

It is impossible now to calculate the number of hours of service Bertie Coleman has given to Dunmore, but I'm sure it would tot up to a staggering total that would equate with a lifetime's devotion. For this, he has never asked anything in return and is modest about his contribution. If you try to speak well of his achievements, you'll quickly find he is far more interested in discussing the countless others doing the same type of work in clubs from one end of the country to the other. He is truly a team player.

# Mayo's Cruach Phádraig and the tradition
of the Reek

How many people have climbed Mayo's Croagh Patrick since the venerable shepherd/missioner Pádraig settled at the top for forty days and nights of prayer and fasting more than 1,500 years ago? Judging by the numbers that make the ascent during the annual 'Reek Weekend' in July the figure must be astronomical; no matter what people might say about changing attitudes towards religion, the attraction of Connacht's Holy Mountain is set to continue. For many, the Reek is the most significant event of the year in the west of Ireland and there are those who would aver that its popularity exceeds even that of the annual Connacht football final or the Galway Races. Better leave that call to counsels wiser than the saint himself, but one way or another it is wonderful to see the great tradition being honoured year after year.

In the sixties I once made the climb on the Friday preceding Reek Sunday. The day was fine and there was a steady flow of people intent on the same mission. I had the benefit of a good guide, Tom Bowe, now regrettably deceased, who was a friend of mine from the neighbouring town of Louisburgh but domiciled in Dublin at the time. He had made the trip many times before and knew all the lore these pilgrimages gather with the passing years. The statue of St Patrick close to the base of the mountain focused the mind on the task at hand, and gave a good excuse to take the first breather of the day. It was easy to visualize the saint having the same thought as he made his way from Ulster and through Connacht on his preaching mission, with only the prayer of 'Lúireach Phadraig' for protection:

> *Críost liom*
> *Críost romham*
> *Críost i mo dhiaidh*

*Críost ionam*

*Críost ar mo lámh dheas*

*Críost ar mo lámh chlé*

*Críost i mo chuideachta is cuma cá dtéim*

*Críost mar chara agam anois is go buan*

*Christ with me*

*Christ ahead of me*

*Christ behind me*

*Christ within me*

*Christ on my right*

*Christ on my left*

*Christ in my company wherever I go*

*Christ as a friend now and for ever*

I think it would be a good idea if a copy of the 'Lúireach' in all of the many languages of modern Ireland were available for distribution at St Patrick's statue.

Climbing a mountain is never an easy task, but there is always the compensating factor of the excellent scenery that improves with every footstep of the ascent. This is especially true of Croagh Patrick, and many pilgrims take time out now and again to gaze in wonder at the work of the creative master that sketched and placed it all. By the halfway mark we were rewarded with the fine vista of Clew Bay, but my guide, Tom, was not doing too well. He complained that one of his shoes had sprung a hole large enough to admit particles of the rough gravel of that mountainside. I agreed it made progress that bit more difficult, but for sport I drew his attention to the fact that others – either through zeal or piety – were doing the climb barefooted. He did have a great sense of humour, but declined to take that particular option as we set forth once more. Before long he decided it might be better for him to turn back and for me to 'follow the others'. It seemed reasonable enough because he had completed the journey many times, so we parted with the understanding that we would meet later at the statue.

It was a solo run from here up, but there was no danger of going the wrong way as the path is well marked. The final climb to the summit was almost on a par with the Devil's Ladder on Corrán Tuathail in the McGillicuddy Reeks of Kerry, with loose stones on all sides ready to roll without undue impetus. Once I reached the top, the view was simply breathtaking, the most beautiful I have gazed upon from any mountaintop. No doubt the fine day helped, defining and clarifying the scene stretched out below. It was difficult to take my eyes off Clew Bay to the west with its archipelago of 365 islands, all places on a canvas of Atlantic blue water: a tranquil scene to behold. Naturally it was a bit cold at the top, being roughly 2,500ft above sea-level, but the little oratory was an attraction of its own, with people filing in and out silently. A Mass was being offered when I made my way inside and I decided to stay, as much for a rest as anything else. There is something very special about a Mass celebrated at a mountaintop.

I must have been there for at least fifteen minutes when I got a tap on the shoulder and to my amazement Tom the pilgrim was standing there, welcoming me to the top of Mayo's unique mountain. There had been no miraculous cure of the stricken shoe, but the sense of humour was still intact as he explained his surprise return: 'the thought hit me that you might tell everybody during the broadcast of the Connacht final that a Louisburgh man had turned back when halfway up Croagh Patrick.' I could not argue with that! It is my intention to 'do the Reek' again some time, preferably after Mayo wins the All-Ireland.

Tom was fond of racing of all kinds, with dogs and horses his particular favourites. We discovered that a local race meeting was taking place in Clifden one of the days I was in the west and as a gesture to 'diversion', of which I am a pupil, we made for the town. Before the meeting ended we had learned that it was even more difficult to pick winners in Clifden than it would have been any day in Saratoga Springs, but it was still most enjoyable, as local events usually are.

We did have one stroke of luck just before the last race, however. I had never seen a race like it at a meeting catering for horses, cobs and ponies: it was a motorbike race. The bikes were being warmed up and raced to the left, right and centre from the moment the horses left the stage after the last four-legged contest had been decided. Tom and I stood there in a quandary: how does one judge bikes and the 'jockeys' aboard with absolutely no form available? Just then, we were visited by Lady Luck. One of the bikes pulled up not far away from where we stood and the rider uttered the following words to an interested party who was obviously awaiting instructions: 'I have never sat on a bike like this before.' We had heard enough – *is leor nod don eolach* – and as the rider sped off, raising a cloud of dust, we could see the words 'The Black Eagle' written across his broad back. In less than a minute we were beside a bookie with 3-to-1 on offer on *The Eagle*, and he went on to win in the style of *Arkle* when he took his third Cheltenham Gold Cup in a row at the price of 20-to-1 ON!

The west is a wonderful place and the people who live there are infinitely better at coping with the absence of certain facilities than those who live on the High Streets of big towns and cities. I got a good example of that in Louisburgh one time, when Tom Bowe and I were discussing backing a certain horse. Somebody had told me there was no bookmaker in the town at that particular time, but Tom assured me there was no problem: 'the chemist will be going in to Castlebar or elsewhere and he will carry the money.' There was even a stand-by in case of emergency: the man who rang the Angelus bell was never one to see anybody stuck who wanted to have a flutter. This explains why visitors to the town were sometimes amazed upon witnessing the surge of pious fervour that was summoned by the opening three peals of the Angelus bell. That's organization for you!

# Joan O'Sullivan, the lady from Ballycroy, Co. Mayo

You meet GAA people everywhere and nobody would dare say that Mayo is an exception. Mayo people, and those from outside who settle there, are very interested in football as a rule – in that county the word means Gaelic football and nothing else. They are a sporting people and enjoy victory when it comes, but there is always the desire to win with panache and quality style. This is not easily accomplished, but the initial disappointment that defeat habitually nurtures withers quickly in Maigh Eo: followers are forgiving; they have an understanding nature and prefer to look forward to the next opportunity rather than lose faith and be miserable. There is a lot to be said for that attitude: when the fulfilment of the dream is realized, it makes it all the more memorable.

The truth of the matter is that Mayo teams rarely deserve being classified as 'bad', in fact they can be spectacular at times, but All-Ireland finals have not been kind to them over the past seventeen years. They have appeared in four since 1989, plus a replay in 1996, but have ended as losers each and every time. Still, it was good to see that the support was as strong as ever when they battled with Kerry for All-Ireland supremacy in September 2004.

I had been down to Mayo in the weeks leading up to that final and there was no shortage of people who believed their great hour was about to dawn. There was one lady supporter whom I did not meet on that round, so I rang her number on the Friday before the final to check whether she was travelling. I had met Joan O'Sullivan on several occasions in Mayo. She was a Myers from Kerry before marrying Michael O'Sullivan from the Spa area of Killarney and eventually settling in Ballycroy, in Mayo. There was no response to my first phone call on the Friday, nor to the second or third. As Joan was living alone in Ballycroy and in her ninety-third year, I was beginning to feel a little anxious. My worries proved unfounded, however, when the lady herself answered the phone call close to 9.30pm. She told me she was excited about the match, intended to travel on Sunday and had been in Castlebar all afternoon getting her hair styled for the big day. She had got two tickets from President Seán Kelly and had an interest in both sides: her sons had played for the county, Kieran at Minor and under-21 levels and Michael in all four grades; while both her father and brother had won All-Ireland medals with Kerry. We spoke for a good while and my parting words to her were: 'Sure, I might see you in Croke Park on Sunday.'

Final day came, as all days do, given time. Mayo lost yet again and for some time after the final whistle I was busy writing and recording reports, among all the other things that need attention on All-Ireland final days. The stands had more or less emptied by the time I was finished, but when I looked about me, who did I see down on the pitch looking all round only the lady with the hair styled for the occasion – the Ballycroy woman herself.

I made it down to the pitch as quickly as I could and was greeted in a most friendly way: 'You said you would meet me and there you are.' We spoke for a while about the ins and outs of the match, then Joan pulled a green, knitted cap with a gold string from her bag and told me that it was her father's cap and that he had always worn it when playing for Kerry 100 years earlier. I realized how significant that same knitted green cap was: her father, Jack Myers, was a member of the Kerry team that won the All-Ireland finals of 1903 and 1904 and had played on the very pitch where she was now standing and holding the cap he had worn. Her brother, Billy, had also played there and was a member of the Kerry teams that won the All-Ireland finals of 1937, 1939, 1940 and 1941. She also had further connections with the place as her twin sister, Nellie, was married to Dan Kavanagh, who had played at midfield for Galway against his native Kerry in the All-Ireland final of 1941, and in the same position against Dublin the following year before finally winning with Kerry in 1946.

Joan O'Sullivan was proud to be on that pitch and if ever anyone was entitled to be there that day, it was this woman who linked 102 All-Ireland finals with her father's green and gold cap.

As we were about to leave, I spotted Séamus Moynihan coming through the tunnel. The affable Glenflesk man had won his third All-Ireland medal that afternoon, and now he was headed for the entertainment sector via a short cut through Level 1 of the Hogan Stand. I called out to him and he joined us, and was delighted to meet Joan and hear her story. He asked her to remain there while he went off for a few minutes, which we did. When he returned he was not alone: the Sam Maguire Cup came with him, as did Jack O'Connor, the man who had managed Kerry to victory that day, and selector Johnny Cullotty, himself a winner of five All-Irelands with Kerry. Historic pictures were taken and the unexpected guests really made Joan's final visit to Croke Park.

Before we parted, she inquired if I had seen Nellie anywhere about that day, but I had not. It transpired that, due to other commitments, her twin had not travelled to Dublin that day, but she is still hale and hearty and living in Killarney with her husband, Dan Kavanagh, as sound a judge of a footballer as you would meet in any season of the year. Unfortunately, Joan passed away before the end of 2004 after a long and eventful life. She was the last survivor from the cast of a film called *The Dawn*, made by Tom Cooper in Killarney almost seventy years earlier. Her part was that of a courier on a bicycle and I am sure she played the role well, as did her granddaughter, Luzveminda O'Sullivan, in another role when selected as Rose of Tralee in 1998.

*Suaimhneas síoraí dá h-anam chaoin.*

# Margaret McConville of Crossmaglen

One often hears the phrase 'a GAA family', of which there are many, although sometimes it warrants further embellishment and thus becomes 'a great GAA family'. There are many of those, too, and to me the words describe families who have contributed in many different roles to the running of the GAA club in their community, as well as helping out on the broader front that the GAA encompasses. These men and women belong to the volunteer corps: they supply players, are to the fore whenever fundraising is undertaken, give a hand in coaching, help in ferrying about the under-age players, wash the jerseys, make the sandwiches, cut the grass, line the pitch, and so on and so on. For all this they are rightly regarded as the key element in the success story of the GAA. In short, their club's and the GAA's welfare become part of their lives.

When I made Armagh my first stop in Ulster after leaving the west of Ireland, I had no difficulty in locating a member of just such a family: Margaret McConville of Crossmaglen. It would be easy to find others like her in any corner of the land, people whose enthusiasm is always the same, regardless of location or background. Several members of the McConville clan have been associated with the famous Crossmaglen Rangers club, an association that goes back to the very early days of the last century. One finds the surname McConville in the club's ledgers dating back over 100 years and also the name of Morgan, which was Margaret's family name before 'joining' with the McConvilles. Her father James, better known as Jamesie, was a member of the 'Cross team from 1909 to 1923, and his brother Peter played for them as well. Jamesie was a blacksmith in 'Cross and in an era when there were no cars available to transport players, his horse and cart was often used for that purpose.

Margaret told me of an unusual incident that took place in Camlough during the half-time break in a match in which her father was playing. She thinks the year might have been 1909. A messenger came to the transport manager during the first half stating that the horse had just lost a shoe while grazing nearby. The blacksmith didn't panic, he calmly gave instructions to go to his coat, take some nails from the pocket and have them ready for half-time. This was duly done and when the appropriate resting time arrived, Jamesie went to his cart, got out his hammer and before the referee blew the whistle for the start of the second half, the side-show of Jamesie reinstalling the shoe on the horse's hoof was complete. There is a possibility that the blacksmith gave a 'man of the match' performance from then on.

They were different times. The first Friday of every month was the occasion for a horse fair in Crossmaglen, then a regular feature of Irish life for both rural and urban dwellers. It took a long time for motor transport to become the fashion, and until it did horses filled the roll admirably. Cars were so rare that in 1907 it was news worthy of finding its way into the papers when a car was spotted at a GAA match in Thurles, when Kildare beat Kerry for the All-Ireland title of 1905. The Morgans did not require any transport to reach the Rangers' ground, however, because their home was right next to it. There were eleven in the family and it was a proud day for them when Gene lined out at right fullback on the Armagh team that played against Kerry in the All-Ireland final of 1953.

I was at that final, but arrived late as I was required in Radio Éireann's studio in the GPO to give a ten-minute preview *as Gaeilge* before the start of the game 'up the road' in Croke Park. It was a hectic dash on my bike, but there was not a single traffic light or one-way street along the route in those days. My first glimpse of play was the red-haired Malachy McEvoy sweeping majestically towards the Railway end of the ground and scoring a goal for the Orchard County. Of course, I and every other person present remember the missed penalty by Armagh's Bill McCorry at a time in the second half when a goal would have put them

71

back in front. That is one of Margaret Morgan's lasting memories of the day, as is the sight of her brother Gene and the other Armagh players forming a circle around McCorry as they exited Croke Park later that evening. She was seventeen years of age at the time and would experience many more visits to the famous venue during a life that has never been far away from the GAA. Indeed, all the Morgans were involved: Gene played for Ulster and Ireland teams as well as for the 'Cross and Armagh, she herself played camogie and her sister Kathleen was good enough to line out with the county team.

Margaret married Patsy McConville, whose father, MJ, was the local chemist down the street. Appropriately, they first met in the local drama group when rehearsing a play as part of a fund-raising drive for the GAA club. The play in question was *Is the Priest at Home?* and within two years or thereabouts they were asking another priest to marry them.

Their eldest son, Thomas, died tragically in a drowning accident while attending Irish College in Loughanure, Co. Donegal, during the hot summer of 1976. 'He was a very promising footballer and in a way Patsy never got over the shock of the accident, but we had to carry on and do the best for the others as all families in similar circumstances have to do,' is the way Margaret recalled the tragedy. The 'others' in question were sons Jarlath, Jim, Seán and Oisín, along with daughters Anne, Máiréad and Doral.

In attempting to explain the extended McConville connection with the club, Margaret had this to say: 'we were no different to other families. It was easier for us as we lived close by the club, but a true love of the game was the real motivation – it was our life and everything centred round it.'

Her husband, Patsy, was goalkeeper on the team that won the county title in 1947 while Gene, her brother, was captain. Patsy played at fullback later in his career, but was back as goalkeeper on the winning team of 1960, of which Gene Larkin was captain. The late Gene was associated with the lengthy negotiations that went on at many levels to persuade the British Army to hand back portions of the club grounds, which had been commandeered during the 'Troubles'. Few people now know that the problem in relation to the occupation of St Oliver Plunkett Park first arose as far back as 1971, and took the best part of thirty years to settle. The dignified manner in which the Rangers pursued their objective of reclaiming their club property won them many admirers.

According to Margaret McConville, the club was continually planning and plotting improvements: no sooner were upgrades completed than they were fund-raising again for further measures. It is no wonder that the club has supplied a steady stream of stars to county teams down the years. They ran tournaments in the 1970s as fund-raising ventures and got good support from teams in places like Donaghmoyne, Iniskeen, Clontibret. It was a common sight to see people arriving into the 'Glen' on their bicycles, coats fluttering from the handlebars, on invigorating summer evenings.

Margaret got plenty of practice in sandwich-making in those days, doing all the cooking at home and bringing it along to the club to feed the members once the day's activities were over. Once her family had been reared and moved on, she had more time to devote to her favourite pastime and became secretary of the club in 1995:

It was the beginning of exciting times for football as the under-age structure was good, they had won an All-Ireland Under-13 Community Games title and the great Joe Kernan was then manager of the club senior team; they even trained on Christmas Day 1996 and I used to collect nettles and make soup for them.

In spite of the level of commitment, there was no way she or anybody else could have envisaged that Crossmaglen Rangers would go on from there to win ten consecutive Armagh county titles and bring the All-Ireland Andy Merrigan Cup to the club on three occasions. Margaret McConville has seen the impossible happen with her own eyes, and her sons Jarlath, Jim and Oisín played an important part. Jarlath was goalkeeper for five of the successes and the other pair played in all ten, with Oisín having the distinction of playing in every single game during the ten-year run of Armagh County titles.

The first of those All-Ireland titles came on St Patrick's Day 1997 when the 'Cross beat Knockmore of Mayo in the final: 'It was a great day for us, for the town, the club and the county, with all clubs rallying to the cause of Armagh,' says Margaret. 'We were very nervous and I remember Patsy's knees knocking off the seat in front of him.' She described her pride in the club and everybody who had helped and, naturally, in her own lads whose dedication and talent had brought reward:

In any photo ever taken of Jim when he was young, he had a football in his hands. He wore glasses then and once when in Newry for an appointment about his eyes, he remembered that he had left the glasses hanging at the goalpost at home. Oisín was the same and in the National Féile Peile for under-14s held in Galway, he and Damien Cunningham of An Ríocht shared the Skills Award with the perfect score of no miss from frees at varying distances from the centre to the sideline.

Is it any wonder that Oisín McConville has become one of the leading marksmen in modern-day football?

Further All-Ireland Club titles came in 1999 and 2000, which was no doubt what spurred the county team on to the same lofty plane before long. Joe Kernan, the goal-scoring midfielder on the team that reached the All-Ireland final of 1977, became Armagh manager for the 2002 championship. The All-Ireland final day of that year is one that will be remembered and recalled for ever and a day in the county of Armagh.

The Armagh team was facing Kerry in the All-Ireland final and the new Croke Park was awash with moving waves of incredible colour and heightening swells of excitement. Of course, Margaret was there; unfortunately her husband Patsy had died the previous year, but her daughters were there with her for a game that resounded with echoes of 1953. The same teams were on the field, but this time her son Oisín was replacing her brother Gene. Frank Kernan had been on that 1953 team, and now a Kernan from

74

another generation was out there as manager. Sure enough, Armagh were once again awarded a penalty at the same end of the ground, the Canal end, and no one breathed as memories of Bill McCorry rose before them. This time Oisín McConville was the kicker: different player, same outcome. Incredibly, just like 1953 no score came of it as Kerry goalkeeper Declan O'Keeffe saved from the ace marksman's effort:

I slumped in my seat, not fit to say anything, I sat there during half-time and wondered was Oisín going to be remembered for the next fifty years or more, like Bill McCorry, as the man who had missed the penalty against Kerry in the All-Ireland final of 2002. I remained seated and prayed to his father, Patsy, and before long the second half was underway.

That half told a different and wonderful story for Armagh people and many more besides. The most memorable All-Ireland final moment since Séamus Darby's winning goal for Offaly in 1982 came when Oisín McConville put the perfect finishing touch to a move started by goalkeeper Benny Tierney by driving the ball into the back of the Kerry net. The brilliant score diverted Sam Maguire from the rugged lands of Kerry to the Orchard county of Armagh for the first time in its history:

My daughters and all around were on their feet celebrating and calling on 'Mam' to get up also, but my legs refused. I stayed there and thanked God. I made no effort to join in the festivities on the pitch and waited until it was time to be heading out after experiencing the realization of a dream come true. On the way I met former GAA Presidents Jack Boothman, Seán McCague and Peter Quinn and they congratulated me. As in 1953 I met my brother Gene outside and the tears were tripping each other falling from his eyes. We hugged and talked and I thought again of 1953 when Gene and the others came out with that great sportsman Bill McCorry being protected in the middle. I met Oisín and the others at the banquet and we are enjoying the day from heaven since. I will soon be eighty years of age and Gerard Rushe has taken over as 'Cross secretary, but I am the assistant secretary.

As I was leaving the Armagh City Hotel, Margaret handed me a book entitled *The Crossmaglen GAA Story*. Right in the centre I found the official programme for the 1953 All-Ireland football final. In itself it is evidence of the vast improvements that have taken place over the past fifty years. The programme was small and simple, carrying only the minimum of information beyond the line-outs and the name of the referee, who was listed as P. Mac Diarmuda. There was no mention of his native or adopted county, but he was more widely known in the Gaelic world as Peter McDermott, a member of the Meath team that had won the All-Ireland four years earlier. The Cork-born forward went on to captain Meath when winning the All-Ireland final of 1954. The programme also listed the Artane Band's catalogue of music for the day, under the following solemn heading:

## THE ARTANE BAND WILL RENDER THE FOLLOWING SELECTIONS TO-DAY

1. Potpourri of Irish Marches
2. Selections from Balfe Operas
3. Sketch – Swanee River
4. Medley of Sousa Marches
5. Selections of Irish Melodies
6. Medley of Irish Marches

I wonder does Margaret remember the music of the day?

# Maurice Hayes of Co. Down

From Armagh it is east across to Co. Down, the North's mountainous county. Here it is that you'll find Downpatrick, traditionally said to be the burial place of Ireland's venerable patron saint. St Patrick was just the first famous name to be associated with the place; many more have been added in the course of its long history, among them 'Russell, the man from God knows where'. This was, of course, Thomas Russell, who was born near Mallow, in Co. Cork, in 1767 and became a leading member of the United Irishmen movement. He was active in the Belfast and Down area and was executed in Downpatrick in 1803.

Personally, I would place Maurice Hayes with any of the best of the people associated with Co. Down. Nowadays it is possible that people would be quicker to identify him with institutions like the National Forum on Europe, or the Community Relations Council of Northern Ireland, but his name was firmly set in the football context when I first met him, over fifty years ago. Then, he was a breath of fresh air sweeping over the great world of Gaelic football. The Mourne County was an unexpected quarter for change to issue from, but the successes of one of its finest teams have left a legacy that has not yet lost its influence.

Over the years we had many occasions to meet and I was delighted to meet him once more recently to talk about his part in the Down phenomenon. I had heard many a time and oft that he was one of the architects of the development of the county's first really good football team. Hayes has an interesting background, with a Waterford father and a Kerry mother:

My mother left Listowel in 1913 to work in Dublin, where she met her future husband and they were married by the time the 'Troubles' of that period broke out. He had joined the British Army and was soon sent on duty to Mesopotamia, quite a distance from either Waterford or Kerry. My mother then moved to Down and it was to that county that the man of the house returned when his army duties abroad came to an end.

Young Maurice was a Down man through and through, but the family maintained its connections with both Waterford and Kerry and both counties had an impact on his life. He is a fluent Irish speaker, having learned some at school and then improved it by visiting the Ring Gaeltacht in Waterford. Regular trips to Kerry nurtured a love of football, and it helped that a first cousin, Tony McAuliffe, played for Kerry in the 1930s and in the All-Ireland final of 1938 when Galway became the first team to beat Kerry in a replay.

I played minor football for Down in the 1940s, but for a while became more attached to hurling; I played at senior level with the county team and won county championships with Kilclief. I qualified as a teacher and my first job was in the De La Salle school in Downpatrick. I spent seven years there and my life took a different course when I was appointed Town Clerk of Downpatrick in 1955.

Maurice progressed from there to the responsible post of Chairman of the Community Relations Council of Northern Ireland, joined the Civil Service after the Sunningdale Agreement of 1973 and worked in the Department of Health until 1987. His experience made him an ideal choice for the post of Ombudsman and, later, as an appointee to the Patton Commission, which brought about acceptable changes in the difficult question of policing in Northern Ireland. Currently, Maurice Hayes is acting as Clerk to the National Forum on Europe and is a member of Seanad Éireann. By any man's standard he has made an enormous contribution to the public life of Northern Ireland, and indeed to the island of Ireland, but I have always found the vision he had for football in Down to be equally interesting.

Maurice became involved in GAA administration in 1948 when

he was appointed GAA secretary in East Down. By 1953 he was the assistant county secretary and from 1956 to 1964 he served as secretary of the county Board, momentous years for football in the county. Maurice and his fellow Board members worked hard during the 1950s in an effort to put better structures in place for football throughout the county: 'For a start, we felt there were too many teams competing in Leagues that were weak and there was a time when the entire county Board acted as selectors of county teams.' A Barony League was introduced in 1953, based on the Kerry system of divisional teams, and Maurice is of the opinion that this helped to raise standards.

He consulted regularly with Kerry trainer Dr Éamonn O'Sullivan and acknowledges the great help and advice he received from that man. He remembers clearly being advised of the necessity for a type of fitness that would ensure players were fresh for the big occasions, and also of the necessity to treat all players as individuals.

A major decision was taken during the 1954–5 season to pick a county panel of thirty players and experiment with winter training – a revolutionary idea at the time. Danny Flynn, a teacher in Banbridge who moved to a new school in Castlewellan in 1956, became the trainer, Barney Carr was manager with Brian Denvir and I acting as selectors. Dr Martin Walsh was appointed team doctor at a time when few counties provided such a service.

The plan was signalling success as the decade wore on. Past history told no great story: when Down qualified for the Ulster final of 1958, it was only their third time since the founding of the GAA seventy-four years earlier. Derry beat them in that final, but the secretary counselled that the team was making progress and perseverance and patience would bring rewards in time. They were prescient words: euphoria swept the county a year later when the Anglo-Celt Cup was brought home in glory, with a first Ulster senior title for the Red and Black-clad Mourne men. Maurice Hayes, the selector, remembers it well: 'It was a wonderful feeling for all concerned to see our county make that breakthrough because we had seen Tyrone win for the first time in 1956 and Derry two years later – Ulster was waking up.'

As so often happens, doldrums follow high points and there was disappointment for the followers when the team put up a poor display against Galway in the All-Ireland semi-final. I was in Croke Park that day and remember the seven-point defeat they suffered at the hands of the sturdy Galwegians. They still made an impression though, and the enthusiastic dash onto the field from the dressing room before the start of the game was something new. The game was not long in progress when Paddy Doherty swung a beautifully directed left-footed kick over the bar of the Railway goal from the left side of the field; within a few short years I had come to the conclusion that he was the best left-footed kicker I had ever seen. James McCartan was another who announced that day that he was no ordinary player. Placed at centre-back, he showed real battling spirit by going on sorties through the Galway defence late in the game when to many it seemed a lost cause. He showed the same mettle over the next two years, which eventually won him a Texaco Player of the Year Award, by which time McCartan was an outstanding centre-forward.

In spite of the result of that first championship game in Croke Park, the management trio considered that the team had taken a gigantic step forward. The following year put all that had gone before in the shade: six Down men won Railway Cup medals with Ulster on St Patrick's Day and one of them, Seán O'Neill, had the first of a record nine; Down beat All-Ireland champions Kerry in the semi-final of the National League in April; they beat Cavan in the final to win the county's first ever League title in May; they retained the Ulster title by defeating king-pins Cavan in the final in July; they beat Offaly in an All-Ireland semi-final in August that needed a replay; and the sweetest victory of all came in September when they beat Kerry by eight points in the All-Ireland final.

That 1960 All-Ireland final day is one that will never be forgotten in Co. Down, especially by those who were present to witness the football miracle being enacted. We knew they were good, but the quality of the win exceeded expectations; in fact, it all happened a year ahead of the plan.

The vision dreamed up by Maurice Hayes had become a reality: Sam Maguire was in the hands of captain Kevin Mussen and on its way to a historic trip across the border for the first time. A first final appearance had produced a title and that proud record stands to this day. Four more final appearances have seen them take the Sam Maguire Cup every time, beating Offaly in 1961, Kerry in 1968, Meath in 1991 and Cork in 1994. Statisticians await their next final appearance!

As a firm believer in planning for progress in sport, Maurice Hayes's views on the dominance of Ulster football in recent times are interesting. He is convinced that the 1994 ceasefire helped to get more people involved in sport, which involvement itself had a positive spin-off. Politics also helped in part to direct young people's minds towards aspects of Irish culture, and for the young there is nothing as attractive as play. He is in no doubt, however, about the greatest contributor to the upsurge in both interest and standards: that comes from the huge increase in the level of professionalism of coaching in schools, colleges and clubs through-out the province. 'The structures are good, the work is being done where it matters and with that background it is no wonder that the attitude on the playing fields is one of "no surrender".'

He notes the dominance of football in the third-level institutions and the number of graduates prominent either as players or as coaches throughout the province. 'It is a very satisfactory state of affairs,' was his overall comment on the current position of football in Ulster.

It is now almost fifty years since Maurice Hayes, the son of 'blow-ins', proclaimed that hard work and preparedness would one day bring an All-Ireland title to his native Down. The province has claimed ten titles since 1960 – 100 per cent more than had come in the preceding seventy-two years of All-Ireland championships. Ulster's successes should inspire those thirteen counties still seeking to get their names on the All-Ireland football Roll of Honour for the first time: Antrim, Fermanagh and Monaghan in Ulster; Sligo and Leitrim in Connacht; Clare and Waterford in the south; with Kilkenny, Carlow, Wicklow, Longford, Westmeath and Laois the envious of the east.

The more new teams that succeed in breaking down the barriers of tradition, the better for Gaelic Football. On that basis alone should there be an advisory committee established, under the chairmanship of a person of the stature of Maurice Hayes, with the aim of bringing forward a plan that would work like Down's did in the 1960s. It is true to say that the position of football in that county was lower in the mid-1950s than it currently is in most of the thirteen counties listed above. Croke Park now has a National Director of Hurling in Paudie Butler, so why not one for the big ball game as well, with a mission statement to bring all provinces up to the level of Ulster? After all, over the past fifteen years the Sam Maguire has been brought for the first time to four counties in Ulster: Donegal in 1992, Derry a year later, Armagh in 2002 and Tyrone in 2003.

It's a safe bet that the planners in all those counties were aware of how Maurice Hayes went about initiating a football revolution by the Mountains of Mourne almost a half-century ago. The real lesson from that success is that it can be achieved in any county, if a Mauricean Messiah emerges and is prepared to stay the course over the good days and the bad.

# Ken Whitaker and the Development of Ireland

The drive south from Co. Down is pleasant on the eye – past Carlingford, Dundalk and Drogheda. In moving about this country, one does not need to be vigilant to be aware of all the development that has taken place in the last decade or so. The roads are better, motorways are increasing in number, housing is better and industrial estates are mushrooming. At present, Irish society is writing a new chapter in its history as a nation. That history stretches far back into the mists of time, to tales I loved to hear from the time I was a boy. I had a voracious interest in the myths and legends, but one name in particular stayed with me from the accounts of the Norse era, that of Maolseachlann. He was an Irish king who pledged his support for Brian Ború in the Battle of Clontarf in 1014, even though they had crossed swords in the past. Maolseachlann's decision to throw in his army with that of the Dalcassian was seen as putting the national interest first against the invading Danes, a principle that was lauded in the history books.

The ability to put others first is not a natural human quality, but Ireland has been lucky to number many such individuals in its roll-call of influential people. These people have all played a part in pushing Ireland to fulfil its potential, in promoting a belief in Irish culture that has allowed us to progress onto the world stage in our own right. The twentieth century was a period of huge change in Ireland, and the people who fought – physically, economically or politically – for the country must be acknowledged and commemorated. Of all these stalwart souls, I would place Ken Whitaker, former Secretary of the Department of Finance, in the vanguard of those who initiated positive change in the State.

I first met Ken Whitaker at a Golf outing back in the 1950s. We were part of an Irish golf society, An Golf Cumann, the *raison d'être* of which was to combine a pleasant game of golf with socializing through the medium of the Irish language. Ken had achieved fame at the time as Secretary of the Department of Finance, and it added distinction to the society that he came among us. He wore neither airs nor graces, had the frame of a good midfielder and an amiable disposition that made everyone feel comfortable in his company. My guess would be that he won a prize on that golf outing, but memory can no longer confirm it.

I have met Ken on many occasions since then and he has remained the same cheerful and friendly person, in spite of all the wonderful achievements to his credit. The greatest of these were in the economic field, although his informal diplomatic accomplishments were also significant. As a former Cathaoirleach (chairman) of Bord na Gaeilge, I was very proud to count Ken among my predecessors – he was the first Cathaoirleach when the Bord was established in 1974. He is now in his ninetieth year and when I met him a few months ago to discuss some aspects of his life, I was delighted to find that he still possesses the same lively, sparkling mind as when first I encountered him all those years ago.

Ken was born in Rostrevor, in Co. Down, less than eight months after the Easter Rising of 1916 and a week ahead of Wexford's victory over Mayo in the All-Ireland football final in Croke Park.

My father was on the management staff of a small linen mill and when a post-war slump developed in the linen industry he moved to Drogheda in Co. Louth and to similar employment. I had begun my education in Rostrevor by then and one of my earliest memories is of being accompanied to school by Ben Dunne [Snr] who was later to found the empire known as Dunnes Stores. Ben, in his own quiet, anonymous way, became a generous sponsor of art in later life, occasionally on my suggestion.

From the age of six onwards the budding government official lived in Paradise Cottage, Drogheda, and received his education from the Christian Brothers. School was never meant to be Paradise in the early 1920s, but he has fond memories nonetheless, particularly of the scholarship he won and of the hurling he loved to play and for which he collected a Louth Minor Championship medal, though he is humble enough to suggest that he might only have been a sub – perhaps the original super sub! His life was not dominated by books and learning, as one might expect, and he recalls all the normal pastimes of his era: playing marbles, fishing for salmon, which is still a passion of his, and hunting. Drogheda also had facilities for the pursuit of cultural interests and it was there he developed a love of music, archaeology and the Irish language.

He was recruited to the Civil Service in 1934, just a little shy of his eighteenth birthday, and thus a remarkable career as a public servant got underway. He believed in study as the best means to prepare himself for the tasks ahead and that gained him early promotion to the ranks of executive officer, and then to assistant inspector of taxes. At the age of twenty years he was appointed private secretary to the Minister for Education, Tomás Ó Deirg.

His transfer to the Department of Finance in 1938 as an administrative officer would prove to be one of the most fateful decisions ever taken by the Civil Service. He was immediately committed to drafting memoranda for the government on the recommendations of the Banking Commission, the end result being the establishment of the Central Bank. Further study while still a full-time civil servant brought him the degrees of BSc (Econ.) and MSc (Econ.) from London University – 'I enjoyed studying and learning more about systems and how they operated' – and thus he was well equipped to deal with the responsibilities of his office when he reached the pinnacle as Secretary of the Department of Finance in 1956. Finance is the most important department in the system of government and when he was at its head Whitaker had clear ideas of how it should work in the interests of the State and the common good. He believed that 'decisiveness is a vital cog in planning progress' and stressed that point a few times during our meeting. It was one of the many qualities he admired in Taoiseach Seán Lemass, and it was to him he attributed the quote that the 'worst decision of all is the one not to take a decision'. To Whitaker, the man who succeeded Dev as Taoiseach 'was intelligent, he had integrity, he was open to new approaches, he was supportive and was an intellectual revolutionary rather than the stereotyped one'.

It had become clear to the Secretary and others before the mid-1950s that it was high time to change the old order of protection of industry through the tariff system and the other means that had been the norm for Irish industry up to then. As Minister for Industry and Commerce between 1932 and 1948, Lemass had been of the opinion since the end of the Second World War that the tariffs should be dismantled, but his department was not as convinced. The benefits of the old order were being promoted from the early days of Arthur Griffith and Sinn Féin. In seeking to secure government approval for his new approach, Whitaker made sure he was well versed in Griffith's *Resurrection of Hungary*, on which the protectionist theory was based and which harked back to the original apostle, Friedrich List.

The role of the Civil Service had always been an advisory one, and Whitaker's concept of it was that it should be unbiased and that Ministers should be held in great respect regardless of personal relations. In 1958 he produced a document that was to have a profound influence on the development that has taken place in Ireland over the past fifty years, allowing for periodic bouts of economic depression. The report was simply called *Economic Development* and while Ken is regarded as the architect, he insists it was the result of a group brought together for the specific purpose: Charlie Murray, John Leydon, Paddy Lynch, Lieutenant-General Michael Costelloe, Louden Ryan and some others.

In many ways it was a revolutionary document, advocating investment as the way forward and a departure from the old self-sufficiency policy based on protectionism. Ken wrote to Jim Ryan, Minister for Finance, 'looking for a blessing, which I got, and he proceeded to carry it out diligently'. The government subsequently published its New Programme for Economic Expansion and, strangely, in light of the massive launches that

86

feature in modern times, Whitaker recalls that there was 'not even a debate in the Dáil'.

The documents received a lot of attention from industrialists, however, and I recall excitement in certain quarters in UCD, to whom new terms like 'Free Trade' and 'economic efficiency' were appealing. According to Ken, it was time to acknowledge that massive changes were required if there was to be a place for Ireland in the new Europe that was emerging from the ashes of two World Wars. He had the foresight to understand that a successful economic future for Ireland depended on it being part of the European Economic Community (EEC); there were just six Member States at that time. 'We saw the overdependence of the Irish economy on agriculture and the English market and realized that, without a change of outlook, there did not appear to be any gap into Europe.'

It was not a simple matter of joining up, however, as lots of people and government departments needed to be convinced. Whitaker describes the period of 1958–9 as 'the Dark Night of the Soul' and he remembers a spirited correspondence carried on between himself and the Department of Industry and Commerce (those letters might, in fact, be published shortly by An Foras Riaracháin). Meanwhile, teams headed by people like Louden Ryan went to industrialists and explained the need for change and the benefits that would flow from free trade. It was described how grants for the restructuring of industry would be put in place to prepare for the new challenge, a proposal that was very appealing to those in industry. The EEC was attractive to the government because of its market potential for efficient industry and, above all, because it had a support system for agriculture through the Common Agricultural Policy (CAP). Therefore, when Britain applied for membership in 1961, Seán Lemass, on the advice of the Department of Finance, did likewise on behalf of Ireland. Whitaker recalls, 'But Charles de Gaulle vetoed matters, as was within his rights, and the enterprise was shelved temporarily.' According to Whitaker, while De Gaulle's stance might be regarded as 'unreasonable', he understood there was slightly more to it than a legacy of past conflicts with Britain and that the famous Frenchman held to the belief that post-war Europe would be a better place by having a new bloc between the Anglo-Saxon and the Russian-Eastern blocs.

The possibility of entering Europe was raised again a few years later, when it was decided that Jack Lynch, Charlie Haughey, Ken Whitaker and the appropriate ambassador would visit the heads of state of all EEC countries. It was serious stuff no doubt, but Ken is never averse to seeing the funny side of events, especially when matters might not be going as smoothly as hoped. He recalled being a delegate at the Paris meeting and as an example of De Gaulle's unique character, he described his reply to Charlie Haughey's comment that it must be hard to govern a country that produces four hundred varieties of cheese. De Gaulle looked at Haughey and said, 'Three hundred and ninety'!

'President Pompidou was sitting next to me at the same meeting and his main interest at the time was to find out the difference between rugby and Gaelic football, which I gladly explained in French.' The meeting had an unusual ending insofar as, at De Gaulle's request, the French president met all members of the delegation individually. Whitaker's dialogue with him was carried out in French, without the presence of an interpreter.

Time moved on and the day came in 1973 when Ireland was admitted as a full member of the EEC, by which time there had been a major shift in attitude towards the future of the Irish economy. Whitaker's *Economic Development* and the government's acceptance of its principles were the key elements in powering on ambition for efficiency and a new confidence in Ireland's ability to be a player on the international stage. Those traits have lived on and provided the platform for the country's recent fantastic progress. I believe that the greatest portion of the credit for bringing this about belongs to Ken Whitaker; I would therefore place him at midfield, with Brendan O'Regan, on my Allstar team of progressive, practical visionaries.

This extraordinary man from Co. Down was by no means a single-issue intellectual entrepreneur, however. As early as 1957 it fell to this accomplished and rational negotiator to arrange terms for Ireland's entry into the International Monetary Fund (IMF) and the World Bank. He recalls that many of the trips made during those negotiations were by liner from Cobh across the Atlantic, and it was during one such trip that he met Terence O'Neill, leader of the Northern Ireland government, for the first time. Meetings between the two governments arose from that contact, and in January 1965 Whitaker accompanied Seán Lemass on the historic first visit by an Irish Taoiseach to the parliament at Stormont. Great secrecy surrounded the arrangements, so much so that the Garda officer appointed to drive Whitaker and Lemass had no knowledge of the destination until Seán Lemass uttered the words, 'Belfast, Henry', in his inimitable voice. As a rule, Lemass had no time for 'small talk' and the topic under debate as far as the border was 'the separation of powers as in the American Constitution'. The tone changed, however, once they were joined by Jim Malley, private secretary to Terence O'Neill and a man decorated for Distinguished Service to the Airforce during the war. For the remainder of the journey it was poker, horses and Conamara ponies.

The meeting with O'Neill was cordial and the Northern Prime Minister even displayed the label on the bottle of wine being opened, the name of which made everyone smile: Chateauneuf du Pape. O'Neill had not given advance notice of the meeting to anybody in the North and there is a story told about a remark he made to Lemass during a break in consultations. His mind more or less gazed into the future and he wondered, 'which of us will suffer the most?' He was obviously thinking about all the possible reactions and repercussions of their unprecedented meeting.

Taoiseach Jack Lynch paid a visit to the North in 1967 and Terence O'Neill repaid the compliment in Dublin, so there were hopes at the time that a new era of understanding was about to dawn. As a northerner himself, Whitaker had a good knowledge of the views and aspirations of opposing factions in the complicated history of Northern politics. His philosophy in relation to solving the problems was akin to that of Daniel O'Connell or Thomas

Davis: the pen, or word, directed by reason offered the only hope of bringing together people who held divergent views. Later he worked hard, often in the background in troubled times, to get that principle accepted all round.

A seemingly harmless incident took place during Jack Lynch's 1967 visit that foreshadowed later attempts to derail the peace process. There had been a heavy snowfall that year and snow was still banked up around the statue of Sir Edward Carson at the front entrance to Stormont. He is regarded as the father of modern Unionism, although he was also reputed to have been a member of the Trinity College hurling club during his student years there. As the Taoiseach and Ken Whitaker stepped out of their car that cold, snowy day in 1967, they saw two black-clad figures next to the memorial. For Whitaker, it brought to mind the saga of the Táin Bó Cuailgne and the legendary fight over the brown bull from the Cooley Mountains. He soon realized this was another kind of fight: one of the warriors was the Reverend Ian Paisley, armed with snowballs and roaring 'No Pope Here'. Whitaker remembers that 'Jack Lynch was not overly upset and casually asked me which "of us" did the Rev Paisley imagine was Pope.'

Two years later another difficult assignment was handed to Whitaker, now thirty-five years in public service. This time he was appointed Governor of the Central Bank of Ireland. This new position had a link with his first role in the Department of Finance, where he was asked to prepare a memorandum for the government on the recommendations of the Banking Commission. As mentioned, that report led to the founding of the Central Bank, so he was in a better position than most to appreciate its role in the economy. He approached it with the same principles that had governed his entire career, believing that civil servants had a duty to provide an excellent service to the public and to deliver that service in an impartial manner. He spent seven years as Governor and his advice and contributions to key financial policy were always valued, even if they were not acted upon as often as a Governor would have wished.

I have touched on just a few of Ken Whitaker's contributions

With John
Moriarty, the
Aborigine from
Borroloola.

Archbishop Mundy
Prendiville.

A quiet commemoration at Archbishop Mundy Prendiville's grave.
From left to right: Micheál and Kerry footballers Eoin Brosnan, Colm Cooper and
Tomás Ó Sé, with Seán Kelly, former President of the GAA, standing behind the Kerry flag.

The redoubtable
Charles Yelverton
O'Connor.

Charles Yelverton O'Connor's pipeline under construction.

Brendan O'Regan, the man
who will forever be associated
with Shannon Airport.

A GAA stalwart: Mrs McConville of Armagh
with her late husband, Paddy.

A memorable meeting with the doughty Dan Keating.

Mike 'Iron Man' Murphy:
the man who drank cow's
blood for strength!

(Photo courtesy of *The Kerryman*)

A rare image of the three Ring brothers together, on a cruiser bound
for America. From left: Christy, Paddy Joe and Willie.

Dedication doesn't come any greater than this: a spectator and his dog who haven't missed a match in decades.

On St Stephen's Day, the Wran is celebrated in Dingle with great fun and festivities: as you can see, everyone gets caught up in it!

Betsie Konink and Irene Brune (*left*), the women behind Dún Síon's Camphill Community.

Diarmuid O'Connell of Tigh an Oileáin.

Paddy Ó Cinnéide, Micheál and Kerry Captain Dara Ó Cinnéide with Sam at the top of Mount Brandon.

John Moriarty: writer, philosopher, traveller, gardener – and an inspiring man.

(Photo: Don MacMonagle, Killarney)

to the life of this country, in a public career stretching over seventy years. He was in demand as a valued member of several commissions and inquiries, often as Chairman, and served as a member of many institutions, including President of the Royal Irish Academy, President of the Economic and Social Research Institute and Chairman of the Dublin Institute for Advanced Studies. Following his retirement at the age of sixty, he served as a Senator in Oireachtas Éireann and as Chancellor of the National University of Ireland during a period of unprecedented growth.

I have already referred to the fact that he was the first Chairman of Bord na Gaeilge and held the position from 1974 to 1978. His deep attachment to the native language began under the guidance of Peadar Mac Anna in the Christian Brothers School in Drogheda. Enthusiasm was strong enough to drive him, and others, to research the remaining traces of Irish in the town and its surroundings.

A scholarship won at a local *Féis* brought me to the Donegal Gaeltacht, where a new world opened up for me, a world that is part of my life to the present day. I believe my life would have been infinitely poorer without my involvement in all aspects of the Irish heritage.

Long before his involvement in Bord na Gaeilge, Whitaker was the person invited to draft a White Paper on the Restoration of the Irish Language. One of its findings recommended a new approach and the objective of bilingualism; another expressed the opinion than no Irish child would receive a proper education without knowledge of the Irish language. Later, his term as Cathaoirleach was a fruitful one. While nominees to Bord na Gaeilge were made by the government of the day, there was a tradition that people did not bring their politics to the discussion table nor allow them to influence policy. That was how I found it during my tenure there and I would give the credit to the first chairman for laying down good practice.

What does Ken Whitaker think of the Ireland of today, which owes so much to his ideas, promptings and methods as laid down in his 1958 *Economic Development* report? It is typical of him that he delights in the many positive changes that have come about, changes which trip off his tongue in a litany of commendable advances:

He is glad of the increased prosperity for so many;
he admires the progress made thus far;
he has seen the population grow from 2.8 million to 4.2 million, and still rising;
emigration has been transformed to immigration;
the average rate of mortality has been increased by fifteen years since 1930;
there have been immense and measurable improvements in education;
one in seventeen of his own generation went on to third-level; that ratio now is one in two;
the youth of today are competent and confident and able to realize their potential to a far greater degree;
he is impressed and delighted with the response and dedication of the young to good causes;
finally, he believes the future looks positive if we sustain a proper blend of education, guidance and common sense.

On the downside, the high incidence of binge-drinking and drug-taking among sections of society, particularly the young, worries him greatly, as does the apparent rise in suicides among young people. He would like to see that trend arrested and hopes that appropriate steps will be taken.

Ken Whitaker, a visionary who has seen many of his dreams realized, has been honoured in many ways during his long life. He holds honorary degrees from five different universities, and the French government honoured him by admitting him as a Commandeur of the Légion d'Honneur. Now in his ninetieth year he remains the eternal student, and long may it last. Ken Whitaker is my greatest hero in the history of Ireland. What a pity he has never been President.

# Sports facilities

Leaving Ken Whitaker's Paradise Cottage in Drogheda, the old Drogheda–Dublin road is quiet, no longer being used so much anymore as the new motorway whisks you quickly into Dublin. Long, straight roads make for a wandering mind, and as I made my way towards the capital city I found my own contemplating the various stadia I have been in over the years. Whenever I am abroad I always try to go along to see what sporting facilities are available in the different countries. The medium of television means that most people are familiar with leading venues, such as the Millennium Stadium in Cardiff, Murrayfield in Scotland, Old Trafford in Manchester, Stade de France in Paris, and so on. I have been to a few of them and others further afield, and it is natural to make comparisons with Croke Park. In doing so, it is necessary to divorce atmosphere from the judging process because only aficionados of the sports habitually played at a venue can best measure that essential element. That aside, I believe the facilities in Jones's Road top the list as things stand right now.

I had occasion to visit one of Germany's best stadia when on a visit to that country towards the end of 2005. There was great rejoicing in North Rhineland at the time because it was known that Arena Veltins was to be a venue for some of the games in the 2006 World Cup soccer finals. The Arena is situated in the city of Gelsenkirchen, Westphalia, within easy reach of Essen, where I was staying with my daughter Niamh, her husband George and grandchildren Leonidas and Micheál Óg. The stadium is magnificently modern and was opened officially in 2001 and is owned by FC Schalke 04, a soccer club of great renown. The stadium name was visible from afar, but I soon learned that Veltins had a different status from Croke, Semple, Pearse, McHale, Casement, Oliver Plunkett and the many other names familiar to followers of Gaelic games at home in Ireland. I questioned the guide regarding the name 'Arena Veltins', which elicited the information that it represented a beer company that was willing to pay €5 million annually for the privilege. Once more I wondered about the possibility of such a custom catching on in an ever-changing and more materialistic Ireland. It would be a pity if it ever sank to that level, but a figure with a few noughts added on has been known to dazzle even the most devoted idealist in the past.

The next facet of Arena Veltins that came to my notice was the playing pitch itself. To my surprise, I saw it at close range even before entering the Arena: this was not by any sort of magic, in fact I mistook it for an absolutely perfect training ground adjacent to the stadium. Once inside though, it dawned on me that the lawn-like green carpet of grass sitting atop the 6ft-deep rectangle of clay that I had seen outside was the real playing pitch. The guide explained it all in simple terms: 'You see little rails down there? The pitch can be moved in and out electronically underneath the stand any time we like to give it more air or sunshine.'

The guide was a walking encyclopaedia of statistics, one of the most interesting being that the mobile pitch weighed 11,000 tons; thank God for the gifts of electricity and engineering when it comes to moving it! The capacity of the arena is 61,524 spectators in the case of club fixtures, reduced to 53,975 for international events. The reason for this is that for the regular events, like club football, there is standing accommodation for some 18,000 spectators, with 15,000 of them shoe-horned into an area just like Croke Park's 'Hill 16', close to one of the goals. I was surprised that a modern soccer stadium in Europe would provide standing accommodation, so I asked the helpful guide for the reason. I must say that my admiration for FC Schalke 04 rocketed with the forthright reply: 'We believe in capitalism and want to cater for fan culture.' I think he meant tradition, but capitalism was one of his favourite words.

The concept of commercialism dominated the guide's commentary as we moved along: we were told about the several kilometres of piping that sluiced beer to several bar outlets placed strategically throughout the stadium; of the many food stands and the fact that there were no restrictions as to where food could be consumed; the same applied to smoking, which disappointed me because I believe all sporting venues should be smoke-free zones; finally we heard about the retractable roof, which I couldn't help thinking adds to the potential damage from smoke because it is closed during some events. At this point I mentioned the custom that was observed in Ireland's main stadium in relation to such matters. Once more his reply included the words 'but we believe in capitalism', and this time I figured out that the word signified freedom of choice and we were both quite happy to leave it at that and continued onwards again.

The multi-purpose arena cost €191 million, raised entirely from the private sector, and since its opening in 2001 it has been used for concerts of all sorts from rock to classical, musicals, boxing promotions, tennis tournaments, conventions, shareholders' meetings, car racing and many weddings – although it has yet to draw a 'full house' for a marriage. A church is included as part of the facilities in the lower deck and the learned guide solemnly informed us that it is willing to serve all gods, without question. The fittings are mostly of marble and special furnishings for the nuptials can be provided on request. I could see Croke Park entering the wedding market before long – and it might not be a bad idea at all! There is space underneath the stands where a church could be built and just consider the opportunities for photographs, spots like the Hill, the Davin Goal, the Media Centre, or the plush Árd Comhairle Square.

Of course, Arena Veltins has a plethora of corporate boxes, most not as luxurious as Croke Park's it has to be said, but its dressing rooms come out on top on account of the amount of training equipment available. Each room has weights, a cooling pool and ice box, which are very popular with players 'warming down' after a game.

The media centre has all the required conveniences, plus a large interview room close to the dressing rooms. This area incorporates a museum that, understandably, focuses on the history of FC

Schalke 04. I must say, though, Croke Park's Museum is infinitely more elaborate and superior in terms of quantity, variety and sometimes quality. The Germans have included a nice gesture to tradition and local history, however: the stadium is built on a site that was once part of a vast coalmine that contributed to the German Industrial Revolution in the famed Ruhr Valley. In acknowledgement of this, one of the museum's exhibits is a large consignment of coal held together within a rectangle of strong mesh wire. I liked the idea and look forward to the time when the Croke Park Museum displays a mesh container filled with stones from the debris of Hill 16, which was razed to the ground not so long ago – of course, the foundation for the old Hill was the rubble brought from O'Connell Street after the Rising of 1916.

I enjoyed my visit to Arena Veltins and it made me curious about other venues in Deutschland; I am sure there are several spectacular ones waiting to be explored when next I find myself rambling between the Rhine and the Danube.

# Changing scenes in all worlds

Dublin's outward spread is making 'suburbs' of far-flung places, like Drogheda. The new M1 motorway brings you into the city and to a Dublin that has changed remarkably over the course of the Celtic Tiger years. Croke Park itself is a perfect example of steady change – even the 'park', or playing surface, fits the bill: it is now watered automatically and in the event of the soil getting too wet, there is a mechanism in place that alerts a computer that in turn triggers the extraction of the excess water. It has been called into action only once, as far as I can remember, on that evening of teeming rain in 2002 when the Australian Rules players were embroiled in a Test match with Ireland's best Gaelic footballers.

These new innovations mean we will never again see the surface turn brown, as it did during the fine summers of yesteryear when groundsman and Corkman Con Ó Laoghaire was often at his wits' end in his endeavours to soften it up. It was no easy task because in times of real drought, or in anticipation of same, Dublin Corporation banned the watering of lawns and parks in order to preserve supplies. Con was never a man short of ideas, however, and once, in a real emergency, he put to use the water in the canal beyond the southern terrace. He told me about his plans and, true enough, before long he had huge lengths of hose pipe stretched all over Croke Park and attached to a pump by the side of Brendan Behan's Royal Canal. I can bear testament to the result of his brainwave and the fact that I have never seen a happier man that Con as he watched the water gush forth. The pump was a powerful contraption, and you can imagine the look on Con's face when one day a few eels were catapulted out of the hose end and started to wriggle a foreign dance on the sacred brown sod of Croke Park on a sunny summer's day!

Watering became easier for Con a few years later when a diviner discovered a water source at the angle of the pitch and Hill 16. A well was sunk and the supply of fine water was more than adequate – until the arrival of the computer water. For all I know, that well is still functional. By the way, Con's eels were not the only creatures to have frolicked on the grasses of Croke Park. Joe Rock, who worked there at various jobs from time to time, told me once that a previous groundsman, Chicky Curran, had kept hens and chickens in a coop there and the whole Park became their playing, picking and pecking place on weekdays. They were not always alone either because a pony was used to pull a little grass mower and once his chore was completed, what better place to let it recover than the fine open expanse of green field between canal and railway.

Joe Rock lives nearby and has enjoyed a lifelong association with the historic venue where his father, 'Mr Rock', was responsible for preparing the footballs used in big matches played there. He had his own ritual of pumping and testing before the high-point of the pre-match ceremony on All-Ireland final day, when he would march out to the centre of the field, wearing a majestic bowler hat, and present the football to the referee. I recall some of those stately walks and I think it is a pity to see those little cameos of pageantry removed from the proceedings. Bring back the hard hats and swallowtail coats and dispense with the bibs – except when absolutely essential!

Security is a great consideration these days, ushered in by raids that successfully deprived Semple Stadium and, once, Casement Park of their gate receipts. I was broadcasting in Belfast's Casement Park when the raid took place and was amazed to hear a public announcement to that effect. It was stranger still when the 'news' was greeted by a loud cheer from some of the spectators.

In earlier days there was no need for security, according to Joe Rock, whose first job there was picking up the orange and lemon peels dropped on the grass by the players at half-time. He was eight years old at the time, but soon progressed to a job in the dressing room, and so on. He told me that he often left the takings from his stile area underneath a stone overnight, never once worrying that the cash might be gone when he returned in the morning to bring it along to the office; he was never disappointed. Now in his eighties, he is delighted with the changes about the place since he first starting working there over seventy years ago. Many more of his family did so as well and some of the tribe have played there: Barney Rock was a regular member of the Dublin team from the early 1980s and scored many a fine goal there, also winning an All-Ireland medal on that hallowed ground in 1983. It is good to see a member of another generation of Rocks back in Croke Park and, who knows, I might soon be talking on radio about Dean Rock, Barney's son, playing in the blue of Dublin.

# Fine sporting traditions

My annual sporting rambles in Ireland begin with Féile Bríde in the month of February. I have broadcast from venues in all counties of Ireland over the years, but naturally would have a special *grá* for Croke Park, where I began my career on St Patrick's Day, 1949. The media area as it now looks bears no resemblance to what was there when I began. At that time the broadcasting box, or 'Micheál Ó Hehir's box' as it was generally known, stood in isolation on the Hogan Stand side of the ground, between two stands that were surrendered to progress in 1959 when the New Hogan rose to the skies and arched from one end of the ground to the other. The print media were accommodated on the Cusack Stand during that era. I would rate that old broadcasting box as a satisfactory and practical one: it was sufficiently high to give a clear, unobstructed view of the pitch and had a large window that could be opened as required.

Recalling that box now reminds me of the changes that have taken place in work practices over the years. In my early days three people made up the entire team on location for a broadcast, namely a commentator, a Radio Éireann technician who supplied and rigged up the equipment, and a technician from the Department of Posts and Telegraphs who would have installed the broadcast line earlier but came along on the day just in case any problems arose. As a system it worked admirably. The first adjustment came with the withdrawal of the Post Office representative. Rationaliz-ation, as it was called later, was taking hold. The lines were installed as usual, but henceforth there was no presence from the supplier of the line should anything in that department go wrong during the broadcast. There were 'teething problems', of course, and I remember being at a match in Navan once when, despite the best efforts of the RTÉ technician, we failed entirely to make contact with the outside world.

The operation has been revised further since that day in Navan and now quite a lot of outside broadcasting is done without the presence of any technician. Permanent lines have been installed at many venues, so the commentator simply brings along his broadcasting equipment and it is a simple task to establish contact with base. The new system works and enables RTÉ to cover more venues, although thankfully there is still a team of excellent technicians on the RTÉ staff, a few of whom would be on duty over most weekends, which lends assurance all round.

I once encountered an unforeseen problem with one of those self-operated units, which was the cause of me being locked into Croke Park late one autumn evening in the 'swinging sixties'. The match had long since ended, but I was waiting to do a report for a later programme. The arrival of a squadron of seagulls was welcome as it broke the eerie sound of silence as I wrote the report and waited for my broadcast slot. Sunday matches in Croke Park are vital for the survival of northside seagulls because schoolyards are bereft of food scraps over the weekend, so all they really have is Croke Park, Tolka Park and Dalymount. The squabbling and screaming of the land gulls provided entertainment until report time, after which I was glad to head for home. It was then I realized that every door, big and small, was locked tight as a tomb; at that time, the mobile phone was not even in marketing plans. So it was back up to the box with me, connecting lines once more and hoping against hope there would be a voice at the other end. Fortunately there was, that of the reliable Ian Corr, and I breathed a sigh of relief to know that the strategy for my release was now in the hands of a man with a mind trained for strategizing. It took quite some time though, more seagull dramatics and the Gardaí in Fitzgibbon Street before eventually someone was found who had a key to the problem.

On completion of the Hogan Stand in September 1959 all media moved into it, but the new box did not have the presence of the old. It was poorly designed, a little cramped and the gangway leading to it appeared unsafe to those who had never learned how to move about in a small boat. The view it afforded of the pitch was fantastic, however, and that was all that mattered. I had the privilege of broadcasting many hectic matches from there before it too suffered the ignominy of destruction as a prelude to the creation of the modern 'New Hogan Stand'. That edifice incorporates a vast open-plan media area that is comparable to that in any sporting arena in the world. I think it is fitting that it is now known as the Micheál Ó Hehir Media Centre. It is located in a central position in the upper deck of the Hogan, from where the view is brilliant, there are plenty of broadcast berths, monitors and equipment are supplied, the print media are close by but out of earshot, phone, fax and internet access facilities are provided, there is a food outlet where the kettle is always on the boil and, finally, there is a special media elevator that whisks occupants from ground level to upper deck in three seconds flat. Not bad, even for 2006, although we can be certain that the wonder of our age will one day be deemed old-fashioned, out of date and, like its predecessors, fit only for the battering-ram.

All in all, I have worked from five different locations in Croke Park: the three 'official' spots I have described and two emergency 'wards' in use while the respective Hogan Stands of 1959 and 2002 were being constructed. Of all the games I have commentated on, I will never forget the Railway Cup final of 1958. Most of the concrete work for the seating on the Hogan Stand was complete, but naturally it remained out of bounds to all but the Radio Éireann crew and a lone garda on duty. There was neither table nor seat nor chair, only the bare concrete still sickly white in colour. Nothing on earth is as cold as concrete, and on a freezing March day with a cutting breeze coming in from the north-east there was no way I could be tempted to sit down on it. So like those celebrating the Jewish Passover, I stood for the entire broadcast of the first match on the programme that day. I am normally immune to a certain degree of cold, but that St Patrick's Day surely went beyond the limit and I really envied those on the field who could keep moving about.

A different type of problem arose during the second Railway Cup final, broadcast by Leo Nealon who did quite a bit of commentating in those years. It must have got colder still because before long Leo's eyes 'watered up', which made it difficult for him to identify players. It was nightmarish for a while, but I was able to shelter him whenever the ball came to the Canal side of the ground. Every time it was cleared towards the northern end we had to devise another solution, but between sign language and other means of communication the story of that match reached the public, and we both wished Dan McInerney God-speed with the remainder of the work on the stand and, of course, the new box.

My second spell in exile was far more pleasant and lasted for the duration of the construction of the New Hogan Stand. The western side of the ground, close to Jones's Road, was completely out of bounds for safety reasons. RTÉ's corporate box on the Cusack Stand became the new broadcasting zone, or rather the seats in the open area allotted with the box. The view was perfect, hospitality before and after the games was excellent, with Tom Quinn usually acting as host, but the working area was not ideal from the point of view of spectators, who had to endure the annoyance of commentators at full tilt from start to finish of the matches. But everybody understood that we were living through an emergency and it would not be long before the normal serenity would descend on the Cusack once more.

We have all heard commentators speak of 'matches of two halves' in various debates, discussions or relays, but I have a story that tells of the wisdom of ignoring the events of the first half until the second is truly over. It concerns the 2000 Leinster football final between Kildare and Dublin. I had obtained tickets for two friends of mine, who were very loyal Dub supporters. Dublin played brilliantly during the first half and went in for the half-time rest, oranges and peptalk to a fantastic chorus of cheers from the multitudes in blue. I went for a quick stroll at the back of the stand, where I happened upon the pair to whom I had given the tickets and even without a word from them I could feel their joy and great satisfaction. We had time for a few brief words, but before I left they asked me was there any possibility of getting the very same 'lucky seats' for the All-Ireland semi-final when Dublin would be playing Galway.

I admired their loyalty, but their optimism died an extremely sudden death almost before the second-half got underway, when Kildare banged in two goals in rapid succession that laid the foundation of a recovery that won them the title. We even 'missed' those goals on radio as the last advertisement in the commercial break was being broadcast at the time from the studio in Donnybrook. I have never asked the lads if they attended the All-Ireland semi-final between Kildare and Galway, but if they did, I received no request for those 'lucky' tickets.

# All is changed and the pace of change will accelerate

At the GAA's 2005 Congress an historic decision was taken to make Croke Park available for playing soccer and rugby, on certain conditions. The media swooped on the story like those hungry gulls and the pros and cons provided material for a fine debate, which is to be welcomed in the spirit that all individuals are entitled to hold their own opinions. Fears were expressed that it would lead to deep division within the ranks of the GAA and that overall the result of opening up Croke Park would prove to be detrimental. Of course, that will have to be judged by a long-term yardstick, but division was never likely to occur as the people on both sides of the argument were actively involved together in the day-to-day running of the sports and fully committed to a democratic decision-making process.

Prior to this, I had often expressed the opinion that 'opening up Croke Park' was desirable. It is a magnificent stadium, one of which we are all very proud, and the more exposure it gets on a worldwide scale, the better for our country. I have even heard people who have never set foot there boasting about 'our' fine sporting facility, with the emphasis on the adjective meaning Ireland's. I see nothing wrong with that.

My reasons for being in favour of the change are partly influenced by examples from history. For several centuries, dating back to the sixth century AD, Irish scholars and monks went abroad to bring something they considered to be of great value to people in other countries. The gifts they doled out in exile concerned Christianity in the broader sense, learning and spirituality. In essence, they were sharing what they had with others and I think great good came from the efforts of such men, like St Colmcille, St Gall and the many others.

Colmcille was, of course, banished from Ireland almost 1,500 years ago. He didn't put his head in his hands and weep, however; he established a wonderful community on the island of Iona, off the western coast of Scotland. I visited Iona in the mid-1990s and found it a fascinating place, with the restored ruins of bygone glory proving a source of great curiosity for all visitors. There was a little bit of extra excitement when it was noticed that a cordon was being erected hurriedly around a small area, close to where I was standing. I drifted towards the spot and a friendly archaeologist informed me that a dig had led to the discovery of some skeletons, about which they were highly elated. I thought at that moment of the pioneering Donegal man, Colmcille himself, born in Gartan in 597 AD, and I wondered about the possibility of an imminent announcement stating that his remains had been discovered. Some years have passed and I am still waiting for the bulletin.

Back to the fortunes of Croke Park! I believe that by allowing soccer and rugby to be played there, the greater exposure it will attract on TV screens around the world will play a part in the further development of an industry that has become such a vital part of our economy – tourism. In 2005 I went to Australia with the Ireland team for Compromise Rules Test, to Boston for the Interprovincial hurling final and to Singapore for the tour of the hurling Allstars of 2004 and 2005. During my stays in those places I met thousands of Irish people and if there was one common theme to their conversations, it was the pride they had in the progress being made in modern Ireland. The image and concept of Croke Park figured prominently when it came to sport, and I have no hesitation in saying that the citizens of those places would love to be able to see the stadium for themselves, even if it is only via television. Many of the people I met in Singapore had had that experience because during the Allstars tour the local Singapore Gaelic Lions acquired promotional footage of some big hurling matches back home. The ESPN Channel News Asia broadcast those images to a potential audience of 450 million viewers throughout Asia, and even if only one in 100 were tuned in, it amounted to a lot of eyes on the game of hurling, on Croke Park and, of course, on Ireland.

I believe these are important matters and important opportunities and that we should be anxious to utilize them fully. On my return home I met Donal Curtin, then Chief Executive of An Post and Chairman of the National Lottery, who had been in India on business at the time of the Allstar tour. He described to me his utter amazement when he turned on the television in his hotel room and was greeted by a Chinese presenter holding a hurley, with yours truly and Clare goalkeeper Davy Fitzgerald trying to explain the intricacies of the game. The piece was followed by snatches of hurling from Croke Park and overall Donal Curtin thought it was a good promotion.

Finally, it must not be forgotten, in relation to the opening up of Croke Park, that refusing to share the fantastic venue with soccer and rugby would mean Ireland's home matches in those sports would have to be played abroad until such time as the development of Lansdowne Road is complete. That would be an act of economic and public relations suicide.

From its earliest days the GAA had an inclination to let the world know of its existence. All-Ireland championships were played for the first time in 1887, three years after the foundation of the Association, and were as successful as any first venture could expect to be. Of course, it was hoped and expected there would be an improvement the following year, but an amazing decision was taken mid-championship to abandon the All-Ireland championships in hurling and football and go on a promotional tour of the United States. It was extraordinary, if not bizarre, that such a decision was taken at a time when the GAA had little, if any, assets.

Maurice Davin was President at the time, while William Prendergast had replaced Michael Cusack as Secretary, and obviously there was support for the notion that the movement could benefit from bringing the games to a bigger audience. The preparations certainly suggested as much. A group of some fifty people, made up of hurlers and athletes in roughly equal numbers, assembled in Dublin and after a promotional march proceeded to Donnybrook and later the same day to Kingstown (Dún Laoghaire), where they put on exhibitions of hurling and athletics.

The show was repeated on subsequent days in Dundalk, Tulla-more, Kilkenny, Thurles and Cork before the courageous band boarded a liner bound for the USA. Promotion for Ireland was the main purpose of the trip, and there may well have been political undertones as well. Branded 'The American Invasion', the tour was not exactly a resounding success and many explanations have been offered for its failure, primarily the fact that it coincided with an American presidential election campaign and a split between factions of the local athletics scene. It incurred a loss of £450, which was cleared by means of a loan from Michael Davitt, founder of the Land League and a patron of the GAA along with Arch-bishop Croke and Charles Stuart Parnell. The loan was never repaid to Davitt, but almost 100 years later the GAA did contribute generously to the museum devoted to the memory of the patron in his native Mayo.

In 2006 the GAA boasts many outlets in various places all over the world, with a superb array of facilities where Irish people can meet, play games and socialize, the annual championships at home providing the overarching link between all these disparate com-munities. Nominally it might be a national organization, but its tentacles reach far beyond the narrow web of Ireland.

By the way, in the debate that led to the opening up of Croke Park to other sports, there were several references to the extra revenue rentals would bring to the coffers of the GAA. An annual figure of €10 million was mooted, with the promise that clubs would benefit from the windfall. Let's hope this proposal will not be forgotten when it comes to making grants to clubs in the wake of the financial bonanza. It is my view that the money thus generated should go exclusively to the clubs because those of the future will need far more resources if they are to retain their status as leaders in the community.

The climate is now suitable for a major expansion in the role of the GAA clubs' responsibilities. Introducing All-Ireland cham-pionships for Junior and Intermediate clubs has been a great boost to morale, with a day out in Croke Park and an All-Ireland title now a possibility for all unit levels. It is that, and not the opening up of the famous venue, that could in time be seen as the most significant part of Seán Kelly's legacy as President.

I know that a vast amount of good has been achieved thanks to the hard work and tenacity of the GAA's wonderful and vibrant network of volunteers, but the potential for much more is there. The GAA structure covers the entire country and, if properly harnessed, it could be instrumental in eliminating many of the perceived ills of modern society. There is no reason why an enlightened government could not invest money at local level to provide facilities and guidance for communities. I should also note that what I am saying in relation to GAA clubs applies equally to other codes and community groups. I would have faith in them all. So let them have the resources that will come from the opening up of Croke Park and a substantial top-up from central exchequer funds in order to halt the development of impersonal, alienated communities.

All that is needed to kick-start the process is a government courageous enough to take a novel and radical approach towards eliminating growing social problems before they escalate further. The value of a good community base should be obvious to all by now, and the value of investment in communities should not be underestimated.

# Is the era of professional GAA players about to begin?

The question of professional status for GAA players might seem to be a topic of recent provenance, but that is not in fact the case. I was more than surprised to find it mentioned in the first ever book devoted to Gaelic football, which was penned by Dick Fitzgerald, a member of Kerry's winning All-Ireland teams of 1903, 1904, 1909, 1913 and 1914. He captained the sides of 1913 and 1914 and in his time was regarded as one of the greatest ever to play the game, even though only twenty-seven All-Irelands had been played to date. His book was published in 1914, and the fact that the holder of five All-Ireland medals decided to comment on the theme of professionalism must mean that it was topical already. He did not delve into it in depth, but merely commented as follows:

It is hoped that Gaelic Football will always remain as natural a game as it is to-day, and accordingly we trust that, while it will ever be developing on the scientific side, it will never become the possession of the professional player.

It is fair to say that the matter of professionalism for GAA players has never been discussed openly, but sooner or later that too will come about. When writing my autobiography in 2004, I suggested it was time a member of the GPA (Gaelic Players Association) was appointed to the GAA's Central Council. I am glad that has now come about, and I think it is far more productive to have Dessie Farrell on the committee than have him running back and forth with views from both sides of a fence that encloses a common interest.

There are some players who would love to play Gaelic football professionally and no doubt a percentage of officials would agree with them, but at a guess I would say that those favouring the status quo would be far greater in number. As with any issue where opposite sides are the choices for debate, there is no shortage of arguments on either side.

A very strong case can be made for continuing to run the games organization for amateur players: it has been that way from the start and has been the main reason why the GAA has developed into the most powerful sports body in the country. The Association is owned by the people in the sense that it is non-profit-making, with surplus revenues ploughed back to the various units. That is the ideal set-up for any association geared towards promoting community welfare and is the main reason why the GAA is ahead of others by way of facilities at club, county and national levels. Of course, the big support given to the games has been another factor in the size of the funds available for distribution.

The huge input from volunteers is another major contributor to the success of the GAA and it is far easier to mobilize such support when dealing with a community association. I reckon that there are at least a quarter of a million people working with the GAA on a voluntary basis, who would generally see their part as a duty to the community to which they belong. It is those sort of people who have made the GAA the organization it is today. They are a vital part of the community, as are the players, be they county level or club players in the different grades. It is not an exaggeration to say that the GAA is a driving force in much of the social life of modern Ireland.

So we can say without reservation that amateur status has served the GAA cause well over the 100-plus years of its life so far, allowing it to benefit the community at large. However, the question that will be asked in a direct manner at some time in the near future is whether or not that blessed state can, or should, continue.

It is not so long ago that the number of Irish people earning their living through sport was minimal in comparison to what it is today. If one takes 1950 as a benchmark, the personnel of professional sportspeople comprised soccer players, some jockeys and a few golfers. The numbers have increased dramatically since then, with more in each of the above categories plus an influx of rugby players, athletes of many disciplines and a few from some minority team sports. The level of financial rewards on an adjusted formula for professional sports people has increased substantially, and it is easy to understand why some GAA players might cast envious eyes on the big earners while they themselves play for the love of the game and the honour of club and county.

As I have said, I think a debate on the question would be both interesting and illuminating if sufficient research were conducted beforehand to take both sides of the argument into consideration. Furthermore, it would be in the interests of the GAA to carry out a survey at this time with the assistance of experts in the field. I am sure other sports bodies would be willing to co-operate and they must be in possession of a vast amount of information that would be of assistance in arriving at proper guidance if, or whenever, the problem presented itself to the GAA in reality.

From my observations of professionalism in rugby, it has raised the standard of the elite players significantly, but has done considerable damage to the fabric of many grassroots clubs. They will admit freely that fund-raising to pay professional players has become a strain, forcing the phasing-out of teams in lower divisions. It is not too long ago since I attended the annual dinner of the Old Wesley Rugby Club in Dublin, a club that traditionally catered for players of non-Catholic religious persuasion. In a way it resembled a GAA club: covering a particular area and drawing on players who had attended Wesley College. Many of the members present were very definitely of the opinion that professionalism brought ill-tidings; it meant their good players would be recruited by and attracted to the bigger and more successful clubs, thereby eroding the very ethos that had been dear to them for generations. They counselled me that small GAA clubs would suffer the same fate if ever professionalism became the order of the day for the country's biggest sports organization. That is actually what is happening at the moment in the Dublin GAA circle and in other parts of the country. It is not a new phenomenon entirely – a percentage of players from outside counties have featured in Dublin club football over the years – but we are witnessing a change as the trend grows for them to join Dublin clubs that traditionally drew members from their own localities.

Another point that needs to be clarified is the sources of the funds that would be required if GAA players were to be paid a salary. My understanding is that most of the money necessary to keep in operation the Ireland rugby squad and the teams taking part in the Heineken Cup comes from television rights via foreign channels. Professional athletes spend most of their time outside Ireland and compete on circuits that do not include us, and while there is a good living for professional club golfers at home, the big names earn their euro, and other currencies, overseas without any recourse to Irish governing bodies. Prize funds in golf are made up of sponsors' money and a percentage taken from other PGA revenues.

By and large, Ireland's leading soccer players earn their living in England's Premiership or elsewhere, but there are more who play either on a full-time or part-time professional basis with League of Ireland clubs. They get paid for their efforts, but now and then that arrangement leads to financial problems for the clubs and is one of the main reasons why facilities for soccer are not of the same standard as those of the amateur GAA.

The GAA's case is entirely different because none of the lucrative television deals available to rugby, for instance, would be there for the national games. One natural reaction to that fact would be to say that the money should then come from the revenues of the Association itself, but there is no way that would be sufficient to maintain the number of senior hurling and football teams that play annually in the All-Ireland championships and leagues. Plus, where would that leave the principle that all profits are to be ploughed back into the organization?

One thing is for sure: now is the time to begin a proper study of both sides of a situation that is, as yet, no more than hypothetical; but this is a problem that won't go away – it's a landmine planted in the future of the GAA. Perhaps there is an Irish solution out there for this Irish problem. I think everyone would probably agree that it would be nice to see players able to earn a living from their sport, if that could be achieved without undermining the basic tenets and desirable qualities of the GAA. So far there has been no clamour from players for payment for play, but that is certain to come in time and it would be foolish to think otherwise. Some unease has already been expressed about loss of earnings due to time spent in training, about expenses incurred in treatment of injuries and about anomalies that arise from time to time. A pointed discussion will have to be had sometime about the players' position, although hopefully having a representative of the GPA on the Central Council will make it easier to arrive at an amicable arrangement.

I have always supported the view that inter-county players should not be out of pocket on account of their football or hurling activities because they are the principal generators of the revenue. That said, they are usually looked after in a fair manner by the County Boards, with provision made for meals, playing gear and agreed travel expenses. Most teams now also enjoy an annual holiday at no cost to themselves and, even though old-timers might say that current players are being 'spoilt', I think the trend is to be welcomed. A few years ago the GPA attempted to bolster the position of inter-county Gaelic players by trying to get them included in a scheme under which other elite athletes qualify for tax rebates. The relevant government department did not warm to the idea, but it might be worth revisiting, with some amendments. The awarding of sports grants is another avenue of 'compensation' that has made headway insofar as it has made an appearance on the floor of Central Council and thereby is on the media production line.

I have yet to see a problem that could not be helped, if not cured entirely, by debate. Even when such discussions carry the label of confrontation, ongoing talks nonetheless tend to lead to more understanding and a mellowing of attitudes when the participants see that appropriate changes are taking place. There are plenty of ideas out there to help solve this problem, we just need to encourage people to speak up and make suggestions. In that spirit, I would like to put forward an idea for debate. The thought has struck me more than once that a system of vouchers, as operated successfully by the Golfing Union of Ireland (GUI) for many years, might work for the GAA. The GUI has approximately 300,000 registered members, all of whom pay an annual subscription to a club, purchase their own equipment and then play away as regularly as they wish. The GUI caters for amateur players, but acceptance of vouchers as prizes is allowed provided they remain under the stipulated ceiling for such prizes. Most golfers have won vouchers at some time or other; indeed, I recall getting a table and six chairs in Clery's of O'Connell Street in Dublin in exchange for one such voucher when I was furnishing my first house! I'm sure there are plenty of GAA players who have received similar prizes in golf clubs, but has any of them seen a GAA voucher?

This kind of scheme need not be too costly and could attract a sponsor. On the basis that it would apply to senior players only, a sum of approximately €5 million would allow for each member of All-Ireland winning teams to be given vouchers for €20,000, beaten finalists €12,500 with beaten semi-finalists each receiving €10,000, and so on a reducing scale as far as the provincial championships. It would be a nice 'thank you' to players and nobody could begrudge them the small rewards that would accrue to them infrequently over their playing days.

I am aware that some people in positions of authority in GAA circles might be of the opinion that players do not have genuine grievances, but as long as the players hold a different view there is a need for dialogue and willingness to work towards a solution. We all know the players, and I have never found them other than reasonable people who deserve to be listened to.

At base, I do not think full professionalism would be a successful move for the GAA because I feel the likely outcome would be an All-Ireland championship for an elite group of ten or twelve teams. Perhaps it is time for President Nicky Brennan to put in place a committee or a commission with terms of reference broad enough to embrace all views on a topic that is, and will continue to be, of major interest to senior, young and aspiring players.

# The GAA and the national problem
## of alcoholism

It is generally agreed and is obvious to most people in Ireland that our society has an over-emphasis on the consumption of alcohol. 'Binge drinking' has entered our normal vocabulary and blaming our heady new prosperity is far too simplistic because social history tells us that the same problem existed in the mid-nineteenth century, a time when extreme poverty was the norm for the majority of the population. Campaigns for temperance by people such as the indefatigable Fr Mathew did have a positive effect, however, and as the century drew to a close the topic faded from the limelight for a considerable span of time. The work of the Pioneer Total Abstinence Association (PTAA), founded by Fr Cullen in 1898, played a notable part and it is a pity that the movement was not non-denominational, or that it did not become so at a specific juncture when religious ecumenism was gaining ground.

My own generation was no stranger to alcoholism, but it certainly wasn't as widespread a phenomenon as it is today. At the age of ten I took the 'pledge' at confirmation, as did all my peers, which was a promise to abstain from alcoholic drink until the age of eighteen. After that it was up to the individual whether to extend their promise by becoming an adult member of the PTAA, and many did so. The 'pin' that announced one's abstinence was worn on the coat or dress and was a common feature of adolescent life right up to the 1970s and is an interesting presence in most photographs of teenagers during those times. When I was growing up in the 1930s and 1940s it was a very rare sight to see a person under eighteen taking an alcoholic drink and regardless of the reason – be it parental control, lack of money, or devotion to the pledge – I believe that was a better scenario than that we see today.

The PTAA has a current membership of about 200,000 and has

a special section dealing with the twelve- to eighteen-year-old age group. The work of its youth unit merits greater support because that is the gestation period for most drink- and drug-related problems, but so far no major government programme has been put in place to address this issue. Under-age drinking, or rather the abuse of drink by a section of our under-age population, is for me one of the saddest features of present-day Ireland and leads to all kinds of social and personal problems. A cogent, intelligent attempt must be made to reverse the trend, which I believe can be achieved if enough parents and associations get involved. Good example by way of responsible drinking by adults can be the most powerful force of all; modern teenagers are only imitating the social habits of older age groups.

I have always been a member of the PTAA and never considered myself at a disadvantage at functions or events on account of not taking alcoholic drink. It has been my choice and in all my years nobody has ever tried to 'convert' me. I have nothing against drink, or drinkers; if it was undesirable in society, Our Lord would never have changed water into wine at the wedding feast of Cana. Now and again people have commented on the 'pin', which I always wear. In fact, quite recently it led to an unusual request. I was getting my photograph taken in a studio and at least three people were involved in the production: one for lighting, another for set-up and one to take the actual snap, even though that might be too simple a word for the operation. Everything seemed to be grand until the photographer had yet another reconnoitre through the lens, then immediately stood to his full height and asked me did 'that little white object on the coat have any significance'? He was an honest Englishman, who possibly felt that the 'white object' did not match the colour of the coat, or something like that, and would thus diminish his handiwork. I had to explain, without going into any detail, that it was almost a part of my coat and within a second or two the masterpiece had been taken, offending white object and all.

I remember another occasion when that affable Corkman, Mossie Keane, father of the famous Roy, was introduced to me at a function. He was holding a pint glass that was half-full or half-empty, depending on one's innate attitude. He was a friendly man and rightly very proud of his son, on whose behalf he had accepted an award earlier in the evening. He remarked that he had heard tell that I 'never took a drink' and wondered could that possibly be true. I simply told him that I had never had any great desire to do so, and that alcoholic drinks did not even look attractive to me. With that he lifted his glass in contemplation, viewed it from all angles and then turning solemnly towards me said, 'Do you know, Micheál, I have an entirely different opinion.' I have always believed in the value of diversity of opinion and I now knew that Mossie did also: he had given full consideration to all I had said before making his pronouncement. Socrates would have been proud of him!

The connection between drink and sport has a long history in many places, Ireland among them. There are legendary tales of the drinking powers of rugby players, Gaelic players and several categories of the sportsmen of the past. Post-match celebrations were ideal occasions for imbibing, and in the days before sports associations were founded barrels of beer were often given as prizes for winners of sporting contests. I often heard a neighbour of mine in Dún Síon, Big Peetie Farrell, recount the story of a day long ago in his cousin's pub, Longs, in Dingle. A woman put her head in the door and called for 'forty pints for forty Fairhill women'. They had just arrived from Cork in a lorry for a drag-hunt, and soon they all trooped in the door for sustenance before going out to cheer their beagles, or 'bagles' as they were called in Dingle. That call for forty pints for forty women remains the single biggest order ever in Long's to this day!

While the link between sport and drink has survived, I have noticed an immense change over the past four or five years, with a far more responsible approach to drinking now among leading sports people. Trips abroad, post-match celebrations, and so on, are no longer excuses for a skite. Most players nowadays place great emphasis on maintaining fitness and that is perhaps an aspect worth bringing to the attention of our young people. While in

Australia one time, I noticed that Australian Rules players were paid to promote an anti-smoking campaign. It was a good idea. Sports stars could play a huge role in campaigns to minimize the fad for alcohol abuse and they should be utilized as much as possible and paid to do so. It would be a good investment.

The change in players' lifestyles was described succinctly by former President Seán Kelly after a trip to Argentina a few years back. He was asked what he had learned during the adventure and replied, 'I have learned that the big drinking days for players have ended, moderate drinking has replaced it.' *Alleluia!* Why not have them proclaim that from the rooftops so those young people who believe it is fashionable to become intoxicated, especially over weekends, can hear it loud and clear.

I have spoken to schoolchildren about alcohol from time to time, but would never claim that my approach is better than others. The point I would stress is that there is a choice and that independent judgement is preferable to doing something simply because others are doing it. From listening to young people from, say, age fifteen years upwards, I have come to the conclusion that many of them drink alcohol because they feel it is expected of them by their peers. So far they have been let down by a society that prefers to be ostrich-like and hopes that the problems of drink and drug-taking will go away.

It has now reached the point where it is incumbent on all community associations to play a part, and to this end a proper campaign, spearheaded by sports bodies, could be very influential in bringing about a change in popular culture. The GAA has already announced its intention to become active in this sphere following recommendations by its taskforce on Alcohol and Substance Abuse, conducted under the chairmanship of Joe Connolly, captain of Galway's All-Ireland winning hurling team of 1980. Brendan Murphy has been seconded from the Department of Health and appointed as National Co-Ordinator of the Alcohol and Substance Abuse Prevention (ASAP) programme.

The GAA is a good vehicle for such a programme as it has units, and therefore structures, in every parish in the country. In the past the Association has given great service to the country's youth by providing worthwhile and enjoyable pastimes, something that has been greatly appreciated in many communities. The same is true of other sporting codes. Now we are facing a modern world, where children are bombarded by a thousand influences a day, and we need practical measures to combat this problem. If the programme is to be successful, it must percolate down to local level.

We should see the ASAP programme in full swing by early 2007, as the National Co-ordinator has now completed his consultations and briefings in all counties. He was received with enthusiasm everywhere, but it must be remembered that sustained local effort will be necessary to make the programme work. The ambition is that every single club will appoint a suitable person to oversee an ASAP programme drawn up by professionals in the business. It may sound idealistic, but it's best to aim high. The programme is a great idea that deserves support, but I am disappointed that the funding granted to it is not greater. So far the Department of Health and the GAA are jointly financing it to the tune of €75,000 each, which is a paltry sum. We should be talking in millions, so let's hope that is only a start. And would it not be a worthwhile gesture if all clubs with practical ASAP schemes were rewarded generously by the GAA out of the extra money generated from leasing out Croke Park for soccer and rugby matches?

Let's give a real chance to those born in the twenty-first century.

Of course, there are other groups working within communities towards the same end as ASAP. I am familiar with the work of the NO NAME clubs, of which there are currently about thirty-five countrywide – a small number, but it is increasing year on year. The movement started in Kilkenny in 1978 when local men Eddie Keher, Fr Tommy Murphy and the late Bobby Kerr, along with a Wexford man, Éamonn Doyle, came together with the aim of providing alcohol-free social occasions for young people between the ages of fifteen and nineteen.

Eddie Keher had just retired after nineteen seasons as a Kilkenny senior hurler, during which time he won six All-Ireland medals. His sporting career involved a lot of travel, meeting people, attending functions, speaking engagements and much more, and I am certain the non-drinking former AIB bank manager learned a lot from those experiences. Fr Tommy Murphy had played a good deal of hurling with Eddie and had won an All-Ireland medal with the Cats in 1963, but it was his work as a priest that brought home to him the need for adults to provide something practical to guide young people through those difficult teenage years. The late Bobby Kerr was the proprietor of the Newpark Hotel in Kilkenny and his work in such establishments had given him a clear picture of the social scene and its harmful side. Finally, Éamonn Doyle was a Garda Sergeant who had witnessed first-hand the problems that could beset a wayward youth.

These four men made an ideal committee and the birth of the NO NAME Club was the outcome. It operates according to a very simple principle: *ní neart go cur le chéile* – real strength is acquired only when people co-operate.

The first step in founding a No Name Club in a community is to select an adult committee whose initial function is to recruit a group of young people from the local schools. The next stage is to provide training in leadership for those with a view to becoming hosts and hostesses in the proposed new No Name Club. Once these steps have been completed, the basic infrastructure is in place and work can begin on organizing various social events in the form of discos, dances, quizzes, debates, or whatever might be in vogue at a given time. The vital thing is that the young people themselves are the chief organizers, with back-up from the adult committee.

The NO NAME concept has spread far and wide beyond Kilkenny. I have seen them in action and I must admit it was an eye-opener. They hold regional gatherings as well as local events, with a fantastic annual national get-together at which the national host and hostess of the year are chosen. In 2006 it was held in Ennis, Co. Clare, where Richard Ryan from Ballycallan in Kilkenny and Jenny Murphy from Dungarvan in Waterford were voted host and hostess of the year.

The scheme is part-financed by the Departments of Health and Education and has immense scope for development, possibly in co-operation with ASAP. What is needed for the message to get through, however, is the participation of the entire community. Adults cannot over-indulge in alcohol and then tell their children not to do so: that simply won't work. So let leaders, sports stars and ordinary people in all walks of life be seen to be practising responsible drinking and a total rejection of drugs. This is what the next generation needs from us: example is so much better than talk, and the provision of meaningful financial support from government would be the best example of all.

# Gong Gong of Singapore

Dublin is now an international, bustling city, but parts of it, like St Stephen's Green, have changed little since I first walked there over fifty years ago. The Green is at its best on a good summer's day when people desert the hot pavements and ramble into its cool, tree-shaded paths to wander and feed the ducks. On the far side of the Green is the beautiful University Chapel, and each time I pass by I recall my sister Eileen's marriage to her late husband Mick Devane there in 1955, and my son Cormac tying the knot Irish-style with Maybelle Tan of Singapore in 2005.

Most Irish people born after 1900 would be accustomed to the phrase 'American cousins'; continuous emigration to that continent from Famine times onwards ensured that family ties spread far and wide throughout the United States and, to a lesser extent, across England and Australia. Now, however, the identities of our foreign cousins are changing given that immigration to Ireland has become the norm. The vast majority of the newcomers have come from the East and no doubt it will not be too long before we hear people talking of cousins from places like Poland, Romania, Nigeria, India and further afar in the Orient. It will lead to a different Ireland and there is no reason why it should not be a better one.

Before welcoming Maybelle into our family, I had visited mainland China in 2001. At that time my daughter, Nuala, was working in Beijing on a European Commission Human Rights project and I thought it was an appropriate excuse to make a trip. My son, Aonghus, was working in nearby Thailand so he dropped over as well.

I was not too long in the city of Beijing when I was reminded that Chinese customs are completely different from ours at home. My lesson in cultural differences began when I decided to visit the city's major soccer stadium. To my mind, this would simply entail presenting myself at the main entrance, and thereupon being admitted. I duly presented myself, but was informed by one of the soldiers on duty that I would need to write to the Department of Sport seeking permission to enter the stadium. I tried another entrance, but it was the same story: a pass from the Department was absolutely necessary. I never did manage to get to see that stadium, but perhaps the rules will have been relaxed when next I get there.

The remainder of the holiday went without a hitch. Taxis offered great value and for US$50 we were able to hire one for an entire day. We journeyed far into rural China, where there were none of the signs of wealth so apparent in parts of Beijing. We were taking a photo stop when we heard the familiar sounds of children playing; children at play use a universal language comprised of shrieks of delight, groans of disappointment, but mostly that of high-pitched laughter which sounds the same in every language and dialect. We decided to follow the source of the noise and pay a visit to the nearby school.

We were obviously the source of great curiosity as we entered the play area. The teachers invited us into the classrooms, which had a clay floor and an assortment of old and battered desks that were clearly discards. But I must say there was an air of contentment about the place, and I wished I had an old football to give them in place of the rag one in use in the yard as we arrived.

We spent hours climbing the Great Wall in the company of two guides and even though they had only 'words' of English, no Irish and my Chinese was severely limited, we managed to communicate effectively. One of the guides was a young woman who worked on the land 'outside the wall' and acted as a guide whenever she could to earn some extra cash. She had two children, which is unusual in China, but we learned that it is easier for parents to get State permission for a second child if the first is female, particularly in farming areas. It was a source of wonder and amusement to them to meet somebody who had eight children in the family.

I have always enjoyed my trips to that part of the world, so was delighted when that part of the world came to visit us in the form of our son's fiancée, Maybelle. The Ó Muircheartaigh clan had its first official connection with the East after Cormac was married in Singapore in January 2005, in accordance with Chinese customs, prior to the University Chapel ceremony in Dublin that August. A Chinese wedding is totally different from a traditional Irish one. For a start, it begins very early in the day when all the guests are invited to the home of the bride, but she remains in her room and does not appear for some time. The custom is that guests bring some present for the bride's parents, and research conducted on my behalf suggested that a roasted pig presented by the father of the groom would honour an ancient Chinese custom and be very much appreciated. Accordingly, I arranged to meet the providers on the way and accompanied the roasted pig to the home for what they call a Chinese Tea Party. There were blessings and other rituals upon arrival before preparations began for the bridegroom's entrance. The preparations involved locking all doors and gates in a light-hearted attempt to prevent Cormac from entering until he had passed tests put to him by relatives of Maybelle, who were posted on guard at the gate.

That part took about half an hour, with all the guests lined up inside, watching and listening. After some time, when there appeared to be no correct signal for unlocking the gate, some members of the Singapore Gaelic Lions suggested the gate be 'rushed'. Ultimately, as is the custom, Cormac was admitted, he 'found' Maybelle, and the Tea Party got underway and lasted for several hours. Maybelle's father, David, and I had official functions to perform, principally blessing people and pouring tea. I did mine *as Gaeilge*, while David was more comfortable in his language. The pig was carved and distributed, while Helena and Maybelle's mother, Jennifer, supervised the celebration in the garden under the ever-present Singapore sun. It was my first Chinese Tea Party.

The guests dispersed in the early afternoon to prepare for the official marriage and wedding banquet. This followed a traditional Western pattern, except that the decorations in the hall were colourful beyond description and the ending was unusual in that

it coincided exactly with the time stated on the invitation card –
not, generally, a feature of the average Irish wedding! Precisely at
eleven o'clock all members of the host family took up preordained
positions and on cue from the hotel management everyone else
proceeded in a line to shake hands and say *slán abhaile* in any
language. Five minutes later only the Irish Brigade remained,
and they honoured another custom by finding a place where the
celebrations could peter out naturally, in their own good time.

A few months later we gathered at the University Church,
Stephen's Green, Dublin, for the Irish wedding ceremony, which
conformed to the tried-and-trusted Irish customs from start to
finish. For the Chinese visitors the highlights were the horse-drawn
coach to and from the church and the notion of a wedding banquet
in Slane Castle.

I got a little insight into what life was like in China 100 years
ago from talking, through an interpreter, with a man known as
Gong Gong (pronounced Gung Gung). He is Maybelle's grand-
father and has been living in Singapore since the age of twenty or
thereabouts; he is not entirely sure of the date of his arrival. It
amazes me that he has never attempted to learn English in the
seventy years he has been living in Singapore, given that many
people there are fluent English-speakers.

'I was born in a village in the Guong Dong province of China,'
Gong Gong told me, 'but I am not sure when.' There was an echo
in that of the plight of some Irish emigrants of the 1800s and it
resonated, too, with one of my own memories from childhood in
Kerry when one heard of people writing home from America 'for
their age'. Anyway, Gong Gong estimates that he must have been
born around 1915, but he does know he was one of sixteen
children in the family and that only four survived past infancy. He
remembers being told to call his mother 'auntie', which he later
figured was probably an attempt to trick the evil spirits that were
being blamed for the deaths of his siblings. He attended school,
but it came to a fairly abrupt end when the Japanese invaded
China: 'The war was bitter and there was a lot of killing and one
of the teachers organized an escape for a group of students, and I

was in that group.' He never again saw his parents and it took a while before his group got safely out of the country: 'We moved from village to village, hid in the mountains and were lucky to stay ahead of the Japanese.'

Eventually, through the good work of the teacher, they procured a small boat that took them to a ship and onwards to Macau, then under Portuguese rule. He stayed there for some time and was aware that 'sister number seven' was in Hong Kong. I learned that it is a feature of Chinese social customs that they always know where relatives live, so when an opportunity arose Gong Gong set off for Hong Kong and joined 'sister number seven' and her husband, who ran a restaurant. He has good memories of his time with them, but he had an ambition to go to Singapore where his sister number one was living. There, his rambling came to an end.

In Singapore he became an apprentice in a metal workshop, worked hard, studied engineering manuals and admits that he was fortunate to get a good job in the massive British Marine workshop: 'I did not forget home and sent my first month's pay back to my parents — enough to provide a year's grocery bill for them.' He said that he and his sister often sent packets of rice and other dry products back home with Chinese people they knew who were returning to the Guong Dong region. How the presents reached their destination, I do not know. But wasn't the parcel from America a vital part of the economy for many years in an old Ireland that is now forgotten?

The Second World War impacted on Gong Gong in a big way because the British decided to pull back from Singapore to Colombo in India. He was detailed to go as part of the workforce, but when the time came to leave he was in hospital following an accident and they sailed without him. The Japanese invaded Singapore soon afterwards, but they needed the British workshops and kept Gong Gong on as an employee. He did not like the way he was treated, however — Chinese workers who performed better than the invaders were subjected to slapping and other insults — so he decided to 'stay at home' as, theoretically, nobody could resign. As the war continued he got work with the Swiss Steel Company and was offered his old job back once the British returned. He declined the offer and instead went into business with a partner and prospered. He married a Chinese girl called Pou Pou and Maybelle's mother, Jennifer, is one of his children.

And that is where my connection with him comes in. Even though neither of us can understand the other directly, I feel we have some sort of telepathic communication. When I returned to Singapore in January 2006 for the Vodafone Allstar tour, Gong Gong expressed a wish to come and see the pick of Irish hurlers in action. He was among the spectators at the fantastic show put on in Polo Park and was simply captivated by it. Though over ninety years of age, according to calculations, he was in no hurry to depart once the game ended and stayed on for the Irish dancing that followed. There are times when I truly think he is a Kerryman who happened to be born in the wrong place.

Gong Gong has a simple and admirable philosophy of life, one that can teach all of us a thing or two: be willing to learn, work hard, show respect for one's elders, be humble and don't ever forget the many people who helped you.

# Pano and Irini of Greece

Speaking of foreign cousins, my Greek relatives have also lived an ordinary yet extraordinary life. I refer to Irini and Panagiotis (Pano) Kalaitzidis, natives of northern Greece but resident in Germany for more than forty years now. And how, you may well ask, did I come to have Greek relatives? My eldest daughter, Niamh, is married to Georgios, son of Irini and Pano, hence my connection with both Germany and Greece. In many ways their life story bears similarities to Gong Gong's, and also echoes many an Irish immigrant's story – with a continental Greek touch, of course.

Irini was born in 1933 in a village called Evzoni, close to the Greek border with the former Yugoslavia. She was the third child in a family of six. Her parents were farmers with a holding of sheep, pigs and cows as well as growing tobacco and other crops. When Nazi Germany invaded Greece in 1941, Irini's home village was regarded as a base of major importance due to its proximity to the Yugoslav border. As a result, it had a strong military presence for the remainder of the war. The Greeks were obliged to open up their homes to the German officers and to feed and otherwise care for them as one of the family. A German general by the name of General Miller was allocated to Irini's parents' house. He was a married man with three children, but had a Greek girlfriend during his stay in Greece. Irini remembers it well:

Her name was Evi and she came from Thessalonica. Our rural villages were full of city people at the time – all looking for work. There were massive food shortages in the towns and cities due to the war. Evi managed to feed her whole family back in Thessalonica through her relationship with General Miller. When the war was over she returned to Thessalonica and General Miller returned to his family in Germany.

Irini is happy to report that despite the strong military presence, there was no brutality or abuse inflicted on the villagers. In fact, she credits the German military with saving her mother's leg. Her mother had stood on a rusty nail and her foot became infected. The Greek doctor saw no option but to amputate. General Miller intervened, and Irini recalls the military doctor arriving in the middle of the night and treating her mother's foot. No amputation was necessary.

Despite the hardness of the time, Irini has fond memories, too, particularly in relation to her brother, Stathi. She describes him as being like David Copperfield, with an amazing ability to do magic tricks. Their living room was 'full to bursting' every evening with local people and Germans watching him perform. He was also gifted at making handicrafts from tobacco. Unfortunately, he died at the young age of twenty-three during the civil war that followed the Second World War. Irini's mother lived to the age of ninety-two, but never gave up her belief that 'he would come back down from the mountains', hoping against hope that Stathi was still alive somewhere.

Irini describes the end of the war in October 1944:

We all had our windows boarded up and blackened because of the war and one night there was loud knocking and banging on the blackened windows. It was the Germans coming to say their farewells. The war was over and they had received their orders to leave. They thanked us and left us pictures of themselves and were gone.

Irini's future husband, Panagiotis, was born in 1930 in Agia Marina, a village in northern Greece. The Kalaitzides were also farmers, mainly producing peaches, grapes, pears, apples and also holding sheep and cows. Pano's father died when he was fifteen and, as the eldest boy, he took over the running of the farm.

When Irini was fifteen she and her eldest brother, Thomas, went to Thessalonica, where Irini started an apprenticeship as a seamstress and her brother started an apprenticeship as a mechanic. They spent the winters serving their apprenticeships and during the summertime returned home to Evzoni to help with the sheep and tobacco farming. Irini came to Agia Marina one summer with her cousin to pick cotton. Her cousin Maria had been there the previous year and Irini was determined to join her the following year. Initially, Irini's father was completely opposed to the idea, but she got her eldest brother to persuade him with the promise that she would 'bring you back a lovely shirt when I return'. Thomas intervened as she requested, and Irini was allowed to go.

While they were in Agia Marina that summer it was agreed that it would be a good thing if Maria, who had neither a mother nor a father, were to marry Pano. The young lady herself was in agreement and returned to Evzoni and her elder sister with this happy news. However, when her sister heard that the intended husband was 'somewhat small', she advised against this and the match was broken. Of course, Pano and Pano's family were very upset and an entourage arrived in Evzoni to try and sort things out. Word was sent back that 'he can have Irini'. Not a very romantic start by any means, especially as nobody thought to consult Irini about this! But then, hasn't many a good match been made that way in our own country in the past?

The young couple got engaged four months later and were married in 1955. Koula, their eldest daughter, was born in 1956; Maria in 1962; and George in 1963. Irini says that, unlike many other marriages, their love and respect for each other 'grew after their marriage and during the many years spent together'.

The early 1960s were very tough times for farmers in Greece. There was a glut of farm produce and therefore no demand whatsoever for Pano's fruit and other goods. As Greece had not developed any export markets at that time, the goods were just left to rot. In 1962, in utter frustration, Pano took off on his tractor to his fields and chopped down all his fruit trees. He then set off for Germany, leaving over 30 tons of unwanted apples behind him.

At that time Germany was in the middle of its economic miracle and was crying out for *gastarbeiter*, or guest workers, from Mediterranean countries. Pano arrived in Essen, in the heart of the German Ruhr area. This huge industrialized region with its steel and coal would have been the polar opposite to his quiet, rural village in northern Greece, with its olive and peach trees. He quickly found work at P.A.G. Steel Company and starting sending money home to his family.

A year later Irini followed him to Essen, while the three children remained behind in Greece with Irini's mother. Irini joined Pano working at P.A.G., but was soon forced to stop due to eye problems caused by the chemicals in use there. She then found work as a seamstress. In the meantime, both Maria and George were brought over to Germany to be with their parents. Koula was already in school in Greece and remained there with her grandmother.

When Pano and Irini arrived in Germany, they spoke no German whatsoever. They are proud of the fact that they managed to learn the language over the years and 'never needed a translator. We always managed to make ourselves understood somehow by using our hands and feet.'

Unfortunately, Pano was forced to stop working in 1979 when he was diagnosed with cirrhosis of the kidney. After three years on dialysis he underwent a kidney transplant in 1982: 'Things looked very bad at the time. Relatives arrived over from Greece to say their farewells.' Then, much sooner than expected, a donor was found. Pano knows his donor 'was a young, nineteen-year-old Austrian man who was killed in a motorbike accident' and he often wonders if this young man's family realizes what a gift he received from them all those years ago. Over twenty-four years later, his donor kidney is still going strong. Pano would be a practitioner of Gong Gong's simple philosophy: 'don't ever forget the many people who helped you'. To this day he pays an annual visit to his hospital and the specialists who treated him to deliver a small token of his appreciation for their help all those years ago and through the intervening years. He usually brings them some Greek wine, or homemade Zipuro distilled from grapes pressed in his own backyard in Greece along with some traditional delicacies baked by Irini.

In the same year as Pano underwent his operation, Irini opened her own seamstress shop on Rellinghauser Strasse in Essen. She

ran this shop until the summer of 2005 and it became something
of an institution in the area. She was well loved and known – not
only for her hard work and skill with a needle and thread but also
for her hospitality to customers and passers-by. I myself often had
occasion to visit her shop during my visits to Germany and always
enjoyed some typical Greek snacks, or some German *Kaffee und
Kuchen*. I recall one such visit in particular: Irini was sitting at her
machine, mending the holes in my trouser pockets, while an
elderly German lady who was also relaxing there over a cup of
coffee serenaded us both opera-style.

Now in their retirement years, Pano and Irini divide their time
between Germany and Greece. They winter in Germany's Ruhr
area with their two younger children and grandchildren, and the
summer in Agia Marina in Greece where they can spend time with
their eldest daughter, granddaughter and two great-grandchildren.

Irini has an interesting perspective on their lives now, some
forty-four years after they first left Greece: '*In Deutschland bleiben
wir Ausländer aber in Griechenland sind wir fremd.*' Translated this
means something like, 'In Germany we are still foreigners, but
Greece is foreign to us.' I wonder how many long-term emigrants,
both to and from our own shores, would echo this very sentiment?

# Martin White of Kilkenny: The oldest living All-Ireland medal-holder

Time now once more to summon the mind back home, and what better lure than the game of hurling and a visit to the oldest living All-Ireland medal-holder. An old adage tells us that age is honourable and I would be inclined to add that it is also instructive. For that reason I enjoy listening to the stories of people blessed with a long life as they often present a different slant on matters from that to which I am accustomed.

Martin White of Kilkenny is the oldest living holder of an All-Ireland medal and I count myself lucky that I have met him many a time and oft. When I tell you that it is over eighty years since he first played in Croke Park, you will gather that he has reached that honourable age I have spoken of. He was born in 1909, but experts by the Nore have no difficulty in recalling in vivid detail his achievements for the county on the hurling fields. It was prior to that, though, that he first stepped out onto the famous pitch of Croke Park, as he well remembers:

It was 1925 and I was playing for St Kieran's in the final of the Leinster Colleges championship. I remember clearly the chanting of 'Rock, Rock, Rock' by the supporters of Blackrock College, our opponents in that game. It was a good match and I won't forget Fr Billy Dunne on the sideline: he drove his stick into the ground, pulled off his priest's collar and stuck it and his hat on top of the stick and then started to run up and down shouting at us. We were lucky to win by a point and his running and shouting helped.

The first of three Hogan Stands to be erected in Croke Park was then a year old, but all Martin White remembers of the facilities was that he had to wash himself at a tap outside the dressing room after the game: 'There was nothing inside the room, not even a table or chair, but it was Croke Park. There were grassy banks on both sides of the ground and Hill 16 looked a wilderness.'

He was back a year later, playing in the colleges final once more and, strangely, it was another rugby-loving college that again provided the opposition, this time Dominican College, Newbridge. On that occasion the 'Kittens' had an easy victory and Martin had a reason to celebrate: 'I scored three goals.' (Incidentally the Newbridge college had another claim to fame in the Gaelic world at the time as one of its teachers, Bernie McGlade, a native of Armagh, was on the Kildare team that won the All-Ireland football final of 1919.)

He got his first experience of senior inter-county All-Ireland final action when the Cats and Cork met in the memorable championship of 1931:

It was great to be on the Kilkenny team that year and it is the only final ever that required three matches before it was all over. I played in the first one, Lory Meagher was the big star of the era, but he missed the third match due to rib injuries he got in the second game and maybe we might have won if he was fit to play.

Martin White has been a regular follower of hurling all through his life and can describe the styles of the stars of the past seven decades with great clarity. One of the first to impress him was Dick Grace, who won an All-Ireland with Kilkenny the year he was born: 'I like to boast that I won a county championship title with him on the Tullaroan team of 1930. It was wonderful to win, but it was better when I could say I was on the same team as Doctor Dick and Lory Meagher.' To this day Lory remains an icon of hurling and according to Martin White he had:

. . . a style of his own. He looked a little on the slow side, but that was deceptive because he had the greatest sense of anticipation imaginable; nobody ever saw him in a hurry on the field, but he was the man that was always where the ball landed. He was tall but light limbed, though his arms and shoulders were real powerful. He had delightful hand action and was a beautiful overhead striker. His stamina came from working on the farm, and when you needed something special to pull a game out of the fire, you always turned to him. I remember a day when we were playing a good Dublin team and found ourselves twelve points down. Lory said that if we could get two goals we'd win and he went and got the goals himself and we did win. That was Lory and the glory all together.

Dublin had good teams in White's time and he remembers a day in Croke Park when one of their players, Vesty Muldowney, got a rattle that put him down, but instead of staying on the deck he did a somersault and came up with the ball and carried on. 'In my whole life I saw only one other person do that and he was a footballer from Wicklow by the name of Gerry O'Reilly,' was White's postscript to the little cameo about the Dubliner. In fact, I got to know the same Vesty years later as a member of Grange Golf Club in Dublin, where the former hurler was honoured with the captaincy in 1959. I once beat him in the final of a less-than-classic club snooker competition, which made history by being refereed through the medium of Irish by another club member, Seán Ó Buachalla.

Martin White was a fixture on the Kilkenny team for the 1932 campaign that ended with a one goal win over Clare in the All-Ireland final. When I asked if he remembered getting hold of that first All-Ireland medal, he gave an indirect answer that went as follows:

We won again the following year and I remember being waiting at the Kilkenny station in 1934 to get a train to Cork – we were going on a trip to America. As the County Secretary was passing along the platform he doubled back and asked me did I get anything for the match we won the year before. When I told him I had got nothing, he put his hand in his pocket, produced an All-Ireland medal and gave it to me. He was about to move off when I decided to tell him that I had got nothing either for the match we won in 1932 and without delay he put his hand in the other coat pocket and said, 'There you are now, Martin,' as he handed me another medal. I was delighted, but I was afraid I'd lose them in America.

That trip to America turned out to be a memorable one for him for an unexpected reason, but there were times on the outward journey when all wished fervently that they were at home:

The weather was fierce and the *Deutschland* was heaving and bobbing up and down for long spells at a time. Johnny Dunne and myself were the only two that could eat breakfast and Paddy Phelan often wished he had stayed in Cobh, but we got there and had been given the run of the boat by the German captain.

They were treated royally while in the big city, but for Martin the trip had a wonderful ending, which he explained to me, still with wonder in his voice to think of the sequence of events that took place over seventy years ago:

I knew of my mother's brother, Michael O'Shea, who had not been heard of since returning to America thirty-three years earlier and the feeling at home was that he was dead. Johnny Dunne had spent a few years in America and I told him about my uncle who was a doctor and he began his search right away. New York was a big place even then, but 'Lovely Johnny', as he was known in hurling circles, went through all the telephone books and tracked him down to Staten Island. He spoke to him on the phone, but found him to be very suspicious and not anxious to speak to anybody else. He put me on to him, but the man was not keen on accepting me and gave me some reasons: he said he had been doing well in partnership with another person before going back home on the visit, but found the partner had sold everything and left before his return. I learned more later, but I told him early on in the conversation that I would love to meet him if that could be arranged. He seemed cautious and began to question me as follows on the phone: 'What's your name? What's your father's name? What's your mother's maiden name? Where is she from? What's the name of the field behind the house, etc.?'

I knew all the answers, but I was still not invited, but he promised to ring back. He did so before long and told me to get the ferry to Staten Island at a certain time, but did not promise to meet me, but said his son, John, would be there. I saw no one waiting when I got off the ferry and so I walked out onto the street. I saw a man on his own a bit away and strolled towards him. When I got nearer I thought I saw a likeness in him to my mother's people, the Sheas from Ballyragget, and as I got close to him I said, 'John O'Shea' in the hope that he would say 'yes'. He didn't, but asked, 'How do you know?' and my answer was, 'From your father's people.'

He welcomed me then and brought me to meet my uncle Michael. He was married to a German and they gave me the time of my life for a whole week. He explained that on his return from Ireland, gangsters had got in touch with him with a request that he would become their doctor. When he inquired who told them he was a doctor, they replied that they knew everything and made him a very attractive offer. He considered it for some time, but eventually wavered and decided to disappear to Staten Island and start life all over again.

That explained all the suspicion and he wanted to know then what brought me to America. He hadn't known I was a hurler nor that Kilkenny had won two in a row, or any of the home news. There was no way he would consider ever returning to Ireland, but asked me would I put my mother on a boat, that he would pay all costs, meet her on arrival, give her a great time because 'your mother is a lady'.

She was delighted with the news when I came home, but she wouldn't even consider going on a boat. She wrote to him a few times, but he was dead for a while before we heard about it. Members of his family came to Ireland a few years after that and enjoyed the experience.

Martin has no doubt but that meeting his lost uncle was the highlight of his 1934 American trip, but neither has he forgotten the day Dick Sullivan of Ballyhale brought a few of the hurlers to his farm upstate and showed them black pigs and other pigs that were half-black and half-white. 'We guessed that Kilkenny people at home would not believe that story!' said Martin, laughing.

It was back to hurling soon again and after the disappointment of losing the 1934 Leinster final to Dublin in a replay, the Cats went on to play in the All-Ireland finals of the next three years: winning against Limerick in 1935, losing to them a year later, and losing to Tipperary in the Killarney final of 1937. I felt compelled to ask him about another legend of the ash, the great Mick Mackey, and he was quick to emphasize that the Limerick team of the 1930s and early 1940s deserved more than three All-Irelands:

Everybody talks about Mick Mackey for the past seventy years, some not so kindly. I was very fond of Mick and even if he hit hard with his enormous strength, he himself was hit as often and never complained. He hit me one day and put me spinning. I decided there and then that once was enough, but I had huge respect for him after that. He was an extremely skilful hurler and, like Lory and Christy Ring, he was a man that could cut loose when his team needed a crucial score.

The 1937 final was Martin's last and it meant he had played in six finals over a seven-year spell, and he was quite happy with everything: 'I was proud to have won three All-Ireland medals and to meet so many wonderful people.' At first I was surprised at how little training the players of his era seemed to do for important inter-county matches, but after listening to him talk on the subject I got a new insight into the way of things then:

The question of fitness never arose because we were always fit. From as far back as I could remember we were hurling. There was at least one hurling field in every parish, one of our own fields in Tullaroan was one of them, and we'd be there almost every night of the week until it got dark, pucking, chasing, tackling, tussling and so on among a crowd that included all ages.

It was the same later when I went to work in Waterford, except that on bad nights we'd go to the pictures, but on the other nights we'd cycle the six miles to Doody's hurling field in Granny Knock, near Mooncoin, and hurl until dark. It was a special field because it contained a fine spring well of pure cold water. James Doody always filled a big bucket with water every morning and put a good measure of oatmeal into it to soak for the day. A few mugfuls of that brew was like magic after the hurling and the cycle back to Waterford was no bother to anyone, even after a few hours in the field. It was seldom a match, but hurling hell for leather without a referee while the light lasted. Of course we played a lot of matches with our clubs as well and there were plenty of tournaments at the time to raise funds for building schools and churches. We helped to build a lot of them. We built the school in Ballylinan and there was great excitement the night we beat Clonad in the final of a great tournament.

I remember we got a Cup and there was a bus the same night and someone got an idea to tie the Cup on top of the bus for the journey home, but it must have got caught in a branch of a tree along the route because it did not arrive with the bus and has not been seen since. It might still be up some tree in North Carlow for all we know.

It is obvious from talking to Martin White that he really enjoyed his hurling days and also that he is as informed on today's performers as he is on all the previous generations. He credits St Kieran's College with giving many a hurler the extra bit of finesse that can make all the difference. Naturally he mentioned Eddie Keher, singling him out as a great competitor who had every skill in the game to match his speed and strength. When it came to that legendary Corkman Christy Ring, Martin White had a unique way of describing him:

He was the absolute hurling fanatic and I remember meeting him on the stairs of Hayes's Hotel in Thurles after a match with Limerick one day. He was so anxious to talk about the game that he put both hands on the wall on either side of me and went from throw-in to full-time before he stopped. I say now that he was as good a hurler as only a fanatic can be; he was simply tremendous in all aspects of the game and could not bear to think of ever being beaten. It is fair to say that he did more that any other Corkman to ensure that many victories were gained.

After working with Clover Meats in Waterford for ten years, he moved to Cork in 1939, played with the famous Rockies and stayed there until 1947. He came to Dublin in 1948 and before long he and his wife Peg owned the Boston Bakery, which they ran for a good number of years, himself seeing to the production side of the business and herself taking care of everything else. He retained his links with hurling and was associated with the Crokes Club, then based around Croke Park, where the local kids did their pucking and training with the help of two generations of Currans who worked there: Michael and his son, Jimmy, known as Chick. Martin White was chairman of the Crokes when, through the assistance of Micheál Burke of Kilmacud, the two clubs amalgamated in 1966 to become Kilmacud Crokes. They celebrated in appropriate style by winning the Dublin hurling championship of that year.

Martin White is no longer a young man and suffers from a hip problem dating back to a match in Cork years ago, but he remains very young at heart and was looking forward to his seventieth All-Ireland hurling final when I spoke to him. He had missed a few of them from time to time due to his 'acting hip', but he still enjoyed watching the modern practitioners of the game:

I think that DJ Carey has been in a class apart for a good number of years. He has this extraordinary ability to be both a great team player and a wonderful individual player and knows the role of each. He has done things that, in truth, were nearly impossible and it was wonderful to watch the easy style that led to it all. He has beautiful hands and I remember seeing him for the first time as a corner-forward on a minor team. Joe Hennessy was with me the same day and at one stage I remarked that the young fella was the nearest thing to Paddy Phelan I had ever seen – with that, Joe told me that Paddy was his grand-uncle!

Paddy was the man who was called in from the 'Bank' in Croke Park one day to play in goal for Leinster in the Railway Cup semi-final when Malachy Kelly of Laois did not show up. It was big news because the man who was named as left-half back on the Teams of the Century and Millennium years later had not yet played for Kilkenny at the time.

Fittingly, Martin White's final words were in praise of Tipperary's Eoin Kelly, the player who ignited the championship of 2006 with an amazing tally of fourteen points in the Munster quarter-final clash with Limerick:

It was as good as I have ever seen from any individual. It was extraordinary to watch him position himself perfectly every time in anticipation of the run of play. He scored from all angles with the same ease. He is a beautiful striker of the ball and why wouldn't he be – the finesse was born during his stay in St Kieran's College.

# Tom Cheasty, 'the Waterford Tornado'

The neighbouring counties of Kilkenny and Waterford are known for their rivalry, and crossing the border from one to the other brings you from one area of steadfast loyalty to another, although the gods who distribute the spoils of battle have thus far looked more benignly on the Cats.

One of the likeable characteristics of sport is its ability to abandon the hallowed centres of excellence every now and then in order to direct a beam of glory into an oasis where hope has strong roots, but seldom comes to full bloom. In the world of hurling, Waterford would be one such oasis. The county was supportive of the ideals of the GAA from the start and entered teams in hurling and football for the first ever All-Ireland championships in 1887. Their footballers participated but the hurlers withdrew; it must have been a case of the spirit being willing but the body being weak, or even very weak.

It took a long time before that hurling body was strong enough to win a championship match. It finally came in 1904 when they got the better of Kerry in the Munster semi-final of 1903. Their skies brightened further in 1938 when they brought home the Munster title for the first time. This bestowed a modicum of status on Déiseland, but they were still last in the provincial pecking order because each of the other five counties had annexed an All-Ireland title by then. They became full members of the union ten years later when at last the McCarthy Cup made its way southwards, to the eastern corner of Munster.

The pioneering spirit of those heroes of 1948 took hold and before long another bunch of outstanding Waterford hurlers appeared on the horizon, hell-bent on claiming centre-stage. I saw them in action on numerous occasions and for a period of a decade or more they gave many spectacular displays that powered them into three All-Ireland and three National League finals between 1957 and 1963. They won one of each and with a little luck could have done better. The team had several real quality players whose achievements are writ large in the county annals, as are the deeds of the county's current representatives who have added two more Munster titles to the tally.

I remember being on a committee in 2005 to select 'A Farmer's Fifteen' from the ranks of hurlers through the ages. It was not an easy task, but I had no difficulty rattling off a few 'automatics', the first being an unforgettable Waterford gladiator of the 1950s and 1960s. He was Tom Cheasty from Ballyduff, and in many ways he typified the drive and daring of the Waterford team of his era. Though ill and receiving treatment for cancer at the time, he attended the 'Farmer's Fifteen' to see members of the team being honoured, and as ever he was more anxious to talk about hurling, team mates and opponents than anything else. I met him again as the 2006 hurling season was gathering momentum and it was simply wonderful to listen to him mix farming, hurling, history, folklore and the ups and downs of life in a steady stream of speech punctuated by hearty laughter. It was as if he enjoyed telling a story that I found captivating.

His surname is an unusual one and when I asked where it might have come from, he told me that his brother believed the family had Kerry connections:

There is a place called Tuosist near Kenmare in Kerry and the Irish name is Tuath Ó Siosta – the territory of the Ó Siosta – and that is us. It is said they came from there to Waterford in the seventeenth or eighteenth century to fight a battle out at the Sweep, halfways between Waterford and Kilmeaden. It was a kind of internal war over wine smuggling.

Some of the Ó Siosta, or Cheasty, clan must have survived the wine war and stayed on in Waterford. There is no further folklore available about the clan at that time, but there is an element of sport in the immediate background: 'My father's uncle, Dick Phelan, I always refer to him as Whelan, was on the Ballyduff team that won a county football championship back in the early years of the GAA. They represented Waterford in the first ever All-Ireland championship held in 1887 and he was on the team beaten in Elm Park, Dublin, by Young Irelands of Louth.'

According to Cheasty, his father Geoffrey played 'only a bit of hurling because he was what you would call a dedicated farmer. I wouldn't have much in common with him now, but my brother Edmund would. He is a farmer who played a bit of hurling and I was the opposite, a hurler who did a bit of farming.'

The Cheastys farmed 200 acres of good land that combined tillage, beef and dairying, which meant there was plenty of work to be done at all times. There was employment for three men on the farm while the lads were very young and attending school: 'I went to Waterpark College for two years and I was doing well, but I gave it up; I learned how to play rugby there, but I wasn't impressed. I was fast and thought I would be a good winger, but they put me in the pack because I was strong and I did not like that.'

On leaving the college he went to work on the farm and it was then that he first showed signs of becoming the hurler who did a bit of farming:

We had a workman, Mick Power, and he was a good hurler. I remember late autumn and early winter days when the pair of us would be pulling mangolds and turnips. We would be talking a lot about hurling and we often took a half-hour off here and there to practise and most of the time my father wouldn't know a thing about it, but I was hurling minor and wanted to practise.

Tom was quite content, but after two years spent mostly on the land he got a 'peculiar' offer to return to education. Apparently St Augustine's College had a good football team that year and there was talk of the possibility of winning a Munster title. A neighbour of Tom's was attending the college and he told them about the fit young fellow who was a good footballer. Before long the headman, Fr Murray, was knocking on his door and inviting him to come to the college as a boarder.

He accepted the offer, but told me that he felt like 'that famous man from Dingle, Paddy Bawn Brosnan, who told his teacher one day that football was the only reason for his attendance at school. I couldn't get used to boarding, going to bed early, and it was hard to get into the habit of studying after two years on the farm. Two weeks was enough and so my second scholastic career came to an abrupt end when I went home.'

There was to be no sudden early end to the Ballyduff man's sporting career, however. He played minor football and hurling for the county and was on his club's junior hurling team, playing with the men at the age of fifteen. The best gauge of his loyal service to the game and club is the fact that he played his last game for Ballyduff junior hurling team thirty-four years later, at the age of forty-nine. In between he had a glorious innings as an inter-county player, mostly in hurling. He played for the minors in 1950 and 1951, but missed out in 1952 because he was serving out a long suspension. Before I could ask about the circumstances of that sentence, he hinted that it was best to let it rest in the peace of history. The same suspension offered him a great opportunity to get another hurling distinction, which he explained as follows:

I had strong Kilkenny connections around Mooncoin on account of my mother. Myself and my brother spent a lot of time there. They had a good senior team at the time and they were looking for a player for a match against Tullaroan. I was asked and agreed to play, but chickened out at the last moment as I thought it might cause trouble or confusion in the club. I regretted it afterwards, I had great friends there and the Mooncoin jersey was a great one to be offered.

There was no question of refusing the offer to play for the Waterford senior hurling team when it came during the 1954–5 National League:

I went up to the Sportsfield as a spectator, to see how we would do against Kilkenny. I was in early and after a while the secretary of the East Board came over to me with the news that they were stuck for players as three or four had not turned up. He asked me to play and even though I had trained earlier in the day, I volunteered because, to be honest, I was always ambitious to play senior hurling for the county.

He lined out at centre-forward that day and recalls that he was playing on Mick Brophy and that Waterford lost, 'but I must have played well enough to make an impression because I made the championship panel of 1955 and came on against Limerick'.

Before long he had a reputation on the inter-county circuit, due as much to the fact that Waterford were improving as to his unique style of play. As a player his main assets were great pace, enormous natural physical strength and a relish for taking on defences and breaking through in a line for goal that never became a semi-circle. He described his hurling style to me as follows:

I hadn't a wristy stroke, like a lot of the classy players. I didn't have a big swing either, but sort of pushed the ball away double-handed. I had strong hands from milking cows and other farm work and 'tis never easy to hook a player with a short stroke.' Tis a bit overdone to say I was unorthodox because I thought I was good overhead and on the ground.

Tom has great memories of 1957 when he collected his first of three Munster championship medals when defeating Cork in a highly rated 'spectacular' southern decider. While not complaining, he feels they should have beaten Kilkenny in the All-Ireland final, too:

It was the day actor John Gregson paraded with the Cats as part of the film *Rooney*, being shot in Dublin at the time. He didn't do us any harm and we were leading by six points going in to the last eight minutes. Micky Kelly scored the point that put Kilkenny ahead, but I can still see our forward, Mick Flannelly, in possession on the Cusack side within scoring distance as the ref blew the full-time whistle. It wasn't Kelly's point that beat us at all but Ollie Walsh. It was his first final and he really burst on the hurling scene that day. He was the best at his job that I have seen and a hell of a nice guy as well. Who could forget Ollie at his best, the blocking, catching and the side-stepping of giants heading inwards for the clash and the crush.

Cheasty had much to say in praise of his own team mates: 'John Kiely played his heart out every time he took the field, he was the strongest small man I ever met. Frankie Walsh was a fine captain, good free-taker and there was a sting in his play when a score was needed. Séamus Power could hit a ball, he was good to get a goal, he was a great trier, good hands and clever overhead, etc.' But he was adamant that Philly Grimes was the best hurler on the team and, in his opinion, the second best Waterford hurler of all time:

John Keane was the best, you know. Philly had everything a hurler needed, loads of skill, pace, strength and up against six feet in height. They say he is the only Waterford player with two All-Ireland medals. He played against Clare in the Munster championship of 1948, but emigrated soon afterwards and was away when the team won the All-Ireland in September. He was a plasterer and had cousins in the building business in New York. We were lucky that he returned home in 1953 or 1954 on account of a danger of being called up for army duty with the outbreak of the Korean War. He was the makings of our Waterford team.

'Chasty', as they pronounce the name in Waterford, was rarely short of hurling action given his involvement in club, county and inter-provincial competitions. Farming took second place, though he did throw in the remark that he was a reasonably successful farmer. He won the first of four Railway Cup medals in 1958 and played the first of three League finals in 1959, ahead of the roller-coaster goal-scoring All-Ireland winning campaign of the same year. The team scored nine goals against Tipperary and twenty-three in all, and Tom had the satisfaction of scoring two against Ollie Walsh in the All-Ireland final:

We were much better as a team that year, the resolve was there and the results followed, but we were lucky to get that draw against Kilkenny the first day. Séamus Power came sweeping in from the Hogan Stand side of the Canal goal and his powerful shot took a deflection off the Link Walsh's hurley [and passed] Ollie. They say in Kilkenny that Ollie would have blocked it only for the deflection, but I wouldn't swear to that. Anyway, it was great that it went in and we won the replay by eight points.

Naturally that was the highlight of Tom's hurling career, but he carried on with the county team for a further eight years. They were not without successes, with 1963 being particularly good as they won the National League and finished within three points of a Kilkenny team of legends in the All-Ireland final. An interesting point about the 1963 Waterford team was that ten of the players had lined out in the finals of 1957 and 1959. Tom Cheasty was one of those and throughout he generally played centre-forward, from where the broad-shouldered, light-legged warrior led many an attack towards Ollie Walsh and other brave goalkeepers.

While hurling is his life's blood, he is very proud of the fact that he once played at midfield for the Waterford footballers in a National League game against Kerry in 1954: 'The game was played in Tralee and it was an honour for me to shake hands with the Kerry midfielders, Paudie Sheehy and John Dowling, before the start of the game.'

The more I listened to the Ballyduff man, the more I began to appreciate the term 'a hurler who did a bit of farming'. As far as I could make out, he would be willing to abandon the fields for any type of sport at any time. When Mick White of Dunhill invited him to take part in cross-country running, he gladly took up the new challenge and won county intermediate titles over five miles in 1957 and 1958. He says he really enjoyed it and compared it to National Hunt racing with 'real fences to be jumped'. He did state, however, that in his own opinion he would never have reached the top in that sport as he was not built for it.

On the other hand, he might have reached a high level in weightlifting if he had decided to concentrate on that strenuous calling. His author for that theory was Hugh O'Callaghan, son of Dr Pat, the man who won Olympic Gold medals in the Hammer at the 1928 and 1932 games. Hugh was a top athlete in his own right and held Irish records in weightlifting and the 16lb shot, as well as holding decathlon and boxing titles. Tom met him when both were taking part in the shot at the Kilmeadon sportsfield 'at vastly different levels', although it did result in Cheasty being invited to Hugh's training gym. He was glad to accept because he hoped he would meet Dr Pat there, which he did and which he lists among the great honours in his life. He came to like the weights and under guidance made great headway at the lifting:

I used to go two evenings a week in 1958 and 1959, but I kept it quiet because we were training for the hurling and they would go through the roof if they knew what I was at. I was lifting big weights and in a letter Hugh wrote to the *Cork Examiner* he stated that I could be a champion at the discipline only for the hurling.

The truth was that Cheasty lived for the hurling and, as he puts it, 'the club scene is the part of my career that sticks in my mind'. He had to wait until he was thirty-six years of age before he won his first county championship at senior level, and it came in one of the years when Ballyduff and Portlaw formed one team. When Ballyduff ran solo again, Tom stayed with Portlaw and they went on to win four more 'counties'; he was forty-three years of age when his fifth and final win came his way. All the same, he was destined to finish up with Ballyduff, it was a circle that had to be completed. So when the Juniors needed a manager, he was the willing volunteer and before long he himself was back on the team and played his final game of hurling at the age of forty-nine.

Tom Cheasty is a man with views on most GAA topics. He is grateful to the Association for 'giving me a good lifestyle away from farming, an occupation that could be dull on its own. It also gave me confidence, which is good, and made me, an ordinary man, into somebody who was known and a sort of a personality. Then I made friends in a lot of places, the fellas I played with and against, Eddie Keher would be a great friend of mine, but don't have any doubts Ring was the best hurler ever. I won four Railway Cups with him, he used to pull out all the stops for the Cup, he couldn't relax and he'd be peppering before the game.'

Tom's interest isn't confined to days of yore – he is still an avid spectator of the sport and has great admiration for the skill levels of the players of today. He speaks in wonder about Tipperary's Eoin Kelly: 'his movements are so perfect that fellas just don't get an opportunity to block him or stop him; he is truly exceptional.' But there is no way he will ever forget or underestimate his own generation: 'Shure,' he says with a sort of a roguish smile, 'there is no comparison between the quality of the cameras used nowadays to show hurling on the screen and those in operation in the early days when we were playing.'

Anybody who is privileged to know Tom Cheasty will have a good idea that he has got a lot of enjoyment out of life. He and his wife, Kathleen, are very proud of their family and were anxious to give them whatever education they desired, as far as possible. But life dealt them a cruel blow when their eldest, Siobhán, died as a result of a brain haemorrhage. As Tom spoke about her, he almost became a different person, his voice soft with emotion: 'She was the eldest and we were hoping she would be a good influence on the other three; and she was. She was a great girl and a good student and graduated as a doctor from UCD in 1996. She began working in the Mater Hospital in Dublin and was barely a month qualified when she was taken away. It was so sad and a terrible blow to the entire family.'

They have all learned to cope, though it was hard to accept, and Tom himself has battled his illness successfully. He and Kathleen have retired, though he told me that he fell into a drain a few days before we met when 'wiring off a few cattle'. Meanwhile, daughter Catherine practises as a Chartered Accountant, Margaret works in the National Gallery and Geoffrey, the youngest, continues with his business and legal studies. And I am sure that wonderful tales of the giant of Waterford hurling are related to them whenever people hear they bear the surname of Cheasty.

# The uniqueness of a Munster hurling final

From Waterford, it's a scenic drive down to the centre of Munster. The province is wedded to its GAA tradition and nothing illustrates this more clearly than a Munster hurling final, in particular those played in Semple Stadium, Thurles.

I like to set off early on the day of a Munster final and the journey is made all the more pleasant by being able to take it easy. Once out of Dublin, or any town or city for that matter, the countryside appears to be restful and calm, even if the day is not the perfect ally to the forthcoming event. Rural Ireland looks well in late June/early July, when growth comes without strain. That's when the myriad of green fields surrounding the cornfields begin to blend with the rich golden brown that early August brings. An occasional field shorn of its crop of grass, swept away in bales of silage, looks cheated and dispirited, as if refusing to sprout ever again. There is nothing remotely beautiful about baled silage, it is more natural to think of fields dotted with wynnes of hay. In my mind, those images are always linked with glorious sunshine; the splendour of a Munster hurling final day is hugely increased whenever it coincides with a day when the sun is splitting the stones.

Along the way, at crossroads and corners, people stand in twos and threes waiting to be picked up and transported onwards. Many are displaying their county colours, especially the young, who are getting more numerous every time you make the journey. You rarely see people talking while they wait; they are deep in thought, but ever willing to wave at passers-by who are on the same mission.

One never, ever commits the sin of keeping the driver waiting on the day of a Munster final – it would not matter at all on any other day. A match car is easily recognized on the road, though there have been some changes: once it was four male passengers, possibly wearing headgear; now it is common to see cars carrying both males and females. A sighting of an all-female vehicle has not yet been reported; can't be far away, though.

Traffic increases in volume as Thurles gets closer: that is what you expect and no one complains. By now some cars have pulled in onto the grass verges, their boots flung open, the sandwiches are taken out. The passing cars emit friendly honks, and louder ones for those parked but showing the 'wrong' colours: it is all part of the banter that thrives on a final day. It is best to park a bit away from the centre of Thurles town and walk the remainder in order to savour the unique atmosphere. By now there are people everywhere and all anxious for talk, young and old and in between, male and female, and at least a few from every county in the land and beyond. A stranger could easily imagine that everybody knows everybody else; greetings are being exchanged and acknowledged, the street is being crossed and recrossed, old acquaintances are being renewed, drink is being consumed, music played, chips eaten, programmes bought and all the while excitement and antici-pation are building up as the clock ticks towards throw-in time.

The sight of former heroes wending their way towards the Mecca that is Semple never goes unnoticed and brings cheers from the crowd. I remember once walking behind former Limerick and Dublin hurler, Tony Herbert, as he made his way from the Anner Hotel to the game. A great admirer of his was by my side and exclaimed that Tony should have been the minister and not his brother, Mick, who sadly passed away recently. The loquacious Tony was receiving great attention at the time and his friend's remark caused me to ask for an explanation, which proved simple in the extreme: 'neither Mick nor anybody else in God's world can shake hands like that man.' It was a curious statement, but many more like it are made on days of Munster finals. It is never a day for normality or moderation. And believe it or not, Tony eventually did become a Senator in Leinster House, although I don't think his expertise in hand-shaking had much to do with his election.

If at all possible, one should never pass Hayes's Hotel without paying a visit. I thought of it once during a visit to Calcutta as I watched a steady stream of Indians wade into the waters of their spiritual home, the Ganges River. They had touched base and lingered there in silence, respectfully pouring cupped palmfuls of the healing water onto their upper bodies and the bodies of their children. It's like that with Hayes's: there's some indefinable blessing to be gained by going into Hayes's Hotel on a Munster final day and passing by the billiard room where the GAA was founded by an odd assortment of seven people on 1 November 1884.

It takes time to complete the short journey from the main square to Semple Stadium. On the road you will hear banjos, fiddles and concertinas and there, halfway up the slight incline close to a pillar on the right-hand side, you are bound to see and hear the king of street singers/musicians, The Pecker Dunne himself, along with members of his family. That part of the journey is a special station.

Once you walk inside the ground, the scene changes completely. A corps of willing volunteers is scatttered across all areas and they are well versed in the ways of dealing with the allotted tasks. Groundsman Jimmy Purcell rightly looks proud as he surveys the immaculately manicured playing area, with its flags, goalposts, lines and semi-circles all ready for the tumult that will erupt once the hurling begins. I always pay an early visit to the RTÉ nest, close to the roof of the old stand, but I have never yet arrived ahead of the technician on duty. The view of the pitch from there is fantastic and the sight of a green field behind the goal at the Killinan end fits neatly into the panorama that includes the Sliabh Bloom Mountains, which are visible to me far beyond Ardán Ó Riain, with the enduring Devil's Bit as mystical as ever.

The crowds march in early and the alluring sound of a pipers band, be it The Seán Treacy, The Cullen or any other outfit, is an appropriate proclamation that the great hour is not far away. Talk of the match is the only topic now, with theories often vying with rumours and followers more anxious than ever to propound, speculate, wonder and hope. Some will give messages to be relayed to family members or friends who, for some reason, are not present.

By now the teams have arrived and many of their followers will have waited underneath the old stand to see their heroes enter the dressing rooms to the tune of 'good luck' from all angles. I always visit the dressing rooms to check if there are any late changes, to gauge the tension and mood among the teams and, of course, to enjoy the special atmosphere that can only be found on such days. Soon every seat and standing spot is filled, and what a sea of colour and an ocean swell of goodwill greets the gladiators upon entering the arena.

The preliminaries are important: the limbering, the team photographs, the calling out of the names, the parade, the silence that precedes the National Anthem, all of these are essential because a Munster final means far more than seventy minutes of hurling. Now, finally, it is time for the drama to begin and to dismiss temporarily those memories of the many glorious moments from the past, of Ring, Mackey, Doyle, Keane, Broderick, McGrath, English, Fox, Flynn and so many more. Now there is only the spectacle that is about to unfold on the field. The whistle blows, the *sliotar* is spun into play and one of the year's great spectacles is underway – the magical, mythical Munster hurling final. Even the wait has been inspiring and the world seems a wonderful place.

# John Doyle, the hurler from Holycross

A special place is reserved in the hallowed halls of sport for those who set records, or equal those already established. John Doyle, the hurler from Holycross in Tipperary, just outside Thurles, fits into that category. He first played in Croke Park in September 1947 as a cornerback on the Tipperary minor team that beat Galway in the All-Ireland final. By the time he played his last game of hurling there, two stands had been made redundant to make way for the 1959 version of the Hogan Stand and twenty long years had slipped by.

John Doyle's last stand was staged on another September day, and on this occasion he was attracting more than a fair share of the attention because he was chasing a record: two years earlier he had equalled Christy Ring's harvest of eight All-Ireland medals when the Premier beat the Model County of Wexford in the All-Ireland final. That assured Doyle of hurling immortality, but one more medal would catapult him onto a platform shared only with Cú Chulainn himself. His chances looked good because Tipp were strong favourites given that opponents Kilkenny had not beaten them in a final since 1922.

The form was good: Tipperary had stormed through the National League and beaten Kilkenny by nine points in the home final and then New York in 'the away final'. Later they trounced Waterford by ten points in the semi-final of the Munster championship and Clare by twelve in the final. Analysts read much into the win over Waterford because it was they who had knocked All-Ireland champions Cork out of the reckoning in the first round. Nor was it lost on the gurus that the same young Cork side had beaten Kilkenny in the All-Ireland final a year earlier and that, if further proof of Tipp's credentials was needed, they were then on top of hurling's Roll of Honour with twenty-one All-Ireland titles, heading Cork by one and the Cats by six.

That was the picture in September 1967, as clear as spring water on a sunlit day, when the representatives of Munster and Leinster met to battle for the championship of Ireland and the Liam McCarthy Cup. Of course, that type of day is beloved of the scheming gods and far too tempting to be ignored: to make a story that is now almost forty years long a little shorter, the Cats played as never before and engineered the hurling upset of the century. It gave rise to massive celebrations by the Nore, but there was one terribly sad outcome from the match because the talented twenty-three-year-old Kilkenny forward Tommy Walsh lost the sight in one eye due to an accident in the course of play.

For John Doyle, his joust with history had ended in failure, but he was not a man given to complaining and regardless of what happened that fateful day, he remains, along with Christy Ring, the only other hurler to have won eight All-Ireland medals on the field of play. It is only right to point out that Kilkenny's Noel Skehan holds nine medals, but three were gained as a substitute when his illustrious cousin Ollie Walsh 'kept goals' for the county team.

What manner of man, then, is this giant of the game, John Doyle? I have met him on numerous occasions down the years and always look forward to the next; he is that sort – friendly, roguish, humorous, the best of company, gregarious, loquacious, mischievous and confident. It would be fair to say that he liked the limelight in his day – 'It was good for the game to have as many people as possible talking about hurling and the men who played it' is his way of dealing with the stories and myths that attached themselves to his name. He dismisses them by saying that 'most of them stories are not true at all, of course, but you can't stop people from letting the imagination run a bit wild.'

When I met him in early summer 2006 he was recovering from a back operation, but eagerly looking forward to another championship season. We spoke mostly about his past: he was an only child and his mother died in childbirth; his father passed away when he was twenty-one years of age and, as he put it himself, 'I was never used to having too many people in the house in my young days and I spent a while alone after my father's death.'

He married Ann Reidy and there was hurling aplenty in the Reidy household, too – Ann's brother Ray was the 'talking minor' of the 1950s who played at centre-back in the All-Ireland final of 1954 when Tipperary were beaten by Dublin, and again in the same position as captain a year later when they took the title. He would almost certainly have progressed to the county senior side if he had not chosen the priesthood – in those days, the twain of religion and sport did rarely meet.

We were not long in conversation when I mentioned that final Croke Park appearance in 1967. Was he disappointed that he did not win that ninth All-Ireland medal?

I always wanted to win every game I played in from the very first day I played for the Tipp minors in 1946, but 'tis different once the game is over. Kilkenny were better that day and I had no complaints. I appreciated what I had got from the GAA. I travelled the country for twenty years playing hurling and meeting all sorts of great people. I got trips to England and I was in America twelve or fourteen times. It was great and only for hurling and the GAA, I might never have seen Shannon, never mind New York, Florida and the other places. I never found anything wrong with the GAA and players should appreciate what it does for them rather than the reverse, I don't mind saying that anytime.

He is certainly not a man who believes the talk that takes place about the 'sacrifices' players make for the sake of the game. He offers the view that

anyone involved in sport has to make sacrifices and they are not always the players. I remember some Sunday evenings when myself and the wife would be milking the cows, we had about thirty and it was hand-milking in those days, but it wouldn't stop Paddy Leahy arriving and telling me about a challenge match somewhere later on. The wife often said to me to go and play the game and that she would finish the milking. Wasn't that a sacrifice as much as anything the players of today are talking about?

He also spoke of the sacrifices made by the Irish people he met on GAA trips abroad:

Whether it was in England or America, they always gave us a great time. I know that many of them took time off work to bring us here and there and nothing was too much for them and we should not forget it. Some of them would take their holidays in order to give us a good time and wasn't that something. The same would be true of my neighbours at home who looked after my farm whenever I was away and minded it better than I would myself maybe. They were happy once a Holycross man was on the Tipperary team and hurling anywhere. I remember a time when we spent a whole month in America and came home in a boat called *The Rhyndam*. Jesus, that was wonderful, something else, it lasted for nine days and it was an experience that I will never forget.

When talking to me about his career in May 2006, John told me he felt it was time 'to go' after that 1967 defeat, but added quickly that he was proud of the fact that he had never missed a match during his time as a county player: 'I played in challenge matches and all and was never either dropped or taken off in my life since I was picked on the championship team of 1949.' It's an impressive record. When I jokingly suggested that perhaps the selectors did not have the courage to 'invite' him to come off on occasions, he just laughed and added, 'That could be true too, Jesus, you can never tell what way some selectors act.'

I first met John Doyle in October 1949 in the dressing room in Croke Park before he went out to play against Laois in the final of the Oireachtas Tournament. I was due to broadcast the game on Radio Éireann, my second broadcast ever and my first on hurling, about which, to be honest, I knew very little. It was my first visit to a dressing room as well, and I clearly remember 'calling' in to see the Tipperary men in an old dressing room that was close to the corner near the Railway wall. I am certain that nobody knew me from Adam as I approached Pat Stakelum, who was the captain of the side that had won the All-Ireland a little more than a month previously. The Thurles Sarsfield man was very helpful to 'the new recruit' and he identified all the players for me in turn. I had not attended the All-Ireland final as I was still in Kerry at the time, on summer holidays from the Teachers' Training College in Drumcondra, but I had heard Micheál Ó Hehir's commentary on radio and was fascinated by the idea of a nineteen-year-old on the Tipp winning team. To me, All-Irelands were for men, but it was now obvious that there were exceptions – and John Doyle was one of them.

I was very anxious to see this precocious youngster in the dressing room and my memory of him is that of a bony, square-shouldered *scafaire*, an Irish word that translates as a lively, spirited, athletic young man. I didn't speak to him that day, but I do remember his forceful play, something the public saw a lot of over the following nineteen seasons. In all, he played in ten All-Ireland finals, winning eight, and when I asked about League successes there was a twinkle in his eye as he replied, 'they say I have eleven of them medals'. It is true and is a record collection by a mile. He played in thirteen League finals, counting the home final of 1963 against Waterford, and won ten for good measure, plus he has another medal he won as a substitute in 1949 when he did not play in the final.

Paddy Leahy was a vital man in Tipperary hurling in Doyle's time and he commanded great respect: 'Paddy was the type of man you couldn't say no to,' are words John Doyle used a lot during our chat. Paddy was an All-Ireland winner himself and later chairman of the selectors:

He was definitely fifty years before his time, but I'll tell you one thing, he was the boss, there was no such thing as manager but he was better than any manager. He knew the game inside out from his own playing days and kept in touch with the whole county. He had men in different parts with whom he discussed all the local things that mattered

– knowledgeable people like Séamus Ó Ríain in Moneygall, Paddy Kenny down in Carrick, Bill Moloney above in Graigue and so on.

Doyle concedes that the quality of the players around him on the Tipperary team of the 1950s and 1960s made it easy for him to win titles and medals. He even went as far as to say that, in his opinion, the second best hurling team in the country at that time was Tipp's second string:

I shouldn't say it, but I think our reserves would walk on to any team in Ireland, but they could not get on their own county team and that is a tribute to the men I played with – Theo English, Mick Roche, Jimmy Doyle, Tony Wall, Donie Nealon, Liam Devanney and all of them. 'Twas easy for me to be a winner with the likes of them around me. They had everything, they were able to hurl hard in close quarters, on the ground, or in the air, it was all the same to them. Each knew what the others could do and never had to be told how to play. Most of the modern players cannot double on a *sliotar* in the air, and I suspect they might even hurt themselves if they even tried.

There is no doubting his admiration for the men he played with and against, and it seems to me that he enjoys talking about all of them whenever he gets the chance. He admires the skill levels of many of the hurlers of the present, but fears that some of them are too concerned about 'what is in it' for themselves. In his day there wasn't the same kind of coaching or training at all. These were hard men who went out and performed week in, week out, without the benefit of expert health advice or physiotherapy. Doyle believes that one of the reasons why he never picked up injuries, as one might have expected, was the hard work he faced daily on the farm:

Sure you exercised every muscle and sinew in the body on the farm, whether working with the horse, tramming hay, or hauling beet. You'd be as hard as iron and there was no need for stretching or worrying about hamstrings either, we didn't know they existed.

My strength stood to me and it was a help that I weighed 13 stone 10lbs when fully fit – with that weight, you'd fear nothing, but I think that determination to win is the most important thing of all for a player. I wanted to win everything, even if it was only for a box of matches. Barring a few Wexford men and an odd other person, I can't remember meeting any hurler that was stronger than myself. It was good to feel that way at least. I always kept an eye on the fellow that would be coming towards me after the throw-in – in those days the forwards lined up at midfield for the start of a game. Whenever I saw a small man coming in I'd sort of smile to myself and say, I'm right for today anyway, though a small man could surprise you now and then. But them Wexford men had real physical strength, sure you might as well be hitting a tree as trying to tackle Ned Wheeler and the same went for Philly Grimes of Waterford. But I'll surprise you now and say that the strongest man I ever met was Eddie Keher of Kilkenny, Jesus he had a pair of hips on him and if he hit you with those hips you'd never forget it.

He has many memories of Christy Ring and their glorious battles during the 1950s and 1960s:

He was different to anybody else, he had everything, in a way he was a class of a freak and he lived for the game. The only thing we could do was try and stop him. You'd be at your wits' end marking him and he was so quick on the pull that I decided at one stage that the only plan for me was to make sure never to be more than a half-inch away from where he was. We finished up having fisticuffs one day in Limerick when the going got rough, but it was harmless and over in four or five minutes.

Even though he never played against Mick Mackey, Limerick's greatest hurling legend, I asked him how he compared the Ahane man with the pride of Cork and Cloyne, Christy Ring. I was not expecting him to reply decidedly in favour of one or the other. He pondered for a while before giving me an answer that could be interpreted in many ways:

I'll put it this way, you just could not compare Ringey to anyone else, but from what I could make out, if you were two points down and needed a goal, Mackey would be your man, but if you needed a point, Ring would get it for you.

The popular perception of the hurler John Doyle in action was that of a fearless and powerful force, always on a mission. He was not accustomed to wearing a welcoming face on the field and though a talkative person when in street clothes, his countenance could resemble a mystic on retreat when on the field of play. I put this to him, and he was very quick to assure me that he had never injured a player in his life and there was absolutely no truth in the myth that a few small hospitals in North Tipperary had closed down when he and a few of his colleagues retired: 'everyone knows that it's just a story composed by somebody for a bit of fun.' I thought it best not to dwell on that story, but it gave me a cue to mention another famous myth – the branding of the Tipperary fullback line of himself, Mick Maher and Kieran Carey as 'Hurling's Hell's Kitchen'. He told me not to believe a word of that either:

They wouldn't touch anybody, not at all, Michael Maher never hit anyone, he was a big strong man and intelligent and Kieran Carey was just the same. The talk about Hell's Kitchen is only old pishogues. Mind you, they were strong men and you wouldn't fancy going in tipping around among them. It was not all one way either, you can be sure of it, and there were strong men coming in too and we had to be able to mind ourselves and not get hurt and that was all we ever did, but we did it in the style of the old Tipperary hurling tradition.

I accepted the pishogue story without hesitation and it was a neat reminder that there are two sides to every story, but I feared that if we stayed with the topic for another while he might have convinced me of the torture that he and other defending angels had to put up with in their hurling days!

Doyle is totally against the modern practice of referees using 'them coloured cards' in the course of controlling games and believes strongly that the old system was fairer to players:

In my time you were put off for a serious offence and players had a good idea what was serious and what was not. Referees had the courage to send off the offenders and that was that. The yellow cards are destroying the game and the confidence of some hurlers. A player is shown one for a minor matter and from then on he's afraid to hurl in case he gets the second. I've seen players sent off after a second yellow card when they wouldn't have done much wrong, overall that worries me.

Considering the great rivalry that has always existed between his native county and Cork, it was interesting to hear the Holycross man extol the virtues of Frank Murphy as a referee:

The best referee that I know of in hurling over the past fifty years is that Corkman. He came out there and refereed every match as he saw it. He wasn't taking instructions from the office or anything like that and if you did anything that deserved being put off, he took action. He didn't need cards, but nowadays you have the poetry book first, then the yellow card and maybe another and you're gone. Frank Murphy was in control of the game from the word go, he was an honest guy and it didn't bother him what teams were playing. A good referee is heard but not seen. Now 'tis gone the other way and some referees think that it's them the people are looking at instead of the game. Frank Murphy was not like that and I'd have been happy with him even refereeing games between my own county and Cork. I have no doubt about it he was the best I ever saw.

John Doyle never took up the whistling role in the GAA himself, but he did serve in the administrative side and was his county's representative on Central Council for fifteen years and a regular and popular figure at the annual GAA Congresses. He had an interest in politics and stood for Fianna Fáil in the general election of 1969. His farming duties meant he did not have that much time for canvassing and as a result he failed to win a seat by 'a couple of hundred votes'. He was elected to Seanad Éireann on the Agricultural Panel in that same year and served there for five years. He liked the political scene and viewed it in an unusual way: 'All the wrong things would be good about it. 'Twas a different way of life and you learned all about how the country worked. Ray McSharry and myself shared the one office for four years. He was a lovely man, interested in economics and government, but not that much into sport at all. But there was no shortage of talk about sport in Leinster House during my days.'

Active sport and politics are now well behind the Holycross man, but there has been no diminution of his interest in both. He accepts the views of the majority of GAA members in relation to Croke Park being made available for soccer and rugby during the development of Lansdowne Road, but would have queries if little had happened by way of rebuilding in a year or two. The natural Doyle edge comes out when he says: 'Croke Park is magnificent, I went and saw every bit of it, but that is not all – look at the provincial grounds and even every GAA club in the country has done wonders in development, they all have stands and good dressing rooms. What have others been doing when the GAA was investing in development?' The Gaelic Grounds in Limerick is his favourite venue and the reason is a valid one: 'you develop a *grá* for a place where many of your great battles took place and twenty-three of my games in Munster championship hurling took place there, fourteen of them against Cork. We had great days in Limerick.'

It seems almost a crime that a man who lived within a few short miles of Thurles only played championship hurling in Semple Stadium on three occasions during a span of nineteen seasons. But at least he can say that he was never a championship loser there: Tipp beat Limerick in the semi-final of 1951, Waterford in the final of 1958 and, sweetest of all, they defeated Cork in the final of 1960 'on the pitch where every hurler wants to play' and before a crowd that was a mere handful under 50,000. It was a high-scoring game – 4-13 to 4-11 – and accounts have rated it the toughest ever Munster hurling final. These are some of the words from Pato's article on the game, which appeared in *The Irish Times* the following day:

A packed throng of enthusiasts witnessed a brilliant hour's play – played at lightning pace – Cork's best display since 1954 – a thrilling finish and if we accept a few brief disturbing incidents between leading players in the end, a good sporting spirit prevailed – one of the Cork players who was involved in a heated argument was escorted to the dressing room by the Garda – John Doyle, Jimmy Doyle, Tony Wall and Mick Maher played brilliantly for Tipp – Christy Ring gave the big Cork crowd much pleasure with some delightful touches.

Enough said about 1960, except to point out that Christy Ring was forty years of age at that time; is it any wonder that John Doyle said he was a freak and that it was his greatness that made him so! Provincial finals were almost a predictable annual outing for John Doyle: he played in fourteen in all, winning ten of them, the most chaotic of those being that of 1961 in Limerick. Memories of Thurles a year earlier had boosted the pre-match hype to an unprecedented level, so it was no surprise that the official attendance of 61,175 was the highest ever to witness an Irish sporting event outside of Croke Park. The figure does not tell the full story, however, as records show that the gates leading into the standing areas were opened during the minor game on account of the dangerously swaying masses on the terraces. In real terms, that meant thousands more gained admission. There was much confusion on the Ennis Road, which was so packed with people that the cars bringing the Cork team from a city-centre hotel could not make any headway at all. The players, already in their gear, had no option but to get out and walk to the 'Park', arriving in small groups. That is how Christy Ring clocked in for his nineteenth and last Munster final.

Tipperary won that day and John Doyle was destined to go on and play in five more finals before driving a nail into the back of the door and hanging up the boots for good. He had won

All-Ireland medals in three different decades – an honour he shares with the unrelated Tommy Doyle from Thurles, who was on the Tipperary teams of 1937 and 1945 and a colleague of John's in the successes of 1949, 1950 and 1951. Again, we must tip our caps to Noel Skehan of Kilkenny, who was a winner on the field in the finals of 1972, 1974, 1975, 1979, 1982 and 1983 and a substitute on the champion sides of 1963, 1967 and 1969.

Holycross Abbey is known to many tourists the world over as a delightful place to visit, but for the majority of Irish sporting people who pass through the pleasant hamlet outside of Thurles town it is the birthplace of John Doyle, a charismatic hurling character whose fame transcends generations. In other ages the Poet Laureate would have been commissioned to proclaim the achievements of such a sportsman!

'Come all you loyal heroes . . .'

# Munster medals lost and found

The Gaelic season now runs almost right through the twelve months of the year, even though the Autumn All-Ireland finals bring open inter-county activity to an end until National Leagues resume with the coming of spring. The hiatus is filled by club and inter-provincial action and subsidiary competitions, and followers certainly don't object. Each year provides its own highlights, often from unexpected sources, but nevertheless the calendar of fixtures that circulates in winter helps stoke the anticipation of all types of titanic clashes that are possible between then and All-Ireland final days in September.

Each person will have his or her own favourite venues and competitions in the season, but for me, when I watch the slanting February sun and think of the games ahead, I still relish the thought of the Munster hurling final, which has been part of my Irish summer for many years now. I have already described Thurles on final day, and if I had my way it would be staged annually in Semple Stadium and would never move from there. It would be inconceivable to move the Masters Golf championship out of Augusta, the Gold Cup out of Cheltenham, or the Grand National from Aintree, and so it is for me and Thurles. I know there are business and other reasons for moving the Munster finals about, and that there have been great and magnificent finals held beyond Semple, but Semple Stadium has a spiritual connection with hurling because it was here that the magic first took place.

It could be said that the clashes between Cork and Tipperary in the championship of 1926 sowed the initial seed, which has since blossomed into something that has held an addictive attraction for followers of the game. That final coincided with a growth in interest in hurling and football, and a crowd in excess of 25,000 – a massive crowd in those times – came to the Cork Athletic

Grounds that year to see Cork take on Tipperary. The 'Park' was not able to cope and the match had to be abandoned mid-way through the first half, whereupon it was decided to stage the re-fixture in Thurles.

Preparations for a big crowd were made, this time under the stewardship of Tom Semple, winner of three All-Irelands with Tipperary and captain in 1906 and 1908. As the Irish proverb says, *ní raibh barr cleite amach ná bun cleite isteach*, which is a novel way of saying that the arrangements were perfect – the game ended in a draw and was rated a classic. The excitement of the day was brought home to a much bigger audience than those present because the infant national radio station, 2RN, had broadcast it, with P. D. Mehigan commentating. This was just the second such broadcast: three weeks prior to this the station had broken new ground with the relay of the Kilkenny/Galway All-Ireland semifinal from Croke Park. The replay, again in Thurles, assumed the status of a national event: another massive crowd attended; Cork won; and Thurles claimed a special niche in the hearts of hurling lovers that has never been challenged. Most hurlers love to play in Semple and it remains their choice as the best hurling pitch in the country. Many a grandchild has been told that it was in Semple Stadium the heroics were performed 'the day the grandfather won the Munster final'. Every medal won in that hallowed place is cherished, especially a first or last.

I believe that the gods take special care of those medals ever since I was accidentally associated with one at the National Ploughing Championships staged at Rath, Co. Offaly, in 1997. I was wandering along through the masses, as people do at the ploughing every year, when I was stopped by a couple with a five- or six-year-old child in tow. They showed me a medal the child had seen on the ground by chance and picked up. The parents must have recognized me and thought perhaps I would know what to do with the find. I had a look at it and saw that it was a 1936 Munster hurling medal; on the reverse side it said *Luimneach a bhuaigh – G. Howard*.

By a quaint coincidence I had known Garrett Howard, winner of All-Ireland medals with Limerick in 1921 (when the Liam

McCarthy Cup was first offered), 1934 and 1936 and with Dublin in 1924 and 1927. He had lived into his nineties and was the only person ever known to me who fell and broke his hip coming out of a confession box. 'Twas a savage penance! He had since passed on, but once I told the finders that I knew his daughter, Liz, who was then well-known as PRO of the Tipperary County Board and is now President of the Cumann Camógaíochta na nGael. The keen-eyed child's parents were happy to leave the medal with me for a subsequent reunion with some member of the Howard family.

That was the beginning of what would lead to another amazing chance meeting. I headed on to the Public Address chalet, where I learned that a 'distressed lady' had called earlier inquiring if anybody had handed in a medal that she had lost. After making a few announcements that must not have been heard, it was decided that I would keep the treasure-trove and return it to the rightful owner in due course. It was now getting late in the afternoon, so I decided to head for home.

Sometime later, while walking along in search of my car – in the wrong field, as it turned out – I was again greeted by strangers, this time two athletic-looking teenagers. 'You were at my grand-father's funeral,' remarked one of them almost immediately. Failing to recognize the boys, I asked who the grandfather in question was and was astounded to hear the reply, 'Garrett Howard'! Before I could say anything further, the boy added that his mother was gone almost 'demented' because she had lost the last Munster medal he had won and had almost given up hope of ever again laying hand on it: 'We have been all over the place and she has now sent us back to where we parked the car in order to retrace our route from there to the stands and other areas with strict orders to keep looking at the ground all the way.' With that, I produced the famous medal! I would say it did not take long before the lads' mother, Jo Needham (*née* Howard), was once again in possession of it. I had made a note of the finder's name and I'm told she received a pleasant reward long before grass had grown again in that field in Rath.

# A Weekend to Remember – Cork in 1983

As the medal in question was won in Munster, I am now paying a visit to a city in that province that boasts more All-Ireland medals than any other – Cork, the city by the Lee. It reminds me of a very special occasion that took place there.

From a spectator's point of view, sport is meant to be entertaining and enjoyable more than anything else. I generally find it that way myself, but when I am asked now and then to nominate my most satisfactory match experience, it's never an easy task. It is not a question that suggests a quick response because there are so many matches and sporting occasions that merit consideration for the title. However, more often than not I settle for the weekend of 27–8 August 1983 in Cork City, destined to become the European Capital of Culture twenty-two years later. Culture, of a sort, certainly invaded the city by the Lee that weekend in the 1980s and I am sure there are many who can still see it in their mind's eye as if it happened yesterday. Yes, it was special.

It was a football weekend, but the long lead-up to it is relevant. Donegal had won Ulster for the third time in the county's history, while Galway had retained the Connacht title. By then, Galway were seventeen years without an All-Ireland and it had been fifteen years since Down had brought the All-Ireland to the North. How different the Ulster scene of today is: back then, there was almost general consensus that the destination of the Sam Maguire Cup was a matter only for Leinster and Munster.

Real surprises had sprung from those provinces that year. The big news in Leinster was that Kevin Heffernan was Dublin manager, but as the championship got moving Offaly were the team to watch as they had sensationally beaten Kerry in the All-Ireland final of the previous year with a captivating late goal by Séamus Darby. That meant they were hunting down their fourth Leinster title in a row when lining out against Dublin in the provincial final. Once again a team managed by Heffo succeeded in causing a major upset by dethroning the champions.

There was another shock down Munster way when a late Cork goal by Tadhg Murphy deprived Kerry of a record nine consecutive provincial titles. I remember the occasion well and the scoring of that goal by Murphy. Kerry had a team of legends on duty, with the vast majority of them holders of four All-Ireland medals apiece, the others with five and John O'Keeffe on seven! It was a stunning combination of skill and experience. Jack O'Shea was the captain and had been training with me for the previous eight years, so it was a special year in one sense. Fully expecting that the nine-in-a-row would be achieved, I had Jack prepared to make a speech as well as to play his usual midfield role as Munster final day approached. We travelled together to the match in Páirc Uí Chaoimh and to make doubly sure of details, we enacted a rehearsal of the presentation before we reached Cork. It was perfect – *cuireann sé áthas orm* . . .

The match followed and what an exciting finish! It had echoes of the previous year's All-Ireland final when Kerry were leading Offaly by two points in the dying minutes of the game. Then came Offalyman Darby to shatter what would have been a new record of five All-Ireland wins in a row. It was the same in Cork this time round, with Kerry leading by two points and going for another record as the game was drawing rapidly to a close. Cork were awarded a free well out the field and Dinny Allen was shaping up to take it. Tadhg Reilly was standing nearby and made a quick decision to take the kick himself, and that spur-of-the-moment reaction paved the way for Cork history: the ball dropped to Tadhg Murphy in front of goal and he drove it into the back of the Kerry net.

Another Kerry dream had been blown apart, but I believe there is a positive side to every story. One of my most vivid memories of the day is the sight of Dinny Allen surrounded by Kerry players as soon as play had ended, and all congratulating him heartily. For him it had been a long wait for his first Munster medal. He had scored two goals in the final of 1972 in Killarney, but Cork had still ended up as losers. He then opted for soccer over the next two years and won an FAI Cup medal, but in his absence Cork won the All-Ireland in 1973 and retained the Munster title a year later. He returned to Gaelic in 1975, and by 1983 his hand was practically worn out from congratulating his neighbours year after year on Munster final day. Dinny was well known to the Kerry players and had won four Railway Cups in their company, with Munster, in the intervening years. And now, all of a sudden, he was a winner at last in a Cork jersey and nobody could begrudge him the belated turn of luck. His luck held, too, and his was the honour of captaining Cork when winning the All-Ireland title of 1989. In the end, Fate looked with favour on a fine footballer and all-round sportsman.

Incidentally, Kerry forgot to bring the Munster Cup with them that day in 1983 – I suppose, having held it for the previous eight years, it must have been a part of the furniture in the Kingdom! It meant the Cup presented to Cork captain Christy Ryan was far from being the real thing. It was one found in an office press earlier in the afternoon and hastily polished up, but Cups are mere tokens after all and it did the needful just as well as the World Cup itself would have done. Few noticed the difference and fewer cared – all the glory belonged to the Rebels.

That Cork win in 1983 closed the page temporarily on Kerry captain Jack O'Shea's well-rehearsed speech, but it was useful when he climbed the steps of Croke Park's first Hogan Stand, relocated later in Limerick's Gaelic Ground, where the mid-fielder accepted the National League Cup the following May.

When Cork put the ball in the Kerry net, the pairing for the second All-Ireland semi-final was then known – Cork v Dublin – with the winners certain to be the overwhelming favourites to win the All-Ireland title later that year. The date was set for 21 August, by which time Galway had qualified for the final after a one-point win over a game Donegal side. It is an amazing statistic that Cork had never beaten Dublin in championship football, but on that August day they looked booked for history when leading by five points late into the second half of the Croke Park clash. As sometimes happens on the crunch occasions, a lot of action followed in a short space of time. Barney Rock scored a fine goal for the Dubs, for starters, but then another point on the board for Cork looked enough to see them through. Then Dublin's cornerback, Ray Hazely, finished off a good move with another goal that levelled the accounts. Delirium took hold on Hill 16, but few of those ardent Dub supporters could have even dreamt of the greater excitement still to come.

The replay was fixed for Cork on Sunday, 28 August and a terrific atmosphere built up as the week rolled on. The weather was brilliant, inducing general good humour and encouraging a huge Dublin following to make the long trek to Páirc Uí Chaoimh – the county's first All-Ireland semi-final outside of Croke Park since going to Tralee for a replay with Kerry in 1941. Travelling afar to a football match was still a new experience for Dublin followers then, but many decided to head south-westwards on the Saturday.

There was a carnival atmosphere by the Lee that night and I saw several make the trip out to the 'Park' just to see this far-flung venue. There was music and friendship aplenty and the warm air made it seem like there was no need to go indoors at all. The atmosphere was wholesome, with people eager to stop and talk about the match and anything under the sun.

It was the same on Sunday morning as I headed for the grounds. I was pretty early, but thousands were there before me, just sitting languidly on the grassy slopes by the River Lee as if captivated by a visiting sprite from Hy-Brassil. The ground filled up early and, having arrived in plenty of time, the Dublin team went out onto the field and lingered awhile in their street clothes before retiring to the dressing room. The proximity of the pitch to the stand and terraces meant the fans were really close to the players, a fact both sides appreciated and enjoyed.

Cork were the favourites, but Dublin were well prepared – as

I had learned during the week from a chance meeting with Kevin Heffernan. He had an unusual slant on the upcoming game and put it to me somewhat like this: 'Having led by five points near the end of the drawn game, Cork may be led to believe that they are five points a better side, and the home venue might seem to them as being worth another few points, but if some of those scores do not show up on the board early in the game, doubts might begin to creep in.'

As it was, Dublin got an early goal and went on to play fantastic football and recorded a shock eleven-point win. The celebrations went on well into the night and progress back to Dublin was slow, with groups stopping in most towns for more chat, views, verdicts and *craic* amid unprecedented camaraderie. It was that type of rare weekend. I made several stops and I have a particular memory of one in Durrow, where I saw the late Vincent O'Dea of AIB fame directing traffic in the centre of the street well into the late hours of a balmy early autumn night. The friendly Clareman and his banking colleague Bob Ryan were the original distillers of meaningful Public Relations.

Four weeks later Dublin won the All-Ireland title in a tough battle against Galway, giving them four out of ten since 1974. Any mention of that 1983 All-Ireland final instantly brings to mind Dublin's battling dozen – sometimes unfairly referred to as the 'Dirty Dozen' – holding on until controversial referee John Gough blew the final whistle. Red and yellow cards were unknown then, but the Antrim official sent off three Dublin players in the course of the game – Brian Mullins, Ciarán Duff and Ray Hazely – and visited the same fate on Pat O'Neill of Galway.

The record books show that Brian Mullins and Anton O'Toole were the only survivors from the team of 1974 and they were winners in 1976 and 1977 also. The 1983 captain was Tommy Drumm, winning his third All-Ireland medal, and I would bet that the trip to Cork in August of that year ranks as high as any of his football memories. It bordered on being a spiritual experience and it will stay with me far longer than the final played in Croke Park, which took place in atrocious conditions, although it was notable for the outstanding performance given by the lightly built Dublin defender Pat Canavan. So that semi-final football match in Cork, all told, was the finest sporting mix of entertainment and enjoyment I've had the pleasure of witnessing.

# Willie Ring

Men may come and men may go but Ring and Mackey go on for ever. They are synonymous with hurling, and long will that be the case. In Co. Cork, there is always plenty of good talk about the great game of hurling; they love their own and revere the name of Christy Ring, but in fairness they throw in the name of Limerick's Mick Mackey frequently when the very best are being scrutinized. Other than hurling, there is no sport I am aware of where the names of just two individuals hold a uniquely privileged position whenever a discussion gets underway on the greatest ever practitioners of the game. It almost seems to be an *ex cathedra* truth that Ring and Mackey were the greatest that ever swung a *camán*, and the teasing question is often asked as to which of the pair was the 'superior' in the confraternity of hurlers. More hours of debate than any computer could log have been devoted to the exploits of the pair, but I suspect that few ever wish to reach a definite answer and actually prefer to keep the matter in the 'unsolved' file.

In my view that is where it should remain and hopefully the debate will go on: I never tire of listening to people talk of the divine duo who thrilled followers of the wonderful game in another era. For that reason I took a notion recently to detour through Cloyne, in East Cork, when on the way from Daingean (Dingle) to Dublin. The little town is undergoing development at the moment, like many another town throughout the country, but big or small it will remain forever famous as the birthplace of Christy Ring. His brother, Willie John, still lives there and I spent a few very pleasant hours in his company as he reminisced about his renowned brother and the game of hurling that meant so much to both of them.

The word 'prodigy' was never mentioned, but it entered my mind in relation to Christy when I heard Willie say that his teacher,

Jerry Moynihan, 'copped on to him very early and thought that he was exceptional'. Nor was he the only local expert who predicted greatness for the boy: 'Pad Ahern was leaning on the wall one day, watching us hurling. Christy was no more than eight or nine at the time and smaller than the run of the lads, but Pad said that day that the small young fella would play for Cork in Croke Park yet.' It turned out to be the understatement of the century from the shrewd Pad Ahern. From Ring's first appearance in Croke Park in the minor All-Ireland final of 1938 to his last, twenty-five years later when he won his eighteenth Railway Cup medal with Munster, he was a regular at Croke and often the drawing card at the GAA's headquarters.

Willie was born in 1917 and was three years older than Christy and a fine hurler in his own right. The game was always played in the locality, but the Cloyne Club was largely inactive in the early 1930s due to lack of training grounds, until Jerry Moynihan fired interest to a level that brought re-affiliation. Willie recalls the great excitement as the hurling club began to do well and the fun of travelling out of Cloyne in a convoy of side-cars with good-humoured banter flowing as they passed leisurely through 'enemy' territory. Those memories mean a lot to him and thankfully he has recorded them and much more in his *History of Cloyne GAA*. He and Christy played on the 1939 Junior team that won the Cork championship, but it was the older brother who was prominent on many occasions and who was the star of the East Final with three goals to his credit. I came across a reference to both in a preview of the county semi-final against Newtownshandrum and it gives an interesting angle on the part Christy had played in the previous match with Clonakilty:

The cleverness of the small Ring on the Cloyne wing turned the scales in favour of his side. What a player he would be if endowed with an inch or two more in stature. His brother Willie is also very useful.

Both were very prominent in the semi-final and final, but unfortunately a serious knee injury at the age of twenty-four ended

Willie's sporting career, although he never left hurling. He wasn't so interested in recounting his own innings, being more anxious to speak of his famous brother. He stressed more than once that Christy was never boastful nor inclined to belittle any man who played the game he was in love with, or any game for that matter: 'We were always very close and we both trained together. He was an absolute perfectionist and he said to me once if he practised a thing a hundred times and if it came off once in a match, it was well worth it.'

As youngsters they often trained for four hours or more at a time and Willie says his younger brother practised everything, frees, line cuts left and right depending on the side of the field, and he would not be happy until he had mastered every single skill:

'Tis a quare thing for me to say, but it was impossible to hook him and if he was hooked, he'd cry, but he mastered it and was never hooked again in his life. He'd stay out there in the field practising until we'd be worn to the bone from it, never a thought of coming home until me mother or sister came for us. Our young brother Paddy Joe didn't come with us, he was a bit young, but hurled later and was good – he won a county. Our father was great for instructing us when we were very young and it was a great pity that he did not live to see Christy play for Cork. He was a good hurler in his time and he died a young man at the age of forty-five.

Christy first wore the Cork jersey in the minor championship of 1938 when the Rebels beat Dublin in the All-Ireland final. Interestingly, he was a defender in those days and won his minor medal as a right half-back. He scored a goal from a 21-yard free that day and had the courage to go up and volunteer to take it, knowing that he was good at the art. According to Willie, he never failed to score a goal from the 21-yard line anytime he went for it during his long career because he had practised that specialist shot assiduously. He also studied traits of defenders: 'Never aim towards the goalkeeper,' he used to advise, 'he is the most likely to stop it, aim for a spot left or right into the corner and hit it hard and high.' That was his technique and as for being able to pinpoint a target spot, Willie remembers him demonstrating to young kids how to hit the ball accurately and hard:

There was a garage above our place and the windows were boarded, but in halves, and there was a chap, Mossie Cahill's young fella, and he used to wet the ball at the tap and bet that Christy wouldn't hit the eight-inch by somewhat panel from twenty-five yards and sometimes thirty. But he always did and you would see the wet mark on the panel. It was something he practised year in, year out every night while he was here in Cloyne.

Such a man deserved the distinction of being the first to win eight All-Ireland medals on the field, while his eighteen Railway Cup medals outstrip all others by such a distance that it is the greatest measure of his extraordinarily long career at the top of the scale. What, in Willie's view, were the reasons for his survival, and indeed dominance, in such a competitive environment for almost a quarter of a century?

It came from a lot of things. He was good at the game, but more than any one thing it was his great and passionate love of the game of hurling and that love stayed with him until the day he died. His determination to try and win every single game he played came from that and it drove him to prepare and to practise right through the years. He often said that you must never underestimate any team or opponent. He never drank or smoked and wasn't a man for going to dances on the way home from matches. He didn't know whether it was a church or dance hall he was passing – hurling and playing the game was his life.

It is easy to understand that loyalty to the game. It was another feature of the man that whatever jersey he happened to be wearing ranked highly with him. Willie recounted a story about how Christy once reprimanded a player who was making a habit of holding onto his jersey by saying to him, 'Whatever about myself, leave that jersey alone, I would die for it.' Hurling was more physical in those days and he picked up his quota of injuries, but he never believed in bringing grudges or the like with him to the next game because they would break the concentration needed and the focused determination that often brings victory. 'He got his jaw broken twice,' said Willie, 'and he got six or seven stitches. He told me he got blackouts going for the ball, but he carried on. That was his way, he loved to be hurling no matter what.'

Like most players, there were times when he had to leave the field due to injury. One memorable photograph shows Christy with his arm in a sling on his way to the sideline, but casting a backward glance towards the umpire, who happened to be the legendary Mick Mackey. There has been much speculation over the years about the words that may have passed between the gods of hurling at that moment, but Willie told me that Christy would not even tell him what had transpired. Apparently, Ring and Mackey made a pact soon afterwards to carry the secret to their graves, as they did.

Christy never boasted about particular achievements, but was always happy when things went well. Willie cannot remember ever hearing him say that he got the better of this opponent or that. Nonetheless, he was fully aware of his own abilities, as instanced by an aside about line cuts, or sidelines as Willie sometimes calls them:

The *Sunday Press* used [to] have a forum in those days featuring one player, hurling or football, each week. Séamus Bannon of Tipperary, a grand fella and a fine player, was on one week and he was very famous for line balls. Christy's turn came and when the reporter was driving him out to the Mardyke to get some shots, he happened to say that Séamus Bannon had said that you need grass for the sidelines. With that Christy asked him to stop the car and before long he had placed the horse-skin ball in the centre of the road and cut it nearly as high as the trees. The reporter was amazed and said that he wouldn't believe it only for seeing it. Christy then told him to go back and tell Séamus Bannon that they don't grow grass in the middle of the road in Cork.

He did most of his club hurling with Glen Rovers and there was hardly any way out of it but to play for a city club once he got a job in Cork, twenty miles away from Cloyne: 'He was lucky and delighted to get the job at a time when whole families were emigrating. There were no cars then and he could hardly cycle in and out of Cloyne every day, but he cycled home every Saturday and made nothing of it.' Not only did he make little of twenty miles on the bike but he always joined in with the Cloyne lads for the weekly training. 'That would be followed by a match between ourselves,' says Willie, 'and he would be in the middle of it.'

He was spotted by a visitor one Saturday, on the eve of a match with Tipperary, 'and when he asked was that *himself* playing out there, he was told by Bunty Cahill that it was and that if he came the following morning, he'd be out there again.' He was a great man for the home according to Willie, and was very fond of his mother. 'She seldom went to matches, but said the Rosary so that nobody would get hurt and he would ring her after the matches or whenever he could.'

I was beginning to understand how extraordinary a man Ringie was. The stories about him seemed endless, each one drawing him larger and finer in my imagination than the last. I learned of another episode that demonstrated his huge desire to play hurling. Apparently he left Cloyne on the bicycle one day, heading for Cork to play in a suit-length tournament match. These were popular matches at the time and so-called because the winners received a suit-length of fabric each. 'The suit-length tournaments were great,' said Willie, 'they were the only way we'd get a suit in those days.' As usual, the hurley, boots and socks were tied to the crossbar of the bike, as they were hours later when he cycled back into the town with a suit-length on the carrier.

Winning was what meant the most to Christy Ring, to use his skill, speed and intelligence to outwit his opponents – that's what mattered. He wasn't dazzled by medals or prizes. As Willie says: 'Winning the medals, that gave the satisfaction, but after that he didn't have much to do with them, they were put away or maybe hung up and that would be that, no boasting or anything like it, even when he was selected as Texaco Hurler of the Year at the age of thirty-nine.' When I inquired about a particular medal he had given away one time, Willie explained how it came about:

They were collecting for St Augustine's Church and a priest came to Christy asking for a subscription. He was a very charitable man, a great man for visiting people in hospital – you know Con Murphy, who played many a game for Cork with Christy, he was the President after, a great man all his life, and he told me that the first man in to see him in hospital when he was sick was Christy, even though they had a difference one time. Well anyway, he said to the priest who was collecting for St Augustine's, 'I will give you the most precious thing I have, my eighth All-Ireland medal'.

The priest was more than grateful. As Willie observed, it took a Corkman to win the medal and a Tipperary man to take it from him! The priest later had the medal moulded into the bowl of a chalice.

Naturally, Willie spoke more about hurling from the early 1940s to the mid-1960s than other eras. The great names tripped easily from his tongue, as did the great battles with Tipperary and the clashes between Christy and likeable characters such as Mickey 'The Rattler' Byrne and John Doyle. He believes Jimmy Doyle was the best from that county he had ever seen, and he said the same of Eddie Keher of Kilkenny: 'They were the masters of the skills of the game. Look at DJ Carey over the past fifteen or sixteen years, and I remember tough defenders from there, too, Mark Marnell, "The Diamond" Hayden and Peter Blanchfield and many more.' He has a special regard for the great Wexford team of the 1950s and could name them all: 'A very fair team, the three Rackards, Nicky, Bobby and Billy, they were a grand team.'

When I mentioned modern-day hurling, Willie agreed that it was fast and the players were very fit and could lift big weights and so on, but he reminded me that it is different from the old-style hurling:

Christy would never do the type of training they do now, but he was strong and fit, he worked hard, he kept his eye on the ball and had great faith in skill, judgement and anticipation. I'll give you an instance of his way of looking at things. He told me about playing a big match one day and somebody came up to him saying that the fella he was playing on was terrible fast. Christy said he just looked at the speaker before telling him that Landy of Australia was the fastest man in the world and had won the Olympics, but that he couldn't hurl though. He told him also that he felt he could beat the fastest man in the world to the ball – there's more to hurling than hitting a ball up and down a field, there's judgement and other things.

Willie deplores the lack of pulling on the ball in present-day hurling and feels that former players were good at that skill because they practised it:

It was one of the hardest things in hurling, say, if you were playing full-forward and the ball was dropping five or six yards short, to be able to run out full belt and double on it and score a goal. I saw Christy do it for the Glen one day against Imokilly, a team I was training. 'Twas very near half-time when he ran out, never caught it but 'clung it'.

Willie said he asked the full-back at the break why he did not go with Christy for the pull and his answer was that he thought he'd miss it. Willie's retort was that if he had missed, he would have cried!

He got many a goal with pulls like that during his long career and I wondered did Willie ever advise him that he should retire when he was say thirty, or thirty-five, or forty years of age? He told me that he never did any such thing, not even when Christy was forty-six years of age: 'He scored a goal and a point against Mount Sion in the Munster Club championship and they wanted to chair him off the field, but he wouldn't let them. He decided himself when to go, he told no one and never said to anyone that such or such a game was to be his last.'

Christy Ring's death on 3 March 1979, at the age of fifty-eight years, was a shock to the people of Ireland within the sporting arena and beyond. It is estimated that 60,000 people attended his wake and funeral. His great friend and hurling colleague Jack Lynch later said that it was very moving when they were waking him in O'Connor's funeral home: 'All the old women from Blackpool came in minibuses to pay their respects, they were all round him and they were saying that they would have no one to look after them now.'

My visit to the home of Willie Ring in Cloyne was a most pleasant experience and I thoroughly enjoyed listening to tales of the life of the maestro from such a personal angle. I can also tell you that there are few people who can tend a fire or make proper tea like Willie's wife, Hannah. The time came when I had to take my leave of them, and on my way out of town I stopped to take a look at the beautiful sculpture of Christy Ring that stands at the entrance to the club grounds. The stonework on the base and surrounding walls was all done by Willie and it is an impressive tribute to Cork's finest ever sportsman. I stood there and admired it. It was one of those cold, wet March nights when the wind blew relentlessly from the Arctic North. Inside the club grounds the floodlights were on and sounds of encouragement and frustration were coming from the playing field. It didn't seem right that it was football they were playing on that particular night, but then, didn't Christy win a Cork County title at football with St Nick's to go with his fifteen county hurling medals, his eight All-Irelands and eighteen Railway Cups?

One way or another, I felt sure that any young person who has walked in or out of the Cloyne field over the years has taken inspiration from the man on the pedestal.

# The Stations of Sam Maguire

Before leaving Cork, I would like to dwell a while on another famous Corkman, or more precisely on the most famous 'Corn' in Ireland, which is named after the Dunmanway-born Corkman Sam Maguire; it enjoys a special relationship with devotees of Gaelic football. Sam Maguire played for London in the All-Ireland football finals of 1900, 1901 and 1903; he was captain in 1900 and 1903. The Cup was first presented to the All-Ireland football champions in 1928, Kildare being the initial holders of a trophy whose fate it was to assume a magical aura of its own with the passing years. There might be a little permissible delusion in comparing the respect it is accorded with that of the Jules Verne trophy for world soccer, the Claret Jug that goes to the winner of the Open Championship in golf, or the Cheltenham Gold Cup or steeplechasing's Blue Riband, but I think it is allowed. The Sam, long perceived as having its own distinct personality, has gone in glory to sixteen counties: Cavan, Down, Donegal, Derry, Armagh and Tyrone in Ulster; Galway, Mayo and Roscommon in Connacht; Kerry and Cork in Munster; Kildare, Dublin, Meath, Louth and Offaly in Leinster. All-Ireland titles had been recorded by Limerick, Tipperary and Wexford before the famous trophy, crafted in likeness to the Ardagh Chalice, came on the scene.

There are many stories told about the adventures of the Cup in its rambles through parts of Éire and beyond. Bill Squires Gannon was the Kildare captain of 1928 and the brand new Cup must have been a great curiosity on that September day in 1928 when the Lily-Whites scored an exciting one-point win over Cavan in Croke Park, down the road from the Short Grass county. One folktale mentions that Bill milked cows later that afternoon after the historic win, although it does not go so far as to suggest that he milked them into the Sam Maguire!

I saw it filled to the brim with champagne once, honouring a custom that dates back into the depths of history. As far as I can remember, the night of the 1970 All-Ireland final was the champagne occasion and it took place in a hotel that is no more – the International Hotel in Bray. A Kerry follower, home from England for the match and in high spirits on account of the Kingdom's success, which had netted him a good deal of money on a bet, made the gesture of 'filling the Cup'. I have a hazy notion that it cost £35, the equivalent of €3,500–€4,000 in today's terms.

There is no doubt but that the Sam Maguire Cup holds the record for most miles travelled in celebration. Counting the original and its replacement, which has been in circulation since 1988, the Cup has visited Kerry on twenty-six occasions. Joe Barrett was the only Kerryman to take it twice, and it must have felt lonely when it was left in the dressing room under the Cusack Stand for a night after Kerry won the final of 1959 with 'Team of the Century and Millennium' mid-fielder Mick O'Connell as captain. The glamour of today was not attached to it then and it was not missed from the Kingdom's Sunday night function, because everyone believed it had travelled to Kerry with Mick O'Connell, who took an early train to the south shortly after the game finished. Maybe the gods had ordained that it was appropriate for the Cup to spend a night in a dressing room as Mr Maguire himself had togged out and played in the All-Ireland final at the same venue when Kerry won its first ever All-Ireland. The famous Cup was calm and comfortable when discovered by cleaners on that Monday morning in September 1959.

Thirty-three years later, sometime before Christmas 1992, it went missing again, this time from a very special banquet held in the Great Northern Hotel, Bundoran, to present newly crowned All-Ireland champions Donegal with their All-Ireland medals. Sam was growing accustomed to the north-western hill country by then, but was brought back to Dublin on a Friday to add lustre and decorum to the stage of the Burlington Hotel during the annual Allstar extravaganza. It was scheduled to travel northwards again on the Saturday for the historic and biggest GAA night ever staged in Tír Chonaill. The best-laid plans and arrangements can go awry, however, and that was the case on that momentous night in 1992. I was present, but Sam did not make the line in time. The celebrations were *Gloria in excelsis*, as only a first victory can summon, with great praise being lavished on all the players and those associated with that unexpected fine September win over Dublin. Sam didn't make it until the following morning, but no one seemed to mind.

It was not until 1997 that some of the latent powers of the Cup came to prominence. Kerry won the All-Ireland title that year with Laune Ranger's man Liam Hassett as captain. It was the fiftieth anniversary of the Polo Ground's final, when Cavan had scored a four-point victory over Kerry in faraway New York. By the way, captain John Joe O'Reilly was not presented with Sam at the end of that enterprising and courageous venture overseas for the very good reason that the Cup had been left at home in Ireland. It was said that the cost of insurance was the reason why Sam was left behind, but I would call it a lame excuse. What a pity that the exiles were denied the spectacle of seeing a proper finish to a historic All-Ireland final with the customary presentation of a Cup.

Anyway, in 1997 the GAA decided that the opening round of the National League between Kerry and Cavan would be played in New York as part of the Golden Jubilee celebrations associated with the only All-Ireland final ever played outside the country. It was a fitting gesture and all surviving members of both teams, along with representatives of those who had passed on, were invited to travel with the current players on League duties.

The Cup was definitely travelling this time and arrived at Shannon Airport with captain Hassett. It soon transpired that the Laune Ranger had forgotten his passport and had no way of fetching it at short notice, so there appeared to be the makings of a problem. A solution was eventually found by allowing Liam to travel in the company of Sam Maguire, and both boarded the plane together. There was a little anxiety about what might happen at the New York end of the journey, an anxiety that grew to concern when both were taken aside to an office once it became clear that

Liam was travelling without passport. I do not know who did the talking in that office, but shortly afterwards I and many others witnessed both marching straight through customs: Liam smiling broadly, but Sam getting all the attention from onlookers who had never before seen such a lump of silver parading through a busy airport.

The same silver caused a bit of a problem to the Down footballers in 1968 when they were All-Ireland champions for the third time in the space of eight years. They were entitled to be ranked as a really great team, having beaten Kerry in the All-Ireland final as their predecessors had done in 1960 and in the semi-final of the following year. As part of the national acclaim they received in the aftermath of that 1968 win, the team was invited to Belfast City Hall, an institution not known as a bastion of support for Gaelic games.

I would regard the gesture of invitation as a worthy one, but there were people in Ulster who held a different view and in time-honoured fashion they decided to protest against the visit. The Reverend Ian Paisley was among them, and he is not shy to admit, even now, that his protest was more against 'Sam' than the football heroes themselves. You see, Sam Maguire, the man from Dunmanway in the Republic, had spent years working with the British Post Office in London, was instrumental in getting fellow worker Michael Collins into the IRB and had played a significant part in the War of Independence. In later years he was no doubt suspected by some people of being a 'gun-runner', hence that 1968 protest. It was just another chapter in the intriguing history of the Sam Maguire.

Believe it or not, Sam has also been to the top of Mount Brandon, the second highest mountain in Ireland, which stands close to the Atlantic Ocean in the Gaeltacht of West Kerry and rises to a height of 3,150ft above sea-level. Locally it is regarded as a holy mountain because of its association with St Brendan almost 1,500 years ago. Perhaps he first climbed to the top before setting off from nearby Cuas in a *naomhóg,* or curach, on the voyage that led to the discovery of America in the sixth century – almost 1,000 years ahead of the celebrated Christopher Columbus. Tim Severin, a Kent-born explorer, undertook and completed a similar journey in 1977 and his success gave further credence to the story we had always believed about our kinsman, whose birthplace is said to be Ardfert in North Kerry, where he founded one of three monasteries. The date of his death in Clonfert, Galway, is given as 577 AD.

His life is an interesting study and there is an account of his Atlantic crossing, undertaken with other monks, in a Latin tale of 12,000 words believed to have been written somewhere on the continent of Europe around the year 800 AD. The title is impressive – *Navigatio Sancti Brendani Abbatis* – and the work is regarded as Ireland's best-known contribution to medieval literature. It gives the purpose of his Atlantic adventure as a search for *Terra Repromissionis Sanctorum* – the Promised Land of the Saints.

I have often climbed Mount Brandon and on a fine day there are few more spectacular vistas of land and sea to be viewed anywhere in the world. My most recent 'pilgrimage' to the top was on 30 June 2005 and it was linked to Kerry's win in the All-Ireland final the previous September. Dara Ó Cinnéide, whose home is close to the base of the mountain, was Kerry captain for that fine win and thus was the man who had brought the Sam Maguire back to Kerry that September. I journeyed south from Dublin to witness its arrival in and welcome to Ó Cinnéide's own area. It is really only on such occasions that one realizes the magnetic power the trophy holds for the population at large.

Some few weeks later I met the captain again and he was outlining the many places, not all within Kerry, to which he and Sam had been 'invited'. He was anxious that as many as possible should be facilitated, but casually remarked that he would dearly love to bring it to 'Barra Chnoc Bhréanainn' before it was returned to Croke Park the following August for de-programming. I promised to be there for the unique visit in honour of the saint who had been dead for 1,428 years, and sure enough the call came from Dara in mid-June 2005. His own house was our base camp on the morning of 30 June, but unfortunately the weather was not the best with a wind blowing and spilling rain in from the Atlantic.

I had notified a friend of mine, Evan Chamberlain, of the expedition and as he was then compiling a documentary on Sam Maguire he joined us along with cameraman Pat Comer, former Galway football goalkeeper.

The party was augmented further once three more members of my family signed on: my wife Helena and daughters Nuala and Doireann. Three more Cinnéidigh completed the team: Dara's cousin Laurence Kennedy, who had travelled from Dublin, his father Paddy and his uncle John, who did not intend to go all the way to the summit due to failing health. Sadly, John has died since, but he went a fair bit of the way with Sam that day. *Ar dheis Dé go raibh a anam.*

Following suitable sustenance kindly provided by Dara's mother, Ann, Sam was placed in a large training bag, secured on the captain's broad back and off we set on one of the most pleasant climbs I have ever experienced. The Cinnéidigh were familiar with every part of that mountain and had a name for every rock and crevice, flower and plant along the route, all in the Irish language and familiar to the mountain and the elements for eons. Wind and rain did not matter as we slowly made our way to the top, with Dara refusing all offers of help in carrying Sam to a higher level than ever before – except when airborne. As far as the captain was concerned, it was a day for a mission rather than sightseeing. He had no worries about the mountain and at one point, near the summit, picked up a small flower and informed me of the long-held belief that a person never gets lost if they find 'Seamar Mhuire', the blessed trefoil mountain herb.

Sam was released from the bag for the final ascent and Dara and I carried it over the remaining 100 yards or so. It was a spiritual moment when Kerry's thirtieth All-Ireland winning captain wiped the raindrops from the face of Sam and raised him towards the skies at the top of Mount Brandon as a gesture to the saint in whose honour the mountain is named. It almost looked as if Dara had fulfilled a promise made during one of his many climbs along that enchanted way. I was delighted to witness it.

★

Sam was only eight years old when it made its first trip to Mayo in 1936. Séamus O'Malley, a man I had the privilege of knowing well, was the captain of that excellent winning Mayo side. He was an unusual captain in that he was also county secretary at the time. He lived to the grand age of ninety-seven years and continued to play golf at the Claremorris club almost to the end.

Indeed, golf was associated with the team's trip to Dublin for the meeting with Laois in the All-Ireland final. From what I could gather from talking to Séamus, most of the players travelled to Dublin on the Friday and stayed in the Spa Hotel in Lucan, an establishment owned by a Mayo family. Séamus himself came later, after putting in his day's work as a teacher beforehand. The Lucan nine-hole golf course was attached to the hotel at the time; I can remember when the tee shot for one of the holes had to be driven across the main road.

I am sure it was the same in 1936 when the course was put at the disposal of the Mayo team on the Saturday before the All-Ireland final. Most of them had never played the game before, but clubs were provided and in the words of Séamus, 'we enjoyed the experience immensely for a long number of hours'.

I doubt if any of today's managers would allow such a distraction, but apparently it did the Mayomen no harm because they had eighteen points to spare over Laois the following day. Séamus O'Malley had the distinction of becoming the first Mayoman to raise the Sam Maguire Cup. It is almost incredible that to this day, seventy years later, only one other man from the same county has done so and that was Seán Flanagan, skipper of the flamboyant winning teams of 1950 and 1951.

Séamus and his colleagues attended a *céilí* in Dublin's Mansion House on that 1936 All-Ireland final night and he mentioned the possibility that they collected their All-Ireland medals in between dances like *Fallaí Luimní* and *The Siege of Ennis*. Life certainly was less complicated then. Séamus returned to Mayo once the *céilí* was over in order to be ready for school on the following morning. He decided to bring the Cup with him to show to the pupils, but the problem was how to carry it as the school was three miles outside the town of Claremorris. The solution that presented itself to Dara Ó Cinnéide before climbing Mount Brandon was not original; O'Malley was the first man to carry the Cup strapped to his back. Large training bags had not yet been invented at the time of the Economic War, which left Séamus with no option but to use three pieces of rope to fasten Sam to his shoulders and waist before mounting his bicycle and heading for school. What a sight to behold on any road! I'm sure Mayo people would not mind if they witnessed such an apparition in the near future.

Meanwhile, life has changed for Sam, too, who now usually has an itinerary secretary during his stay with champions. Cuthbert Donnelly held that onerous office when Tyrone were custodians, and he was almost on full-time duty ferrying it to functions. It has been overseas more than once and brought great joy to Wales when visiting there for the first time in late spring 2006.

But I don't know if the current security restrictions will allow for any more unexpected adventures for Sam – time will tell.

# Memories of Fitzgerald Stadium

From the home county of the same Sam it is but a short journey to my own native Kerry. And what better place to begin revisiting places and meeting more people than my favourite broadcasting venue: Fitzgerald Stadium, Killarney. It was from there, in 1956, that I did my first broadcast outside of Croke Park when Cork beat Kerry in the replay of the Munster Football final. Neither that nor the fact that I was born in Kerry has any bearing on my choice, however. The stadium has enjoyed a fine history since it was opened in 1936 and named in honour of Dick Fitzgerald, who captained Kerry to win the All-Ireland finals of 1913 and 1914. The Dr Crokes man died in 1930 at a young age and the arena-shaped new grounds were a fitting tribute to his memory. Patients in the nearby psychiatric hospital, in the care of long-time Kerry trainer Dr Éamonn O'Sullivan, helped in the construction of the stepped terrace that runs right along the western side, and it marked a new approach to their rehabilitation. Subsequently, the doctor saw the benefits patients could derive from playing football and he was instrumental in introducing that therapy also.

For as long as I can remember there has been a broadcasting box at the back of the Fitzgerald Stadium terrace and its location may hold the key to why Killarney is my favourite venue. The view from there at any time of year is breathtaking, with a long sweep of mountains taking in Corrán Tuathail, Ireland's highest peak, Mangerton, the Paps of Danann, and the many glens, ravines and folds of forest that have garnered world fame for Beauty's Home. Whenever I have to go there to work, I make sure to arrive early to study that countryside from an ideal vantage point. It is far more than a lovely panoramic vista because the depth of the ever-changing hues and shades on the slopes convey a weather forecast that is rarely wrong. The prospect of rain or otherwise can be gauged accurately by the perceived proximity or remoteness of the hills. I hope any future development of this lovely park does not entail any type of high stand at the back of the mountain goal: it would be a crime against the environment to take away that view.

The All-Ireland hurling final of 1937 was played in Fitzgerald Stadium due to a delay in the completion of Croke Park's first Cusack Stand. Tipperary and Kilkenny contested the final and, considering the pairing, a classic was anticipated. In fact, it proved to be one-sided, with Tipperary running out winners by a margin of seventeen points. However, the story of the broadcasting of the final was unique in itself. The national station had ten years' experience of covering All-Ireland finals, but this was the first outside of Croke Park. Seán Ó Ceallacháin, father of Seán Óg, and Éamonn de Barra were appointed as commentators, but a shock awaited them on arriving at the ground: they were refused admission on account of a dispute between the GAA and Radio Éireann. That presented a bit of a challenge, but they formulated a strategy whereby one of them went into the match, by paying I presume, while the other went to the local Post Office from where the line originated and began to broadcast at the appointed hour. 'Hard' news was then ferried periodically from the field and the listeners succeeded in getting most of the story of the day by means of 'eye-witness reports'.

The stadium is now the regular venue for Munster football finals involving Kerry whenever the draw favours the county, but that practice did not begin until 1945 when Cork won and went on to beat Cavan later in the All-Ireland final. Simon Deignan, a Cavan player of the time, refereed the game – the first of three in a row for the army lieutenant then stationed in Tralee. He played at midfield on that cavan team of 1945 and was in direct opposition to Éamonn Young, another army man and long-serving star of Cork football.

The Munster hurling final of 1950 was played in Killarney and, unlike the All-Ireland final of 1937, it developed into one of the all-time great hurling matches. Tipperary were All-Ireland champions and an inordinately large number of followers gathered at the grounds long before the match. All could not be accommodated, but everybody got in nevertheless because walls were scaled and gates broken down, with the inevitable result that there was pitch encroachment before the game even got underway. It became much worse during the exciting closing stages, but the game was finished and Tipperary won by three points. It marked the end of the inter-county career of Jack Lynch, the only man in the history of the GAA to have won six consecutive senior All-Ireland medals. He was playing at midfield when Cork won four hurling titles between 1941 and 1944, he was the right corner-forward on the successful football team of 1945 and back in his regular midfield role for a further hurling win the following year. He was a member of Dáil Éireann at the time of that 1950 Munster final, and on his way to becoming Taoiseach, so he played very little club hurling afterwards.

Lynch was a close friend of Christy Ring, and the pair contributed much to Cork hurling. On the night in 1999 when Lynch's remains were placed in the North Cathedral prior to burial the following morning, a letter was shown to me that illustrated his attitude towards staying on with Glen Rovers a little longer. The letter was handwritten on Dáil Éireann notepaper and was in answer to a request from the Glen captain of 1951 that he stage a 'comeback' with the Glen in the forthcoming Cork County hurling semi-final. Seán O'Brien, the captain who made the request, was sitting next to me in the Cathedral and it was he who handed me the letter with the remark, 'that was Jack'.

The letter was brief enough. It thanked the captain for the thought, but declined the offer on the grounds that his return would deprive a promising young hurler of a place on the team for the sake of 'giving a has-been another medal'. He did add, however, that he would attend the match to cheer the Glen on to victory.

The following day Donncha Ó Dúlaing and I shared RTÉ's broadcast of the funeral Mass and ceremonies – one of the few non-sporting events that I have covered for RTÉ. Although, to be honest, it was in many ways a sporting occasion in addition to being a State funeral for the former Taoiseach. The high gantry installed at the back of the Cathedral to facilitate the broadcast posed a problem for Donncha, who had a fear of heights. A suitable arrangement was hurriedly made that allowed Corkman Donncha to stay at ground level, where he had a few words from time to time with many of the personalities in attendance, while the religious aspects fell to this high-climbing Kerryman at the next level. I must say, though, that 'in memory of the great Jack' Donncha did climb onto the high platform in the cemetery for the final part of proceedings, thereby showing both spirit and respect. You can bet that the famous Munster final of 1950 in Killarney got a few recalls during the final ceremonies to honour the memory of the great sportsman/politician.

# Centenarian Dan Keating

My next guest has often been to Fitzgerald Stadium, though he was thirty-four years of age when it was first opened; the man in question is Dan Keating of Ballygamboon, two miles on the Tralee side of Castlemaine. Kerry won the first of its thirty-three All-Ireland football titles in 1905, even though that was actually the final of the 1903 championship. It is incredible to think that Dan was almost of school age when that first All-Ireland was brought to the Kingdom at the start of the last century.

Dan Keating is the second person aged 100 years or more that I have interviewed in the course of my travels. The first was the late Jim Power, fullback on the Galway team that won the All-Ireland hurling title of 1923. I remember Frank Burke, Chairman of the Galway County Board, telling me once at some match or other that Jim was then in his 100th year and in excellent shape. I made a note of the birthday and intended calling in to see him when the big day came round. About a month in advance I decided to give Frank a ring. We first spoke about hurling matters, then he solemnly informed me that they had 'bad news about the doughty fullback'. Hoping it might only be a touch of the 'flu' or something akin to it I enquired further, only to learn that the bad news was that 'the County Council says he is only ninety-nine'. Councils often have the final word in such matters, and even though Jim himself had other ideas, the 100th birthday celebrations had to be postponed for a further year.

I called to see him again when the time came, stopping in Loughrea to get a birthday card. I dropped in to a fairly big news agency and asked for an appropriate card with '100 years' or words to that effect on the front. I was informed they did not carry any such cards, and when I expressed surprise at the omission I was simply told that there was little demand for them. I did not give up, however, and in a much smaller outlet, located on a sharp-angled corner, my wish was granted – they had just such a card. It was ample proof that there is still a place in society for the smaller retail shops.

I did not know Dan Keating at the time of his 100th birthday, but I met him two years later in rather unusual surroundings in Dublin's Deansgrange cemetery. It was not a funeral occasion at all, but rather a ceremony to mark the grave of a former Kerry footballer, Éamonn Fitzgerald, winner of senior All-Ireland medals in 1930 and 1931, a junior one in 1924, National Leagues in 1928 and 1930, Railway Cups in 1927 and 1931, and also a member of Ireland's team in the Olympic Games of 1932. Éamonn died in 1958 at the youthful age of fifty-three and was buried in Deansgrange, but he was largely forgotten thereafter and, as sometimes happens, the grave became overgrown and his whereabouts were unknown until 'rediscovered' in 2004.

That in itself is an interesting story, beginning when Weeshie Fogarty of Kerry football and Radio Kerry renown began doing some research on Kerry Olympians with a view to presenting a radio programme on the subject. Naturally the name of Éamonn Fitzgerald figured and his birthplace of Castlecove, in South Kerry, was the logical starting point. Brendan and Carmel Galvin of the Black Shop had plenty of information about the young Éamonn, who in fact spent most of his life living in Dublin. He had spent some time in Padraig Pearse's Rathfarnham school, St Enda's, and later attended University College, Dublin, where his fees and other expenses were paid for by Lady Albina Lucy Broderick, an English lady of privilege and once a loyal subject of the British Empire. Either fate or fortune had guided her to Castlecove in Kerry, where she became fascinated with the cause of Irish freedom and nationalism. The young Fitzgerald was not the only one to benefit from her philanthropy, and in addition she set up a hospital in Castlecove. She reached the grand age of ninety-three, died in 1955 and lies buried in Sneem.

Éamonn Fitzgerald's sporting career was divided between Kerry football and athletics, with the Hop, Step and Jump his speciality.

He was Irish champion in 1930 and again from 1932 to 1934, represented Ireland in the Tailteann Games and was selected on the Ireland team for the 1932 Olympic Games in Los Angeles. He spent some time training in Ballybunion prior to his departure, in the company of other members of the team, which included gold medal winners Dr Pat O'Callaghan and Bob Tisdall, and Mick Murphy from Clare. They travelled by boat to Boston and then in shifts by train across the United States, making a stop for training halfway across. It was while there that the Kerryman picked up an injury to his heel that may have cost him a medal at the games – the first to have the luxury of an Olympic village. Dr Pat O'Callaghan took on the job of trying to bring Éamonn back to fitness and did manage to get him to the point where he was able to compete.

In the circumstances he did exceptionally well, failing only by a matter of inches to win the bronze medal. The event was won by Chubei Nambu of Japan with a jump of 51ft 7in. Fitzgerald's jump of 49ft 3in was his best ever and only four inches short of the bronze medal mark. He had put in a jump of 51ft, an effort that would have won the silver medal, but it was adjudged to be illegal. Nonetheless, he had the great joy of witnessing Pat and Bob take gold medals when competing against the world's best – the doctor with a throw of 53.92m in the Hammer and Bob in the 400m hurdles in a world record time of 51.8 seconds, though the record was not ratified as he knocked a hurdle.

Fitzgerald would certainly have won more All-Ireland medals were it not for his involvement in athletics. He was a teacher by profession, but ill-health caused early retirement and according to Dan Keating, for years a close friend of his in Dublin, he did odd bits of work in Shelbourne Park greyhound track where the boss, Paddy O'Donoghue, was 'very good to him'. Dan also mentioned two young women who lived close to Éamonn in Dundrum and they 'looked after him well for years when he was in poor health'.

I remember being in Shelbourne Park at numerous meetings during the 1950s, but I never heard even a whisper about a Kerry footballer working there, so I assume the Castlecove man must have been a quiet and retiring sort of person. That might also account for the fact that the attendance at his funeral was sparse in the extreme. My informant for that is once again centenarian Dan. He spoke about it when I first met him in Deansgrange that day in 2004: 'Only five people attended the removal, two from South Kerry, Fionán Breathnach and Seán O'Neill, a brother of the republican Maurice, who was executed in 1942, Frank Fitzgerald, a farmer just outside Dublin and a native of Castlegregory; the hearse man and myself, that was all.' Incidentally, Dan also told me that Maurice O'Neill had stayed in the Keating home in Kerry the night before he left for Dublin in 1942.

According to Dan, there was little publicity about Éamonn's death in 1958, but I still fail to understand how so few heard about it. I was in Dublin at the time, as were a good few Kerry footballers from different eras, but in Dan's view the Kerry Association did nothing about it, although he added that it was better the following day: 'Sheehy [John Joe, former leading Kerry footballer who won four All-Ireland medals and captain in 1926 and 1929] and a few more came from Kerry and there might have been up to thirty in all there.' Overall it was a poor tribute to a great sportsman who had represented county and country with distinction, but 'Bally Dan', as he is known locally in Kerry, is proud of the fact that he was one of the five who shouldered his coffin.

A much bigger crowd assembled in Deansgrange forty-six years later, in 2004, to honour the athlete retrospectively. As a result of Weeshie Fogarty's initial inquiries, the Chairman of the Kerry Association in Dublin, Eugene O'Sullivan, undertook the task of locating the grave. Thanks to the assistance of personnel in Deansgrange it was eventually found, the growth of years cleared and suitable restoration carried out. Finally, on a beautiful sunny Saturday morning in May, a fitting ceremony took place: the GAA was represented by Seán Walsh, Chairman of Kerry County Board; the Olympic Council by President Pat Hickey; athletes by Ronnie Delaney – the track star of the 1950s who is still Ireland's last gold medal winner on the track since his great win over the 1,500 metres in the Melbourne Olympics of 1956, Jerry Kiernan – 1984

Olympic marathon runner in Los Angeles where he finished in ninth place in a time of two hours and twelve minutes, and Seán O'Dwyer – it was his honour eventually to break Éamonn's Fitzgerald's Hop, Step and Jump Irish record.

Eugene O'Sullivan, a South Kerry man and driver to Minister John O'Donoghue, acted as MC, Fr Gaughan recited prayers, speeches came from Seán Walsh, Pat Hickey, Ronnie Delaney and Carmel Galvin before her husband, Brendan, laid a plaque on the grave together with flowers and clay from Éamonn's native sod of Castlecove, where he was born in 1903 – a year later than Dan Keating, the proudest man in the graveyard that morning. He had known Éamonn as a sportsman and as a member of the IRA in his early years. All in all, there must have been about 150 people at the 'second funeral' and as there was a sporting and Olympic theme, it was good to see Jimmy Magee among them.

I have met with Dan Keating on a number of occasions since that day in Deansgrange and found his life story most interesting. There are two main strands to it: a lifelong love of Gaelic sport; and a connection with republicanism that stretches back almost ninety years. He was born on 2 January 1902, which means he has been present, either in spirit or in person, for every single one of Kerry's thirty-three All-Ireland football titles. Between hurling – his first love – and football he has seen 154 All-Ireland finals, but is adamant he will not attend again. It has nothing to do with health matters though – he has cut down on his walking all right, but still covers four or five miles each day, except on the very bad days. No, his reason for forsaking Croke Park is to protest against the decision to allow games other than Gaelic to be played there, something that would not sit easily with his republican beliefs.

Dan's father emigrated to America and saw action in the Spanish-American War, for which he was granted a pension. He returned to Ballygamboon, took up farming, married a girl who lived a few fields away and reared a family that never went hungry, thanks to farming and the American pension. What amazed me about Dan was the accuracy and clarity of his recall of events, regardless of time. It made no difference whether an incident related to the early 1900s, the early years of the present century or anywhere in between, Dan was able to paint the picture and supply the facts. For example, he could clearly recall his first day at school:

At the age of six I was taken to Ballyfinnane school by an older girl from up the road. The principal teacher was Joseph O'Shea and Julia Burke was the assistant. They were good teachers and I had no trouble during my six or seven years there. I never got ill-treatment, but the teachers had big rulers for punishment purposes – you'd hold out your hand and they would come down heavy. I suppose they were tough times all round.

After primary school he headed for Tralee CBS, but did not stay too long because 'I got a lucky break. My father was a County Councillor by then, he had influence and succeeded in getting an apprenticeship to the licensed trade for me with Gerry McSweeney in Tralee'. Dan spent three years with the McSweeneys and most of the rest of his working life was in the same business, although there were several interruptions on account of his republican involvements.

He went to Dublin in 1919, saw his first All-Ireland final, was sworn into the IRA in Drumcondra at the age of seventeen, got a job in one of Mooney's bars, but had to leave betimes due to his IRA connections. He returned to Kerry and again got caught up in IRA activities until his arrest in Tipperary in 1922. That was a prelude to seventeen months in prison, first in Portlaoise and later in the Tintown Camp in the Curragh. He had taken part in ambushes, including, as he put it,

the biggest one in Kerry, 'twas there just beyond Castlemaine, on the road to Milltown. A group of fourteen, some Black and Tans among them, went to town that morning, the first of June 1921, and they were destroyed coming home in the evening. Eight were killed and three wounded. The wounded fellas went into the local women and they cleaned and bandaged them and gave them tea; nobody minded them doing that, Christ, anyone would help a wounded man.

He also took part in an ambush in Tralee and another in Gortalea and took the Republican side in the Civil War. He has his own views on that tragic episode in Irish history and says it was 'a war for nothing – both sides were wrong'.

Dan remained a member of the IRA until the mid-1960s, with another spell in prison in the 1940s. He spent time in the famous huts in the Curragh during the Civil War and while there was a member of the team that won the 'football championship'. He was back in the same place for 'four years and a day' in the early 1940s, one of 600 internees being held there.

After his release he returned again to the bar trade and picked up on his regular visits to Croke Park. He missed nine All-Ireland finals due to that term of internment, but still clocked up that record number of 154 finals attended. He is the only person I ever met who had seen players from all of Kerry's winning All-Ireland sides in action. Kerry's first win was that of 1903 and four members of that team lasted into the next decade, and Dan saw them playing. He had great regard for Dick Fitzgerald, who was on that 1903 team and who captained the winning sides of 1913 and 1914. Dan first saw him play in 1915 and was very impressed by his physique and natural ability – 'he was a great fielder and had any amount of skill'.

I would be willing to bet that the Ballygamboon man has more detail about the stars of the past ninety years than anyone ever born. He considers the Kerry team that beat Monaghan in the All-Ireland final of 1931 as the best he ever saw. Though I find it hard to believe, Dan is adamant that Monaghan were favourites, even though Kerry had won the championships of the previous two years. He asserts that General Eoin O'Duffy, Garda Commissioner at the time and a Monaghan man, had drafted in a fair few Garda footballers to Monaghan stations for the sole purpose of winning the All-Ireland. As Dan tells it, the plan misfired badly in the final when 'everyone was waiting for this explosion from Monaghan that never came'.

He rates the Kerry team that beat Dublin in the final of 1978 as the second best team he ever saw and went into raptures in describing the first of Eoin Liston's three second-half goals. He is willing to concede that Dublin were the better side in the first half, though they did not show it on the scoreboard, and for that he gives credit to John Egan for 'getting a goal out of nothing – typical'.

It was fascinating to listen to Dan talk in great detail about the stars of ten decades, and the name of the heavenly Saviour was invoked frequently as he recounted the deeds of men like Con Brosnan – 'a great friend always, even if we were on different sides in the Civil War' – Paul Russell, Joe Keohane, Mick O'Connell, Mickey Sheehy, Mick O'Dwyer, Jack O'Shea, Maurice Fitzgerald, Colm Cooper and so on. I noted that they were almost exclusively Kerry names, but that was understandable in a way as he was an 'exile' for most of his life. From the time he first went to Dublin, in 1919, he had seen the Kingdom win twenty-eight All-Irelands and play in fourteen other finals. He feels he has a special affinity with the Green and Gold and that he owes them loyalty on account of the great pleasure and excitement they have brought to him over his long life.

He was by no means oblivious of the prowess of other counties, however, and still remembers with pride the style of Kildare's Larry Stanley in the final of 1919. When pressed, he has no bother rattling off the great names from other counties, particularly Seán Purcell of Galway and the 'three-in-a-row' side from the same county. But be sure of it, the motto that Kerry is the Kingdom will be his for ever.

There was a wider vista to his hurling world, maybe on account of the fact that Kerry's lone All-Ireland in that code came before he was born. Lory Meagher of Kilkenny remains a firm favourite of his and he described the star of the 1920s and 1930s as 'one of the greatest, a big man who tried to play the ball all the time, there was no dirt in him, no foul stroke and he liked a game to flow all the time.' He seemed to know a lot of the Cats' players and he remembers how another great Kilkenny man, Paddy Phelan of the 'Teams of the Century and Millennium', once 'got me safely out of the county when I was wanted'.

He had a great regard for Cork hurling from the beginning and went 'numerous times' to see Christy Ring play, and the Cloyne man seldom disappointed him. He told me that 1931 was the best year of all: 'I had four All-Ireland finals that year – Kerry won the football and it took three great games before Cork beat Kilkenny for the hurling title, God it was a great year.'

Dan knows the geography of Offaly almost as well as that of his native Kerry and Kinnity is a favourite of his. He rates the Faithful County's contribution to hurling over the past twenty-five years as magnificent and informed me that there have been several marriages between Kerry and Offaly people; and, even though it had nothing to do with hurling, he suggested that there are many 'safe houses' in that county. Then he skipped back to the hurling once more and began with a question directed at me, 'What was it about Johnny Dooley?'

When I exercised my right to silence, he was quick to supply the answer himself: 'God he was great, he'd get a 21-yard free and 'twas no bother to him to score a goal or point, then he'd get a free 80 yards out and 'twould be the same thing – what kind of wrists he had, no one knows.' And then, as if to educate me further, he threw in the gem that Johnny had two brothers who were 'just as good, Joe and the farmer Billy'.

His love of the game of hurling when it is well played is very obvious and he took particular delight in the 2005 All-Ireland semi-final between Kilkenny and Galway. He spoke as if he were relating the story to somebody who had not heard about the classic: 'God, they got great scores. Kilkenny scored four goals and eighteen points, but Galway got five goals and eighteen points and won the game – 'twas a great one.'

When Dan mentioned a pub in Kinnity owned by a Kenmare man by the name of Raymond Glendenning, I immediately threw in a similar name associated with BBC horse racing broadcasting. He was familiar with that man also and added, 'Jaysus, the man who got the weakness when the Queen's horse did not win the Grand National. He was leading by twenty lengths when all of a sudden he fell on the flat. Glendenning got a fit, he wanted the Queen's horse to win, he was knighted, you know.'

Dan did not take kindly to my remark that there was talk the Queen might one day attend an All-Ireland final in Croke Park: 'God forbid that the day would ever come,' was his way of dismissing it. I did gather that he had regard for the late Princess Di, however: 'She rebelled, you know.'

In the course of our long discussion in his Ballygamboon home, Dan told me an amusing story about an interview conducted in the American Embassy in 1950 when he was trying to secure a visa to the United States. He had been refused one to emigrate after a local sergeant 'gave me a bad reference'. All of his siblings emigrated: one brother returned from America after a short while and remained at home for the rest of his life and is buried in Ballyfinnane; three others are buried in Chicago; one in Detroit; and three are buried in London. In many ways the Keating story is no different from that of thousands of other Irish families before the wave of prosperity hit the homeland in relatively modern times. It is no wonder that from time to time Dan considered emigrating to the States, which was what brought him to submit an application for a visa to the American Embassy. He was given an appointment for the day after St Patrick's Day and duly presented himself. His account of the interview is detailed, even though it took place more than fifty years ago:

I was conveyed to this hall, there was a long green table at one side with a man sitting at each end and I was put in the middle. One of the men read a book and alerted me right away.

'Is there any reason political or otherwise,' and he emphasized the word *political,* 'why you should not be granted a visa?'

'Nothing that I know of,' said I.

'Were you ever in jail?'

'I was in every jail in the country. I was in Tralee, Limerick, Cork, Portlaoise, Mountjoy, Arbour Hill and the Curragh.'

'Why were you in jail?'

'I couldn't tell you. I was never convicted of anything. I didn't answer questions, I was convicted for not answering questions.'

It was up to them then and they knew that his brother, Gerry, was sponsoring him – a sponsor being a requirement in those days: 'Gerry served with the American Army against the Japanese in the Far East during the Second World War and received a decoration, for what I don't know, and I felt that the Embassy more than likely was aware of that.' It did him no harm because before he left he was told, 'you have been very frank with us and I will recommend that you be granted a visa.'

A few months passed by before he heard from them again, but in the meantime he came into a 'sum of money' willed to him by an aunt who had died in America: 'It came in useful. I bought a house, got married to a Waterford woman and then a week later I got my visa, but I did not emigrate as I was settled and had a good job in a bar at the time.' He did mention that he enjoyed four trips to the States subsequently.

As I was preparing to leave, Dan suggested we drop down to Gally's, a pub/restaurant on the road into Tralee. He told me how the Kerry team had refused to play in the 1923 All-Ireland final 'unless Gally, real name Galvin, was released from custody. Fair play to opponents Dublin, they supported Kerry and Gally was released. The match was then played and Dublin won.' And so we went to Gally's, where everyone greeted Dan as 'Bally'.

Whether he is Dan, Bally, or Bally Dan, the Ballygamboon centenarian is great company and for those of you interested in the lifestyle that has kept him so fit, you will find it is extremely simple: regular walking, no smoking and relatively little drinking. He was fifty-seven years of age when he took his first drink and that was by way of a protest, as he explained in his own direct manner:

Paddy Cooney, the Minister for Justice at the time, wanted to increase the opening hours for pubs and he called a meeting to test support – the Barmen's Union was against it, as was the Women Workers' Union, but the Licensed Vintners were in favour. It was then up to the Pioneers and they came out in favour. I was mad, took off my Pioneer pin and threw it across at them while saying something – the Minister said I would have to apologize – I refused, but said I would leave the meeting. I left, bought a glass of sherry and drank it.

I wonder was he the first person on Earth who turned to drink as a protest?

# Diarmuid O'Connell and Tigh an Oileáin on Valentia Island

Dan Keating is a great admirer of Mick O'Connell, one of the people behind a venture that culminated in Tigh an Oileáin on Valentia Island, a purpose-built house for people with special needs. I had a running invitation from Diarmuid O'Connell to call and see An Tigh at any time, so I chose the week preceding the meeting of Kerry and Galway in the 2006 Allianz Football League final in Killarney.

At the time, South Kerry held the title of County Champions and thus Dromid Pearses man Declan O'Sullivan was captain of Kerry for the year. Purely by coincidence, Kerry manager Jack O'Connor came from the same club, so it was a good time to be in Valentia Island, or anywhere else in the vast region of South Kerry. In such an environment it came easy to people to talk about football and the year ahead, and the possibility of Declan O'Sullivan becoming the fourth man from that part of the county to lead the Kingdom to All-Ireland glory. Phil Sullivan from Kenmare was the first in 1924, followed by the Island man Mick O'Connell in 1959 and another Kenmare man, Mickey Ned O'Sullivan, sixteen years later. Whatever about the lure of football, golf or anything else, I wanted to visit Tigh an Oileáin during my brief stay in the south of the county.

I was aware of the existence of this house, built for those in the community with a mental disability. It is in keeping with a trend that is now growing across the country, whereby care for people with special needs is understood to be most effective in small units that are located as close as possible to their own family homes. Tigh an Oileáin is one of the latest to provide that very commendable service. I have known Diarmuid for quite some time now, and there is nobody on Earth who extends a greater welcome to a visitor. He is the son of Mick and Rosaleen O'Connell and copes extraordinarily well with his condition of Down's Syndrome. His parents take him to many events and are to be complimented for this. Diarmuid really enjoys meeting people and getting to know them, especially sports personalities. His love of sport surely comes from his father Mick, the legendary Kerry footballer who won All-Ireland medals in three decades. Diarmuid's memory for names is amazing: he has often been my assistant when I have been acting as MC at functions that involved moving through a banquet hall to chat with various sports representatives. Even though Diarmuid likes the ambience of hotels and the excitement that goes with big occasions, he has told me on several occasions over the past year that 'Tigh an Oileáin is the best place of all'. Now that I have seen the Island House he refers to, I must agree with him.

The history of the house is interesting; completed recently, it has created a perfect prototype for a facility that would benefit every community in the country. The desirability of having 'a house for people with special needs' came to the O'Connells during Diarmuid's school years at St Mary of the Angels in Beaufort, close to Killarney. They, and other parents in the same position, were appreciative of what was being done for the children at St Mary's, but were all too aware that all but those with severe disability would have to leave upon reaching the age of eighteen years. Parents did not mind caring for them, but as Rosaleen said,

The Kerry Parents and Friends of St Mary's saw greater problems down the road once their generation would pass away. We had all known cases of people with disability being well looked after while their parents lived, but finding themselves in a near-hopeless situation once they were no longer there, or beyond being able to do the caring. The future of the dependant would have been almost a constant worry to parents in their last years.

The Parents and Friends group had acted as fund-raisers for St Mary's for a good number of years, but the changes taking place in Irish society prompted them to consider the idea of becoming service providers. They purchased Mount Eagle Lodge in Tralee, guided by the new philosophy of providing a place convenient to communities in as many areas as possible that would care for adults with learning disabilities. Great development has taken place since then and at the moment it has spread to Listowel, Rathmore, Killarney and Valentia Island. The emphasis is on small facilities in order to preserve the culture of individual care as far as possible, and in some cases there is more than one centre in the bigger towns.

Tigh an Oileáin caters for the Iveragh Peninsula and the beautiful residence is built on land donated by the O'Connell family. Diarmuid is exceptionally proud of the place and was delighted to show me around every part of it. It is well designed and tastefully decorated, with the overall feel being of a family home. Diarmuid lives there and, like the other five residents, he enjoys his own *en suite* bedroom in very comfortable surroundings. Three other people live with their families but come daily to Tigh an Oileáin for classes, training and other activities. I could detect a great sense of confidence among the residents and Diarmuid was in his element as he entertained his father, Mick, and myself for the duration of my visit. His initial greeting to me came in Irish – '*Fáilte romhat, Micheál, go dtí Tigh an Oileáin.*' Before long we were offered a choice of tea or coffee, made and served by himself, and I was introduced to his friends as they came along. He answered the phone when it rang, identified base as Tigh an Oileáin and then after a brief conversation told the caller that he had visitors. I could not imagine people like Diarmuid being so communicative if they were being catered for in bigger institutions, where opportunities for personal development would be more limited.

Tigh an Oileáin operates seven days a week, but sometimes the residents decide to go home for the weekend. Fran O'Flynn, a nephew of Johnny of Showband fame, acts as Tigh manager, which means the place is no stranger to music. It is run on the basis of four full-time jobs shared by seven people in a ratio that depends on needs. There is great variety in the learning activities and they include projects with the Valentia Weather Station, art tuition and demonstration, computer use and looking after the birds and animals that belong to An Tigh – the donkey being everyone's favourite and the hawk being the enemy. The hungry hawk has already taken a few feathered friends as prey, but at the time of my visit they were in communication with Dublin Zoo seeking information on hawk-deterrent nets. I'm sure a solution has been found by now. An Tigh also boasts a Green Flag for excellence in recycling, granted by the Department of the Environment and displayed as one of their proudest achievements.

It is the objective of the Parents and Friends of St Mary's to have as many such houses as are needed among the communities of the county. It is good to see the progress that is being made. Like sports facilities throughout the country, there is a common thread running through all these successful and commendable projects: a big input from the ever-dynamic volunteers. My visit to Tigh an Oileáin was an education in itself and further proof for me that money spent by government departments on such places is an investment in community life. Groups like the Parents and Friends of St Mary's will carry on fund-raising, but they must not be left to carry the full burden.

# South Kerry's 'Iron Man', Mike Murphy

Before ever reaching Valentia Island I was led on a pleasant detour by Cahersiveen butcher and golfer Jimmy Curran to meet somebody known as 'the Iron Man' on account of his exploits as a cyclist back in the1950s. Cycling as a sport was gaining popularity back then and the annual stage race around Ireland, An Rás Tailteann, now known as the FBD Insurance Rás, was responsible for a great deal of it. The Rás attracted huge media attention from its first staging in 1953 as a two-day event from Dublin to Wexford and back. The Christle brothers, especially the late big man Joe, were the principal organizers and their motivation came from a nationalistic fervour and a love of all aspects of Irish culture. They were inspired by the legendary status attained by the Tour de France and had a vision of developing such a spectacle in Ireland in their time. There was a surge in republicanism in those years and many of the people engaged in promoting the Rás would not have denied their allegiance to it.

Joe Christle was a great character and a brilliant organizer and I cannot recall an occasion when we spoke other than in Irish. He was married to a French lady, Mimi Battutt, who studied in UCD during my student days there and she too took a great interest in everything Irish. I don't think she ever mastered the Irish language but she did profess an understanding, as I found out when I met her in O'Connell Street one afternoon. Joe had been in court earlier in the day and sentenced to 'a few months' for some 'political' offence, and Mimi told me about the wonderful speech he had made. When I asked what he had spoken about she told me, with suitably French gesticulations, that the speech was 'in Irish, but I felt that he said all the correct things'. Years later I taught Mel Christle, one of Joe and Mimi's three boxing sons, when I was on the teaching staff at O'Connell School in North Richmond Street, Dublin.

Joe served a few prison sentences due to his involvement in republican causes, but he remained as Rás Director until 1972. The whole family served cycling well but one of them, Ando, was sadly killed near Tralee following an accident during the Rás of 1954. He had returned from England to help in the running of the race and was driving a motorbike out of Tralee to watch his brother, Colm, in the closing stages. The leaders had already crossed the finishing line, but Colm had had a day of puncture problems so he was well behind; concern for him was the reason for Ando's drive out of town, which finished in that fatal accident. Understandably, all members of the Gate Club, which included the Christles, retired from the race.

Joe had a great sense of humour and it is said that he as much as commanded that either Colm or his friend, Phil Clarke, win the inaugural Rás in order to save the Director the embarrassment of having no prize for the winner. The loyal brother obliged and the first link in an unending chain of Ráiseanna had been launched. It became an eight-day event the following year and continued so thereafter, with Gene Mangan of Killorglin in Kerry and Shay O'Hanlon of Dublin emerging as the consistent riders of the 1950s and 1960s. Gene was the 1955 winner, while Shay claimed the title on four occasions between 1962 and 1967. Mangan's 1955 win and his spectacular riding created huge interest and generated sponsorship, though not much, from the GAA and Bord Fáilte and the future of the Rás seemed safe.

The 1956 event was won by another Kerryman, Paudie Fitzgerald from Lispole, and this turned out to be the most 'political' contest of all with scuffles between the Rás people and members of the RUC in Northern Ireland and the capture and recapture of flags a feature. I remember the 'rescued' Tricolour being displayed everywhere during the celebrations in Kerry following Fitzgerald's win and the sight of a Union Jack being burned in Tralee, an act that increased the tension generated by the politicizing of a sporting event.

Those thoughts from the past were on my mind as Jimmy Curran and I approached the home of the Iron Man, Mike Murphy, a unique type of champion who hit the headlines in a major way in the course of winning the 1958 Rás. He spent years abroad working in England and Germany, but he is now back home in his own place, Sú Gréine, close to Cahersiveen. When I entered the house I was expecting to see mementos from his sporting days, but the opposite was the case. Conventional furnishings were spartan, in keeping with his lifestyle of the past sixty years: books, magazines, newspapers and an assortment of timber planks took up most of the space and he kindly fixed up a wooden seat for us, which was comfortable. Time did not seem to matter and I felt he was far more anxious to talk about topics other than cycling during our stay. I would naturally have preferred the reverse, considering it was cycling that had made him famous, but I let him speak as he wished and still managed to get a good insight into his cycling escapades.

He was a man who had left school early and had learned how to read and write from his mother, but he amazed me with his detailed knowledge of the Habsburg dynasty in Europe and the Royal Family of Spain and how they had influenced the history of Europe. It was the same when it came to the Papacy; it soon became clear that this semi-mystic had read a lot.

He is conscious of the benefits of a good diet when in training and maintains that this knowledge helped him in his cycling days: 'raw foods are best – meat, eggs, cheese, vegetables, honey – and I always took quantities of cows' blood when I felt it was needed.' He told me how he always carried a penknife with him and knew how to extract blood from a cow's vein without causing any damage.

He was anxious to tell me about his circus acting, something that started by accident when he was very young:

My neighbour, Joe Burke, performed with touring circuses that came this way now and then and he took me on as his assistant at the age of twelve. I was very interested in their training methods, weights and all of that and before long I made my own gym here in the house.

With that, he invited me to have a look at 'the room behind you there' and I must say it was fascinating. An incredible number of weights of all sizes, obviously home-made with concrete, were on display along with the iron bars required for lifting and squatting. They certainly played a part in his fairytale rise to the position of champion cyclist of Ireland in 1958 because he was known as a man with phenomenal strength, but he seemed more interested in telling me about history and his circus life before talking about the bike racing:

I learned how to move along upside-down using my feet, going from rung to rung of a ladder suspended above a stage. I could balance objects on my chin. I was a fire-eater. I could walk on my hands and performed those tricks on the streets of London and in other places years later when I needed money. One time a man in London issued a challenge to race hand-walking from Brighton to London, taking rests every now and then. I volunteered to take him on, but he never showed up.

We eventually got around to talk about cycling and by then Jimmy Curran was concerned that our host, Jerry McCrohan in The Moorings in Portmagee, might be kept waiting. When he mentioned the time, he was politely told to remain seated and listen. By then I had spotted a small photograph of a man on a bicycle above the fireplace and I went to inspect it. It was a photo of the Iron Man with the following words written underneath:

> They helped him onto his bike
> they put his hands on the bars
> they strapped in his feet
> they held him up until the start
> and then they pushed him off.

I learned later that this, the only visible souvenir, referred to a stage of the famous Rás of 1958 when he confounded the cycling world by winning.

His interest in cycling developed from attending carnivals and sports meets all over Kerry, where prizes were offered to the winners – sometimes in the form of cash. Distance was not a problem, as he explained himself: 'I remember leaving here on a common bike one day to cycle the sixty miles to Camp to take part in a cycle race. I won the race and cycled back home again.' Sometimes he might not return but stay, set up circus acts, sleep rough and prepare for a meet coming up shortly in another town.

From his circus connections he got the latest information on training techniques and by 1956 he had decided to try and take on the best in cycling. Training then became more intensive, but due to his day job as a farm labourer he did a lot of his training on the mountains by night. The final preparation for the 1958 Rás was carried out in a private camp close to Banteer in Cork, where he was working as a labourer. He created another 'gym' in a quiet wooded spot, trained as never before, gave up work, did stunts in Cork City and felt really ready for the Rás. He had been selected on the Kerry team following a good stage win in Rás Mumhan earlier that year.

As usual, the Rás Tailteann began outside the GPO in Dublin and the 1958 race was the longest ever staged – 1,494km over eight gruelling days. 'I believed in striking to the front any chance I got and defied others to beat me,' was how Mike explained his pre-race plan to me. He was not too concerned about team tactics or race customs: 'I had confidence in myself.'

I now give a brief summary of Tom Daly's account of the race as given in his excellent book simply called *The Rás*, which charts the history of the race from 1953 to 2002:

STAGE 1: *Dublin to Wexford*
Won by Dan Ahern of Kerry with the unknown Murphy claiming second place.

STAGE 2 : *Wexford to Kilkenny*
The Iron Man disregarded established etiquette, rode solo away from the bunch and arrived in Kilkenny on his own. It was a performance that left the Rás astonished. The Race leader's Yellow Jersey was then

his. Legend tells that he then rode off that evening wearing the Yellow Jersey, did a thirty-mile training spin, stopped at a stone wall and with selected stones 'did weights' for an hour before drawing blood from a cow and returning to base. It is believed he did the transfusion three times during the Rás.

### STAGE 3: *Kilkenny to Clonakilty*
A remarkable stage, with Murphy well ahead of a scattered field on the climb at Watergrasshill outside Cork. But disaster struck when his bike failed on the run into Glanmire. He was at a stand-still and the field swept by and disappeared from view. Suddenly a farmer appeared at a gap holding on to an ordinary bicycle. This gave the Iron Man an idea and in a jiffy he was on the substitute, leaving a startled farmer behind holding another bike. In time the team car reached Mike and gave him the spare racer. He chased for forty miles and caught sight of the bunch close to Clonakilty and was with them at the finish and safely holding onto the Yellow Jersey.

### STAGE 4: *Clonakilty to Tralee*
It was familiar territory to him, but he struck a bridge on a downhill bend near Glengarriff and fell heavily, damaging a shoulder and hip as well as putting his bike out of commission. Gene Mangan realized the gravity of the situation and gave Murphy his bike, on which he finished in a wrecked state in eighth place. He was taken to hospital but appeared for the next stage the following morning.

### STAGE 5: *Tralee to Nenagh*
The words accompanying the photo mentioned above are descriptive of his condition at the start of this stage. It was not a memorable stage for the injured warrior, but he did clock in six places behind the winner, Gene Mangan.

### STAGE 6: *Nenagh to Castlebar*
Mangan won again, but Murphy pulled away from the main bunch shortly before the finish and gained a little on his rivals and held onto the Yellow Jersey with comfort.

STAGE 7: *Castlebar to Sligo*

Murphy started well in this stage and had a minute's advantage when he crashed near Castlerea. On remounting he rode the wrong way for a while, possibly suffering from concussion, but he soon turned and finished with the bunch, with the irrepressible Mangan winning once more.

STAGE 8: *Sligo to Dublin*

Though showing signs of injury, the Iron Man refused to ride conservatively over the final stage and attacked early on with the Meathmen Ben McKenna and Willie Heasley. They were joined before the finish by Gene Mangan, and it was he who crossed the line in first place to create a record of four stage wins in a row that still stands to this day. But the Iron Man from Sú Gréine, Caherciveen, was a comfortable overall winner of the Rás by 4 minutes and 44 seconds.

Murphy was now a celebrity in the sporting world, but he remained the private, enigmatic figure he had always been. Both work and money were scarce, but he did compete again in 1959 and 1960. He recalled his defence of the title in 1959 as follows: 'After getting to Dublin, I slept on the street and then took my place at the start the following day. I won two stages.' He finished third overall in 1960 and was crowned King of the Hills as well.

Like many others he was forced to emigrate to England in 1960, which really ended his career on the bike. 'I worked hard there as a bricklayer and could deal with as many as a thousand blocks a day and I kept doing the circus acts as much as possible.' When work got scarce in England, around 1990, he moved to Germany and in his own words 'we built that country' – by *we* he meant another ten or eleven in the group as well as himself. 'I stayed too long,' he admits with a tinge of regret, 'I got a fall and was not fit for that work again.'

He is now back where his life began, but whether home or away the 'Iron Man' will never be forgotten as long as the romance of bike racing lives on. God only knows what else he might have accomplished if the sponsorship and training facilities of modern times had been available to him, that dedicated, natural competitor.

# Dancing and the dance halls of yesteryear

It is only 12 miles across Dingle Bay from where Iron Mike lives to where I grew up and my first trips to Cahersiveen were by boat. The journey by road is some five times longer, with Killorglin – or 'Puck' as it was more commonly known, on account of the annual three-day fair celebrating the legendary puck goats that run wild on the mountains – marking the halfway point. The 'Puck' was always a big attraction, with the all-night dances a feature that particularly appealed to us during our many visits to the August Fair. Dancing as a pastime was very popular throughout the country for a long number of years.

I have seen many changes in forms of entertainment over the years, with sport remaining among the few constants. There was a time when dancing possibly occupied second place, behind sport, and there were dance halls of varying degrees of grandeur and sophistication in almost every parish in the country. I have a clear recollection of the first dance I ever attended, the venue being conveniently close to home. It was unusual insofar as it was a daytime *céilí* that was organized as part of the celebrations when our school, the Christian Brothers School in Dingle, was presented with a shield in recognition of being the best school in the country in the promotion of Irish. The excitement was terrific as Tadhg Ó Tuama, a visiting Chief Inspector from the Department of Education, handed over the shield to one of the pupils, my own next-door neighbour Frank Farrell, who then led us on a parade of the town with the prized shield held aloft. Frank had his Leaving Certificate at the time, but he stayed on in school until joining the De La Salle Brothers, with whom he spent the rest of his life. He worked mostly in Mauritius, off the coast of Africa, where he is buried and awaiting the call of the Angel Gabriel, who will one day summon the greatest gathering ever known in either Heaven or Earth.

The *céilí* came later on that rare day off school and the girls from the local convent were also invited to attend. It was held in the town's regular dancing spot, a place close to the centre of the town called Jameen's Hall that belonged to Jimmy O'Connor. I was under the age of fourteen, so that was my first visit to the hall. I can visualize the scene yet, with the boys all on one side and the girls all on the other and the supervising adults experiencing great difficulty in getting the twain to meet. I'm afraid I was a mere observer and didn't take a single step, but I did enjoy the singing of 'A Dhruimfhionn Donn Dílis' by a girl from the other side of the Conor Pass; I think she was one of the Dowds whose brother, Seán, came to Coláiste Íosagáin during my stay in that establishment.

Dance halls were commercial propositions then and the era lasted well into the television age, which began in 1962. There were cases of people returning from America or England and investing their life savings in building a dance hall. Such a one existed in Ventry, close to An Daingean, and it was in the owner-ship of the Martin family. Its style was to be found all over the country: simple structures with just the basics – a dancing floor with a bit of a spring to it and a stage of some sort for the band. The floor was deemed good if it was made of wood, regardless of whether it was smooth or not. I remember proprietors like Thomasheen Keane and Willie Moriarty of Lispole Hall fame sprinkling paraffin oil on the wood before spreading some type of crystals that would soon be ground into dust by the pounding feet, thus creating a dancing surface fit for Fred Astaire and Ginger Rogers.

Of course, Dublin was a haven of dance halls when I arrived there in the late 1940s and as students and young teachers we often danced on four or five nights in the week, as well as keeping up with the worlds of cinema and live theatre. There must have been at least ten dance halls round Parnell Square alone – The National,

The Teachers, The Galway Arms, The Irish Club, The Ierne, The Balalika and Conarchy's among them. The latter was a favourite of ours on winter Sunday afternoons if there were no match in Croke Park. It was frequented by nurses and student nurses from Temple Street, the Rotunda and the Mater hospitals, so naturally the boys came along in big numbers.

In those days most halls prominently displayed a sign that said 'JITTER-BUGGING AND JIVING NOT ALLOWED' and the slightest breach by showing a bit of enterprise in dancing meant expulsion from any 'respectable' hall. I could never understand why innovation in dancing should have been frowned on and, thank God, such was never the case in Dingle. There the opposite prevailed and many a time, especially on big occasions, I saw space being cleared on the floor so that local modern dance experts Paddy Cronesberry and his sister, Mary Ellen, could outdo the movements of stars like Bill Haley and the other idols of the times.

Dancing was such a part of the culture of those days that a trip from Kerry or some other distant place after a Sunday match would not be complete without a bit of a dance somewhere along the route. Cruises Hotel in Limerick was a favourite of ours, as was Mrs Lawlor's in Naas, and I remember finishing up at a carnival dance in Borrisokane late one Sunday night after taking a wrong turn in Roscrea. It seems to me that people were not in such a hurry to get from one place to another in those days and a detour was never looked upon as a type of misfortune but rather as an additional adventure.

For those living in Dublin it was almost a 'must' to go as far afield as the Arcadia in Bray or Bar B close to the Woodbrook Golf Club from time to time, where dances went on until 2.00am and often later. All of the halls were 'dry', which meant no alcohol was served, a custom that was acceptable to all-comers whether they were drinkers or not. The humble tea, coffee and lemonade were in vogue and nobody faulted them as a means of socializing between dances. Those that needed the sustenance of alcohol made sure to take their quota on board before entering the dance hall, but I don't recall drunkenness ever being a problem. It is interesting that all of the big modern dance halls that sprang up with the phenomenon of the showbands in the 1960s and 1970s were also 'dry'.

Former Taoiseach Albert Reynolds, a non-drinker himself, was associated with many of those new dance halls. I met him at a Young Pioneers Rally in Roosky a few years ago and he told me how it had come about that he had once been charged with being drunk in charge of a car. Apparently it was a custom for owners to bring some drink along to the halls occasionally to give it to members of the band. Albert was driving home one night after a dance and had the spare alcohol in the back when a crash occurred. There were no injuries, but bottles got broken and when the Gardaí arrived the driver's clothes certainly smelled alcoholic, which led to the pioneer being charged. It never went any further, though, once the real facts emerged.

For a brief spell I actually considered getting involved in the organizing of dances. In fact, in partnership with a friend, Patrick Kavanagh – or PK for short – we booked the Ballerina Ballroom, which then stood next to the Gate Theatre in Parnell Square, for the purpose of running a dance. Our business name was The Liffey Serenaders and the planning went fine – tickets were printed, some publicity arranged and Frankie Blowers plus band booked for the venture on a February night in a year that I cannot put numbers on.

I had learned from my business studies that there are risks attached to all forms of enterprise, and the Liffey Serenaders were soon to receive a practical demonstration. Snow began to fall on the evening of our inaugural dance and while it was not a blizzard, it was enough to cause a drastic reduction in the passing trade we'd hoped would be attracted indoors for a dance. Queueing was part of Dublin life at the time and sometimes people gauged the scale of entertainment on offer inside by the length of a queue outside. So, with a little persuasion, a few of our loyal friends lined up outside the door, even though there was more than ample room inside at the time. It was one of the few queues in Dublin that night and it may have been responsible for the net profit of £11 accruing to each of us at the end of the night. The partnership was dissolved shortly afterwards, with both of us professing to be cured of whatever symptoms of a dancing disease had visited us temporarily!

# Age-old cures *agus An Dochtúir*

For generations, if not centuries, the majority of Irish people had no general access to doctors or medical care as we know it in the modern world. In truth, all but a minority were poor in terms of money and the material aspects of life. As a result, they depended on knowledge passed down from generation to generation when faced with the recurring problems of illnesses, be they seasonal, like 'flu', or accidental, like broken limbs, or more complicated ailments.

All communities had a trusted and competent midwife and knowledge of how to deal with common occurrences, like colds, were passed down within family circles. In many cases plenty of hot drinks, mostly milk, were prescribed, but on occasions it was something stronger – a home brew like mulled stout or hot whiskey sometimes worked wonders for the ailing. I remember seeing mulled stout being prepared for such a purpose, and it was quite a simple operation: pouring the required amount into a mug or saucepan, placing a poker in the centre of a roaring fire until it became red hot and then taking hold of the protruding end with a thick cloth before plunging the red end into the receptacle containing the stout.

I doubt the dentists were kept busy in the Ireland of 100 years ago, or even later, because many people had their own systems for extracting a troublesome tooth. One of the most 'popular' methods was to tie a cord around the offending molar and attach the cord to a door handle in anticipation of somebody opening it from the other side. That, believe it or not, was often the means by which a painful tooth was extracted. The same science was sometimes put into practice outdoors by substituting the solid stem of a bush for the door handle.

Broken or dislodged bones have been a feature of life on Earth since the days of Adam and Eve, which is why the bonesetter was a necessary and very useful presence in any locality. My guess is that, unlike the dentists, they were always busy. The first bonesetter I heard of was a man known as Micil na gCnámh – Michael of the Bones – who lived in Com Dhineoil, close to Dún Chaoin, to the west of Dingle. My father had cause to visit him once following damage to his knee after an 8-stone bag of potatoes he was swinging clear of a ridge accidentally came in contact with his knee, causing dislocation or some other damage. It meant a trip to Micil, and that trip had a positive result.

As a rule, 'gifts' such as Micil possessed were handed down, and from their dealings with various cases such people often ended up with quite a good knowledge of anatomy. There were others, however, who had the enterprise and confidence to make a start in the bone business based on theories they themselves had formulated. I knew of a group of three brothers in the Ventry district who believed that several of the aches and pains visited on the bodies of Mankind came about as a result of some sudden jerk, jolt or twist of the body. One might accept that this was a reasonable theory, but the brothers felt they had further enlightenment on the matter and deemed that only a similar action could provide a cure.

Following some rudimentary research, they created a routine designed to call forth a sudden muscular reaction from a 'patient'. Like many of the great discoveries of the ages, it was not complicated in itself. The patient – always a man – would be placed on a comfortable bed, lying on his back and in a relaxed mood. All the lights were put out and, if necessary, the blinds were drawn. By then two of the brothers would have climbed quietly onto the rafters directly above the bed. In an instant, one of them would drop down onto the hopeful 'victim' before rolling onto the floor uttering the words, '*An mbraitheann tú aon ní?*' – do you feel anything?

The object of the fall was to recreate sudden movements of the patient's limbs and muscles in the hope that one of them would replicate the one that had caused the original injury or damage.

Hence the query and the desired response would be a positive one, denoting that the pain had disappeared. If the 'crash' elicited the negative reply, '*ní bhraithim*', the next in line of the healing staff would repeat the jump and the question. There are known cases of cures that brought forth the perfect answer of '*braithim*', or I feel.

When I was growing up in Dún Síon many years ago a Lynch family lived some miles away in Garfinny, at the foot of the hills. Though he had never attended university nor any other institution of higher learning, the man of that house was nonetheless referred to as 'an Dochtúir', or The Doctor. I believe he was entitled to the honour because he was another of those who possessed a unique cure, his speciality being the treatment of a damaged *scéithín*.

Apparently the *scéithín* is a bone, or piece of cartilege, close to where the breast bone is positioned in the human body. In order for it to function as nature intended it needs to be aligned at a certain angle, but never pointing downwards. At least, that was the way it was explained to me once and I was willing to accept the information for the want of better. Quite a few people suffered from *scéithín* problems in my area and I was always led to believe that strain during lifting, pulling or dragging heavy objects was the cause of most of them. The theory was that too great a strain caused this particular bone to tilt downwards, thereby bringing discomfort and a degree of inertia to the afflicted person. A neighbour of ours, the late Edward Farrell, was among the sufferers of this complaint and like most of the others a visit to an Dochtúir was undertaken.

The secret of Mr Lynch's successful treatment of the *scéithín* lay in some product he was able to extract from a particular herb or plant. In turn, this was made into a potion that was spread onto a piece of strong gauze or flannel approximately 6 inches square, which was then placed on the area surrounding the breastbone. It had an adhesive quality that was vital for the cure because the patch had to be kept in place for an indefinite number of days. I have a clear recollection of seeing the patch on my neighbour's chest and we all wondered when it would fall off because that would be the clearest sign of all that the curing process was complete. The patch would actually shrink in size with each passing day due to a latent substance contained in the potion, and this contraction gave rise to greater pressure on the breastbone area according to the theory we all believed to be miraculous. The final phase occurred when the pressure created sufficient suction to draw the *scéithín* back into its normal position. At that point the patch would more or less fall off and in most cases a complete cure would have been effected. There was great jubilation in the local Dingle cinema one night when one of those under treatment announced that the patch had fallen off and that he was again restored to full health.

Yes, there were many people with cures for this, that and other problems in the world that belonged to another era. They were decent people who used the knowledge handed down to them for the betterment of others and it was wrong that, at times, some of them were suspected of witchcraft or other evil intentions and vilified.

In later life I had occasion to turn to one of those 'hereditary' cures when the two children Helena and I had at the time developed a strange and terrible rash all over their bodies. We did the full round from local doctor to hospitals and specialists, but none of the prescriptions seemed to be having any effect. By this stage I had cut the hair on their heads as closely as possible – distracting them with mirrors that showed the amateur barber at work in order to allow me to do so. When some of their fingernails began to fall off I was at the edge of despair, but it was then that *cabhair Dé* called to the door in the person of Fr Timmy O'Sullivan. He was a Killarney man, or should I say a Spa man, and a brother of Donie who played for Kerry for a good number of years and captained the All-Ireland winning team of 1970. Timmy was a priest in England and rarely came 'across' without dropping in for a chat about football and associated topics. On this particular occasion he noticed the rash affecting Éamonn, then aged about a year and a half, and Niamh, who was only six months old, and enquired about the problem. I related the whole sorry story to him and he mentioned a cousin of his living in the Killorglin area who had a cure for skin complaints such as this. He was actually on his way to Kerry and promised to bring back a jar or two of the Killorglin 'stuff' on his return.

He kept his word and in a few days he was at the door again, this time holding two small glass containers filled to the brim with something that looked for all the world like black Vaseline. There were no labels on the containers, but Timmy told me that the 'stuff' within was from authentic herbs whose curative qualities were known only to this cousin of his down by the River Laune in Kerry.

Of course, we were willing to try anything by that stage. The instructions were to apply it liberally over the entire body, repeating daily for as long as was needed. I once again employed the big mirror for distraction purposes as I rubbed the 'black Vaseline' onto bodies that must have been fairly sore at the time. I must say, I have never to this day come across a prescription that worked so wonderfully and so quickly. It almost bordered on the incredible. In a matter of a few days the two heirs to the mortgage were restored to full health, *buíochas mór le Dia*. Ever since then I am always available to propose a vote of confidence in those who dispense the cures handed down from the time of Ó Laoi, the great medic of Irish folklore.

In a way it was a coincidence that it was Fr Timmy O'Sullivan who brought those God-sent containers to our house over thirty years ago because I was accidentally involved in 'curing' his brother Donie of a different type of problem a few years prior to that. This was the sequence of events that led up to it: Kerry were due to play an important championship football match within a week, but there was a strong possibility that Donie O'Sullivan would be unable to play due to an injury I later found out was a haematoma on the quad muscles of his right leg. I was on holidays in the Kingdom at the time and due to meet a Belfast friend, Raymie Eastwood, in Collins's of Ardfert on my way to Ballybunion to play golf. The injured footballer happened to be in Collins's and after speaking about the injury we took a look at it, and even in

233

our ignorance we could see that it was really serious. The doctor had recommended rest, but was cautious about the prospects of Donie playing in the next match. A little while later Raymie called me aside and immediately launched into an explanation of a cure he and a friend, Paddy Tubridy, had devised for greyhounds with a similar problem.

Raymie was a great sportsman and had enjoyed several fine successes in big events in both horse and greyhound racing, including a win in the Queen Mother Champion Chase at the renowned Cheltenham Festival. Tubridy, from Clare and a cousin of RTÉ's Ryan Tubridy, trained most of Raymie's dogs in Belfast. Apparently Tubridy's treatment hastened the recovery of the dogs from haematoma-related injuries. This was brought about, according to Raymie, by applying strong pressure to the central spot of the affected area. He was proposing that we try the same procedure on the injured footballer.

The plan was simple. First, we asked Donie to show us once more where the problem lay. As he did so one of the strongest men present positioned himself at the patient's shoulders as he lay on the couch, with another at his feet. On a signal from Raymie they both pinned their man to the couch and, with instruction from the Belfast character, I applied as much pressure as I possibly could with my two thumbs to the darkest spot on the quad muscle, as roaring that certainly reached Hades' gates emanated from the poor man on the couch. The treatment lasted as long as my thumbs could bear the sustained effort. Subsequent events proved that the experiment was a success – Donie had recovered fully by match day.

I am sure recovery from such an injury could be brought about today in a shorter span of time and with a much greater degree of sophistication. But on that day in the 1960s we were dealing with an emergency and at that particular moment we were the only show in town, so had the theatre all to ourselves.

I often heard from old people that no disease exists for which there is not a cure to be found in one herb or another. The problem is that recipes have been lost with the death of some of the practitioners, but thankfully people like Seán Boylan are still around and devoted to learning all they can about the power of herbs to add to the vast amount handed down through five generations of Boylan work in the field. And if energy is an indication, the next generation of young Boylans will be well capable of carrying on the tradition.

I knew a woman called Roseanne Moriarty who lived in Lispole, and she had a cure for problems like ringworm and shingles. Her house was close to the bridge and we often played cards there while waiting for the 'music' to arrive at the local dance hall. Roseanne passed away a few short years ago and I am not sure whether or not she passed on her valuable store of knowledge.

There was one cure that was very easily learned and never the secret of a few – the common poultice. It was widely used before the onset of antibiotics and, as far as I can gauge, it was extremely effective. It was mostly used for drawing the 'poison' from irritations like boils, to prevent festering, or to eradicate it from skin cuts and wounds. The process of preparing the poultice did not take long – some bread or porridge was placed within a strip of clean cloth in a container of boiling water for a few moments, allowing just a little cooling time before placing it against the area of the body requiring attention. It had a tried and trusted history and in its days worked many a wonder.

# The Dingle Racecourse

Ireland is a small country and one of the benefits of this is that no place is too far from another. I have spent the greater part of my life in Dublin, but as is the case with people the world over, the home place exercises a magnetic pull at times. For me, that is the area around An Daingean, or Dingle, in Co. Kerry and any excuse is good enough to make a return visit.

Dingle has become a great tourist destination in recent times and even though the scenery and Fungie the dolphin are excellent, the greatest asset is the people themselves. They are naturally warm and welcoming and whether it be innate or accidental, there are more characters *per capita* to be found there than in any other part of the world. I always look forward to meeting them during my 'returns' and there are no better occasions for that than Christmas, the annual regatta, the Wren's Day, or the Dingle Races.

Local events contribute as much to the quality of life in Ireland as do the major ones that receive national coverage. Indeed, as one gets older it is those local events that are most vividly remembered. Irish people have had an interest in horses from time immemorial, so horse fairs and races have a special place in their hearts. For me, that place is occupied by the Dingle Races, an event that generates huge excitement and anticipation around the Peninsula.

I once heard a story that the first horse swam ashore in Donegal long before history as we know it was recorded. Like the current breed, he had a noble bearing and showed many signs of untamed strength. The local warriors decided he should be made to submit to Man and at that one of their number leaped onto the back of the beautiful creature. The horse took off at speed and used all the tricks of broncos to try to dislodge the uninvited guest. They raced three times round the coastlands of Ireland in a ferocious contest between man and beast, with control by one over the other the victor's prize. By dawn it became apparent to the tiring horse that his best efforts were being parried, thus he whinnied and slowed to a halt on the spot where the first ever circuit of Ireland had begun many hours earlier.

Horses under the control of humans have been very much part of Irish life ever since, and whether as working beasts or racing wonders they have served the country well. Prior to the arrival of the motor car horses provided the most common means of transport, although there was a time in Penal days when a Catholic was forbidden to own a horse. The old Irish chieftains often travelled on horseback, as did members of the clergy, and there are stories of hurling matches in pre-GAA times being refereed by a man riding on a horse. It is no wonder that racing as a sport developed and is now a thriving industry in this country. Our big festivals in places like Galway, Listowel, Leopardstown, Punchestown and Fairyhouse draw huge attendances and are as much social gatherings as sporting contests. Across the water the big Irish presence at Cheltenham in the month of March each year, or at Aintree a little later, almost qualifies those spectacles to be regarded as Irish events, such is the devotion of the Irish spectators and the success of the Irish owners, trainers and jockeys.

There is another circuit of horse racing that is not run under the auspices of Horse Racing Ireland and other Boards set up specifically for the sport. This secondary circuit is generally referred to as 'Flapping' and the legendary Dingle Flapper Races provided me with my first opportunities to see horse racing. My village, Dún Síon, is less than a mile away from the course in Baile an tSagairt and from as far back as I can remember I have memories of the Races. The very young children from our village, up to the age of four or thereabouts, would watch from the high ground outside the course, which afforded an excellent view of the entire track from the 'Grand Stand' right the way around. Ever since I was two or three years of age I have been thrilled by the sight of horses in full flight and the athleticism and bravery of the jockeys.

We had horses on the farm at home and were well accustomed to riding them to and from the fields, or into 'town' from time to time to be shod in Barry's or Johnny the Gabha's forge.

As with Epsom, Aintree, Galway and all the official racetracks, the Dingle course had its own turns and bends well known to owners, punters, jockeys and other interested parties. At first the horses would sweep past the Stand on a right-handed track before taking on two bends and the rising ground of the Cnuicín, then downhill again towards the third bend at Lúibín A' Pheata before heading for the fourth at Binn Bán, the Tottenham Corner of Dingle and once again the Stand for the finish, or for a second round depending on the length of the race. The real fun at the Races was being part of the crowd, a buzz we enjoyed from the time we were, say, five years of age and over. The Dingle Races involved far more than racing. There was no end to the variety of entertainments: the swinging boats, the wheel of fortune, the sixpenny pick, the three-card-trick man, the toy stalls, the exotic-looking, bejewelled female fortune-tellers, the drinking tents, the ice-cream vendors, throwing the rings and the Bulla Maggies that were hurled at the man in the barrel. Disneyland could not compare!

The 'man in the barrel' was one of the big attractions for youngsters and a contest for the slightly older folks. On payment of the usual charge of, say, a shilling, the applicant was handed four or five sturdy wooden skittles, known as Bulla Maggies, and invited to throw them from a distance of 20ft at the man in the barrel, who would duck his head up and down almost by intuition. The game was to hit him as the head 'appeared', but it was never an easy chore because an expert barrel man would have a tiny hole in the side of his wooden shell, giving him an idea of an opponent's readiness for a strike at any given second. There were far more misses than hits, but there was the occasional strike once somebody realized that the odds were better by firing when the 'head' was invisible and maybe on the way up.

It was a place for enterprise aside altogether from the racing and I remember great excitement one year when one of the many local characters, Dan Leary, was selling tickets for a bicycle that was to be raffled after the final race on the card. He was popular and ticket sales were brisk – until he was seen cycling furiously towards the gate shortly before the start of the last race. A minor chase got underway, but once the bicycle hit the dry road there was no catching Dan. The raffle never did take place, but his popularity actually went up a notch or two in acknowledgement of the enterprise shown and nobody was at much of a loss anyway.

The races thus had to compete with the side-shows for attention, but the Dingle meetings were always regarded as quality events by those on the circuit. Some of the country's leading jockeys rode there in their learning days, although there is a total ban on all horses running 'under the official rules' from taking part in Flapper meetings. It is said that Adrian Maguire is the only jockey to have ridden the double of the Dingle Derby and the Cheltenham Gold Cup, but there may have been others. Nina Carbury has been making a name for herself recently as a superb jockey and was one of the nine, out of a starting forty, who completed the gruelling course in the Aintree Grand National in April 2005. She too is familiar with the most westerly racecourse in Ireland from trips to Dingle in earlier years, during her schooldays. It is even said that the likes of Barry Geraghty rode winners there once upon a time, but I can tell you that local girl Kate O'Brien is a match for any of the stars nowadays.

Betting coups have been successfully brought off there from time to time when an 'official' horse of some quality and familiar with tracks like the Curragh has been cannily substituted for an inferior mount. Of course, the nature of the coup means one only ever hears of the ones that were detected – the success of failure, if you like. One such happened a few years ago, on a day when I was present. A quality horse was imported, his giveaway markings polished over and he went on to run surprisingly well on the way to victory in the big race of the day. Some way or another Horse Racing Ireland got wind of it later and launched an investigation – with disastrous results for both horse and connections.

There are people who will deliberately set out to pull a stroke from time to time, not for the monetary gain, mind you, but for the satisfaction to be gained from beating a system. This happened on occasions in the local race, known as the Barony, which was originally confined to horses, or cobs, whose owners were genuine residents of the Peninsula. There was always terrific interest in this race as most of the spectators would know the animals in question. Sometimes, though, switches were made by finding a perfect match somewhere who possessed slightly better pace. The switch would be 'imported' during the dark of night, and sometimes the venture would pay off.

I came upon information of such a switch completely by accident many years ago. I went into Dingle on a race morning to attend a funeral and, as I was a little early, I went into Barry's forge to pass the time. There was nobody there but Tommy the blacksmith, a man very knowledgeable on every type of horse, and we were soon discussing the Barony. When I asked him for his opinion as to a winner, he immediately mentioned a specific runner and he seemed pretty certain it was going to be first past the post. I then suggested that the said horse was 'common-looking' and a surprising choice from an expert. He agreed with my assessment of the horse, then added that he had never in his life seen the hoof of the horse brought in the day before to have shoes fitted. The unknown horse duly won the Barony at a good price later that day. Maybe the secret of successful gambling lies in being versed in horses' hooves rather than their form.

Horses are brought to Dingle regularly from all parts of Ireland for the open races, with some travelling from as far afield as Scotland or Wales. The Dingle Derby is the main attraction of the meet and usually the race that brings out the big gambling. As Flapper meetings go, Dingle is high on the list and offers a prize fund of approximately €40,000 over the three-day festival. The considerable work involved in organizing and running the races is carried out by volunteers, with plenty of local sponsorship, and the economy of the area is the ultimate and desired winner.

There was never a greyhound-racing track in Dingle, even though a fair few of the animals were always kept in the area;

Tralee was the nearest venue for official competitions. Necessity is the mother of invention, as they say, and I can remember unofficial greyhound meetings being held at Baile an tSagairt racecourse. No electrical device was available to drive or pull the mechanical lure for the dogs, but a manual operation was a substitute that worked. This contraption was extremely simple, the humble bicycle wheel being its vital component. The wheel was stripped of tyre and tube for a start, then a long, strong string was attached to it with an old sock full of straw, or any such matter, at the end. This was rolled back as far as the starting point of a race and on a signal the dogs were released, just as the sock began to hop and move as a result of furious pedalling of the upside-down bicycle a distance upfield. It was a reliable system and rarely failed and there was a winner in every race, although decisions might be questioned sometimes.

These were the days before Bord na gCon, when there were no rules against giving dogs (and possibly horses) a stimulant before an important race like a final. There were experts on suitable concoctions in most communities at the time, but there was generally great faith in the right 'drop' of brandy or whiskey. According to the wise and experienced sages, these tonics worked best if administered at blood temperature a calculated amount of time before the race. Another type of expert was then required to bring whatever substance was being utilized up to the blood temperature of the animal, to which it would be transferred at the proper time. This delicate operation required that the expert not be disturbed. The ritual was that he would pour the required amount into his own mouth and then proceed to swill and toss it about as the temperature rose, while his eyes, with lids closed, remained uplifted to the heavens. No words would be spoken.

Eventually a downward turn of the 'master's' head would be the first indication that the appointed time was almost at hand. A nod from him was the order to open the dog's mouth, whereupon the transfer of the 'help' to the canine gullet was immediately effected. Once the last drop was safely *in situ,* the dog's mouth was firmly but gently closed and kept so for a full minute, or thereabouts. The rocket was then ready for launch. The funny thing is that even if all the finalists got the same treatment, there was still going to be only one winner – still, it was mesmerizing to watch the precision with which the whole ceremony was enacted.

Occasionally an expert got into trouble with a losing owner amid queries as to the possibility that some of the liquid may have found a way down his own hatch during the warm-up process, thereby leaving the dog short of all the necessary sustenance! It was all innocent, however, and created an opportunity for people to have an outing and meet to talk about this, that and the other thing.

I have another vivid memory from my early years and that is of an air show at the racecourse in Dingle that, as far as I can ascertain, was staged in 1938. Seeing as it was close to our home, we went to the highest point in the adjacent field and from there we had a perfect view of the wonders of that display. We had never before seen a plane – the closest we had got were the photographs of Lindberg's *Spirit of St Louis* that had passed over Dingle during its historic flight from America to Paris in 1936. Aeroplanes in flight still make people look up and stare, so you can imagine the excitement the 1938 air show created in Dingle! It was a commercial venture and drew a huge crowd to the racecourse. My recollection is that there were two planes, not much bigger than small helicopters, and for a charge people were taken on flights that ventured out over the bay with the blue plane, as far as I was concerned, being the winner. It seemed to travel faster and go further afield, although the takeoffs and landings were the most interesting bit of all. That was a different time; before very long the Second World War was underway and we grew familiar with aeroplanes from reading about the progress of the war and, of course, from the three terrible plane crashes into the flanks of Mount Brandon.

# Shanks's Mare and other ways of getting about

Of course, travelling by plane or indeed car was very far from our minds as we grew up in Dún Síon. 'Shanks's Mare' was our most common mode of transport. This was a term used for travelling on foot and was familiar to me from my very young days in Kerry. It was widely used, which is hardly surprising given that people did a lot of walking then. We walked the three miles to school, to Mass, to our own fields for work and through other fields now and then to a little shop a mile away in Baile an Mhamhnaigh where a returned 'Yank', Mary Ferriter, specialized in paraffin oil, tea and sugar until the Second World War put an end to her line of trading.

I have since learned from my travels throughout Ireland that it was much the same everywhere else at the time, except maybe that the distances involved were not as great in towns and cities. When people could use horses or other animals for transport, it was of course regarded as an improvement on Shanks's Mare, which could have given rise to the proverb, '*Is fearr marcaíocht ar ghabhar ná coisíocht dá fheabhas*', which proclaims the theory that travel on 'goat-back' was preferable to walking, no matter how good a person might be at the 'footing'.

Horses were used a lot and I can remember my father setting out on horseback to funerals and on other visits. He had a great love of horses, which would be typical of his generation who lived to see tractors arrive on farms. To them, the 'mechanical horse' was a poor substitute for the live show. They agreed that 'progress' was the cause and effect of change, but took time to glance over their shoulders at what was being lost. Dún Síon was once the starting point of a Butter Road that led all the way to Cork, and local lore tells of trips with horses carrying firkins of butter to the Cork market.

My father's brother, Uncle Dan, spent most of his life in New York but he was just the same and rarely sent home a letter that didn't include a photograph of a favourite horse. For a long number of years Dan and his brother, Michael, operated a bar on 53rd Street and Third Avenue and that was when daily opening was allowed for twenty hours or more. The usual arrangement was for Dan to take charge at night to allow him time in the mornings for tending to his horse and riding in the park; he always kept a horse.

My first meeting with Dan was in the very early 1960s when I went to New York on my first visit to a city I have come to love. He had never been home since emigrating in the 1920s because he was an illegal immigrant in the USA, having gone to Canada in the first place when America was 'closed'. From there he made his way to New York in a coal train, with no knowledge of the big city other than an address for one of the neighbouring Lynchs in Green Point. I think it was during General Eisenhower's term as President that he and his likes became American citizens, which gave them the freedom to return home on holidays from time to time. There are thousands of Irish people in similar circumstances in the US today and I know how they miss being able to make visits home for special occasions, be they weddings, funerals, matches or just holidays.

That first meeting with my uncle Dan occurred in the bar early one morning. Before long he convinced me that the first thing I should see in the Big Apple was his horse, *Fancy Boy*. I did so and it turned out he had arranged for another horse to be available for me so that we could canter along the runs in the wooded park where his horse was stabled. The horse meant so much to him that he never wanted to drive a car and was quite content to let his French-Canadian wife Lilian do all the driving. But *Fancy Boy* was always on Fifth Avenue for the St Patrick's Day parade! I often went to the races in New York and it was interesting to note that when my uncle Mickey went it was to back horses, but the purpose of Dan's day out would be to look at the horses.

At home in Ireland, the horse had quite a long reign as a mode of conveyance and up until the end of the Second World War in

1945 it was not unusual for people to ride a horse the thirty miles from Dingle to a fair in Tralee and return by train if they were successful in making a deal – a practice that had gone on for generations. Of course, cars had made an appearance in the early part of the century but were so scarce that they did not impinge on the lives of most people for a long time. I often heard that the MP for the Dingle area was the first person to bring a car to that part of the world, where it was treated as a wonder and probably as a sign of extravagance. Even the humble bicycle was regarded with suspicion for a while: there is a story of one farmer who invested in one getting friendly advice that the 'bicycle would never keep Milltown [Farm] for him' – the danger being that it could even lead to bankruptcy.

As children we rode horses around the place – without saddles, of course – and it was my job to go to the field early in the morning to bring the horse home for carrying the milk to the creamery as soon as ever the cows were milked. Occasionally when a horse was in need of a new pair of his type of shoe, it would be my task to ride him to the forge in Dingle where the whole operation would take place. It was fascinating to watch the process of heating the iron until it became a glowing red rod, the beating and bending as the sounds of hammer, iron and anvil mingled to create a unique musical note in the presence of blacksmith, horse-owners and some passers-by who always had a few minutes to spare to spend in one of the town's real universities. Is it any wonder that some poet once wrote:

*Níor chuala riamh ceol ba bhinne ná ceathrar gaibhne ag déanamh cruite.*

(I have never heard sweeter music than four blacksmiths moulding shoes)

Horses were always well looked after and stabled for the long winter, and an indication of the level of care they received is that someone always went out and gave a look in at them before retiring to bed on a winter's night. The annual clipping of horses was something of a social occasion. It usually took place in the month of October, or early November, shortly after the horses were stabled for the winter. The task would be carried out by a man who owned a horse clipper and who was known to be good at the job.

In the case of our village, such a man was Tom Walsh, or Welsh as it was pronounced, who hailed from Garfinny, a few miles away at the foot of the hill. It was always a job for the night and a good few neighbours might gather in the stable for the benefit of the company of the visitor, relishing news from afar, talk of horses and, as the best of agendas in the corporate world put it, 'any other business'. Young folk were allowed to infiltrate these night-time sessions and were made to feel part of the operation by being asked to hold the lantern, or some such task that made it easier for the clipper to cut in a straight line along the horse's flank, or in a curved manner by the chest or hocks depending on the lie of the massive muscles. It was never a job that could be rushed. Once completed, the verdict would be that it was perfect and that it was great to see an expert at work. Time then for more talk before moving to another stable, another horse and another job.

The opportunities to ride the horses were not as frequent at that time of year, but there was one journey that had to be undertaken every morning – bringing the horse to the water. I have never seen horses 'watered' in the stable, instead they were taken out to a communal pool. It was less that a half-mile away and comprised a dug-out log in a river close to An Tobairín, a well of the finest spring from which I often drew pails of fresh water. There were days when all the horses from the village would head for the river road and drinking log at roughly the same time in the early morning, and the charge could be like the angling for position before the start of the Grand National.

Horses weren't used for longer distance journeys. For that sort of undertaking, the train was the best way to get around. It is one of my regrets that I never got a chance to travel on the Tralee–Dingle Light Railway. It began its working life in 1898 and lasted as a passenger service until 1938. I remember it well as it was clearly visible from our village for a distance of about five miles along the Mail Road between Lispole and Dingle. It was a narrow-gauge system that ran alongside the road, crossing to the other side without warning here and there, all the way to Tralee. The shrill whistle carried a long way and the steam was left trailing and rising at various angles, depending on speed and wind direction. Now and then, when carrying a heavy load, it would fail to reach the top of an incline and would have no option but to slide back to level ground, build up a bigger head of steam and try again. This gave people a chance to race against a steam train and, on a lucky day, to win.

The first passenger bus arrived in Dingle in 1938 to compensate for the loss of the railway service to Tralee. It was a red-and-white vehicle and my father and a neighbour, Jamesie Farrell, were first-day passengers on the way to Dublin. The bus was a big improvement on the train and more people than hitherto began to travel out of Dingle and the surrounding areas to Tralee and beyond. I would say that it also helped greatly in the building of the strong tourist industry that exists in the west of the county today.

The Dingle bus was part of the CIÉ system and I could not say whether it made either profit or loss, but it has survived the passage of time. It helped matters that the Economic War was as good as over in 1938 and that there was a consequent 'stir' in farming, with a desire to increase production and reclaim some fringe lands by drainage. I suppose it could be claimed that the threat of Hitler put an end to the Economic War that was waged between Ireland and England during most of the 1930s. On the advice of de Valera's government Irish farmers had refused to honour annuities due to the British government in connection with Land Acts that enabled them to purchase their holdings from landlords, while in response the British had refused to purchase Ireland's agricultural produce.

The ending of the stand-off benefited CIÉ and the Dingle–Tralee bus service as land reclamation took on a new intensity in the 1940s. One fad was the blasting of stones and rocks in order to make the land more amenable to tillage. It was laborious work, with many stages to it. First, the earth surrounding the rock was cleared away – there were no JCBs to do the job in a short space of time, so there was no answer but the pickaxe and the shovel. The next step involved more science as it involved drilling a hole in the rock or stone to hold the gelignite for blasting. This stage could be excruciatingly slow and progress difficult to gauge if the rock in question happened to be greenstone, the toughest of all durable creations. The hole drilled in the rock had to be one inch in diameter and at least twelve inches in depth in order to hold the gelignite. For this precision engineering a cold chisel and hammer, loads of water and patience were the requirements: placing the chisel on the stone – the rap of the hammer – some little effect – thousands of repetitions interspersed with pouring water into the hole to get the dust out – until all was complete and blasting could finally commence. The thought often struck me that 'hard labour' in prison did mean exactly that!

Every farmer affected by the blasting virus kept a consignment of gelignite, usually in one of the outhouses. As it could not be purchased locally it was necessary to travel to Tralee, where the County Council had charge of the substance, although I never recall any trouble in getting a consignment. CIÉ provided the transport to Tralee for the would-be blasters. Of course, everyone knew it was illegal to bring gelignite on a public bus so there could have been a problem with the homeward journey, but it never arose. The gelignite was supplied wrapped in brown paper – very similar to the type used by butchers the country over to parcel meat in those days. The conductors on the bus were never too inquisitive and one in particular would always greet the carriers of brown paper parcels with the words, 'More meat today, I suppose?' and the pronunciation was always 'mate' – a throwback to the days when the works of Chaucer were well understood in Dingle. In fact, I was often told that the substance in itself was not dangerous if kept in a cool dry place, as was done.

At any rate, people had their supplies and there were days when the countryside would resemble a war zone with intermittent blasts going off and smoke rising to the heavens. Once the groundwork had been done, readying the blast never took too long: fill the hole with the gelignite – attach the fuse – strike the match – run to the other side of the ditch before the flame reached target. The countdown was on and soon the air would be rent with the blast, scattering spalls over a wide area and leaving behind a better field. I suppose it carried a certain amount of danger, which is why it was only practised in fields well away from houses. Fortunately there was never an accident in the locality, even though an odd fuse failed, but caution was always exercised and plenty of time allowed before going back for the second ignition attempt.

I am not sure what extra value was added to the economy by the massive input of human physical labour that went into drainage, blasting and other reclamation schemes in those days. Soon afterwards JCBs and pneumatic drills appeared on the scene and it was possible for one operator to get through more work in a day than a *meitheal* of 100 men in the previous generation. Again, that is progress and similar changes were taking place simultaneously in all the other 'little worlds' that make up the nation.

Incidentally, the first JCB arrived in Dingle in the spring of 1968 and was driven all the way from London – except over the watery bits, of course – by a local man with enterprise aplenty, the late Michael Kavanagh, or Kevane as he would be known through the Irish version, Ó Ciobháin. The route taken was London to Liverpool to Dublin and on to Dingle, and not even a puncture somewhere in Kildare proved a discouragement. That single machine was a revolution in its own right as it, and the apparatus for deep-ploughing that soon followed, turned acres of mountainside into fertile arable land in a short space of time. The days of the pick and shovel in the Dingle area were over – along with the days of the 'mate' package.

# Betsie Konink and Dún Síon's
## Camphill Community

Following that ramble through the Dún Síon and Dingle of my youth, I would now like to return to the present to introduce you to my newest neighbours in the Dún Síon of today: the Camphill Community. At Tigh an Oileáin we saw the benefits of small-scale community care units, and I really believe it is one of the greatest signs of hope for the future of Ireland that opinion now favours local care centres for those with special needs rather that big, central institutions built to service large regions. The Hospice movement is a good example of the new approach and it is spreading and reaching out to more localities. Similarly, older people in need of care are being tended to in towns close to their homes in line with the philosophy that all people belong to their local communities.

It was for this reason I was delighted to see a Camphill Community set down roots near Dingle recently, devoted to serving the needs of people with disability. The Camphill Community is sited close to my home village of Dún Síon. In my young days there were eight families living in the village. Time brings change everywhere and at the moment there are no Kevanes or Griffins left there. Tim, the last of the Kevanes, died over a year ago and not too far off from the ninety-year mark, while Margaret, the only remaining Griffin and in her nineties, passed away in the spring of this year. The village needs new faces and lives, and the new residents, the Camphill volunteers and those they look after, are very welcome additions.

It must be well over ten years ago that I first heard somebody talk about 'Camphill' and at the time I was totally ignorant of the movement's history or objectives. Vincent O'Connor, former Kerry footballer, told me about a golf outing at Cúrsa Ceann Sibéal, with the proceeds of the day going towards a Camphill venture. I later learned that the event was sponsored by a local businessman, Tomás Garvey, and that a profit of £12,000 had given the Camphill project a great boost. The next fund-raising venture that came to my notice was associated with the millennium year. The late Michael Kavanagh, a local building contractor, financed the production of a millennium coin crafted by local goldsmith Niamh Utsch. It went on sale for the sum of £100, with the proceeds also going to the Camphill Community project. I attended the launch of the special coin and gradually came to learn more about this amazing international community movement. Incidentally, sale of the coins brought in an additional £40,000.

The Dún Síon connection came shortly afterwards with the news that farming land right next to the Moriarty/Ó Muircheartaigh holding had been purchased for the purpose of establishing Ireland's latest Camphill Community. It's a lovely tract of land, on both sides of a low-lying road and stretching all the way to the high, picturesque cliffs above Dingle Bay on the edge of the Atlantic. I remember herding cattle close to those cliffs with my brother, Náis, many years ago and sometimes playing cards and looking out and westwards towards America. It was there we scattered a portion of the ashes of our late brother, Paddy, in 1997 because that part of the current Camphill farm was once 'ours', that is until Náis arranged a swap with Michael Francie O'Sullivan.

By degrees I have become very familiar with the philosophy of the Camphill movement and I must say that it is a wonderful development in the way of caring for people with disability. The first ever centre was founded by Dr Karl Koning, an Austrian who was forced to leave his homeland before the start of the Second World War on account of his Jewish connections. He came to Scotland and in a place called Camphill he established the first centre, on which all the centres are modelled. The ethos is that of the Christian religion, but all denominations are accepted and there is never any attempt at conversion or favouritism towards one form or another. The basic idea is that the residents, together with the volunteers, should be part of a community as far as possible, which is exactly the way the Dún Síon project is progressing. It will take a few years before all plans have been put in place, but after visiting the camp and speaking with members of the community I have no doubt but that it will turn out to be a success.

When I visited on a March day they were busy preparing a few ridges for potatoes and as ever Betsie Konink – a native of Holland and the woman at the heart of the development – was eager to explain it all to me. She had been attracted to the movement in her native Holland because the principle of living and working as an equal with people of special needs appealed to her. She had college training in special needs and social work and liked the calling. She worked for a year in a children's home, where she observed that everything revolved round administration: 'There was a scheme, people worked for eight hours and then went home, there was not much time for the children and I thought there must be a different way. I was looking for opportunities and then I came across Camphill.'

She did a 'practical year' in a camp before deciding to finish her college course, but returned again to Camphill without going back to college. I asked her what was the magnet that drew her back and her answer was that something about the place simply struck a chord with her the moment she first knocked on the door:

I remember that first weekend like anything, it was an amazing experience. A girl opened the door and I did not know whether she was handicapped or not, she happened to be so but I did not recognize it and thinking about it gave me a good feeling – being in a place where there was no distinction between the different residents.

So Betsie stayed for a second year and then went back to college, where she had a very different experience. She found college life and the renewal of town life to be 'empty', a void she was happy to escape from on weekends and holidays when she would dash back to Camphill. She feels certain that by then she knew what her life's calling was, but she admits it took a long time for her family to accept her choice.

In the beginning members of her family thought her choice so weird and strange that nobody wanted to visit her. They even discouraged their children from visiting 'in case it was contagious and they might end up in such a place'. It took until 2004 before her sisters visited her abroad. That pleased her because 'they had grown older, I had grown older, we had learned to tolerate each other. They saw I did not worry and enjoyed what I was doing, so they ceased to worry and I think they now quite appreciate what I do.' I am sure they do. Betsie, and the many volunteers like her throughout the country, are in many ways more important than the great sports stars who give us all so much pleasure in a world so different from that enjoyed by Betsie.

Betsie has been working full-time with Camphill ever since leaving college and so far has given seven years' service to the community in Holland, eight years in England, and thirteen years in Ireland. Close on thirty years' service to a cause is a fair effort in any language and she explained her enthusiasm as follows:

It is very inspiring work, incredibly inspiring to see how people settle, how they make progress, inspiring to set up a place like this in Dún Síon. You start with meadows and a little ruin and you can create whatever you imagine it should be, it gives us an enormous amount of freedom and a very high level of job satisfaction.

The 'little ruin' Betsie mentioned was a two-storey, stone building once used by the Farrell family who lived in Dingle town but came daily to the village to work their farm. The house was never a dwelling, but instead used mainly for making simple meals whenever the bachelor brothers, Peter and Mikey, decided to take a break. There was always a cup of tea for passers-by and as youngsters we were frequent visitors to 'Patsy's shed', as we called it. In later years it was inherited by Michael O'Sullivan, a nephew of the Farrells, and though nobody lived there the new owner had a telephone installed – the first such contraption to come to Dún Síon. In a way, it was the biggest public telephone box in the country.

The house has now been tastefully renovated and is the cosy, friendly home of some of the members of the Camphill community.

They have also rented the former home of the Kevanes and another house in the adjoining village of Binn Bán. A wonderful air of peace and serenity prevails in the camp, my nearest new neighbours in Kerry. I believe it radiates from the attitude of the volunteers and nobody can spell it out like Betsie: 'We share life with people with special needs, we live with them, we take our meals with them, we work with them, we do not see it as a job, we don't do it because we are mad, but we do it because we enjoy it and see there is a place for it in society.'

She emphasized to me that theirs is an 'unorganized' life and never a slave to a programme that has to be obeyed from Monday to Sunday. Local people with different talents come in from time to time and give lessons in craftwork, reading, writing and other disciplines, and this brings more life and variety to the community. But it would not be a strange occurrence to see them all drop whatever chore might be on hand at short notice and head for the beach, or into Dingle, with great care being taken at all times of those who need it.

There is flexibility in the residential accommodation, too. Some members stay full-time, others come for the day and then return to their own families for the night, while there is also a lovely custom of inviting non-member disabled people for a restful break for periods of two weeks, or longer in some cases. The community has learned how best to deal with the Health Boards and other service providers, like St John of God and the Kerry Parents and Friends of the Handicapped, and it appears that all work well together: 'We are getting to know them and they are getting to know us without being slaves to a programme.'

The next stage in the development is the building of three houses in one of the fields, one of which will be designed specially for wheelchair-users. The volunteers are very conscious of en-vironmental issues and therefore are examining the possibility of having those houses serviced by wind or solar power. One way or another, the renting of houses will not be required in the long-term as the community moves closer to its goal of self-sufficiency.

Considerable headway has been made on the farm since the

community settled there two years ago. Earlier this year 10,000 trees were planted in five days, bringing about a revival of the old *meitheal* custom. The neighbouring farmers came in and did the digging and planting, with the help of many volunteers from the schools in Dingle and Lispole and even from Camphill communities in other parts of Ireland. The Department of Agriculture and Forestry rowed in with a grant, Coillte donated 9,000 trees and the others were bought, but Betsie says they 'were given huge reductions'. Right now some elder, ash, sycamore, Christmas trees and others are sprouting and beginning their reaches towards heaven, while other sections of the land have produced potatoes, herbs, vegetables and fruits during the past two seasons, all tended by volunteers and people with special needs as a team. A heifer was donated by neighbour Tadhg Moriarty and, given a little time, that heifer will grow to be 'an elegant cow', in the words of Percy French, and the milk will be useful to the community for consumption and for cheese-making.

It is easy to visualize the farm creating sufficient revenue before long to facilitate the growth of the community's numbers to the desired level of about forty-five. Betsie does not favour bigger units than this as they tend to create communities that are more of an island in the area rather than being part of the general community, which in her view is the ideal: 'the bigger the unit gets, the more inward-looking those associated with it become.'

The Dún Síon Camphill Centre is the thirteenth and most recent in the Republic of Ireland and four others are located in Northern Ireland. I was curious how it happened that An Daingean acquired a Camphill centre; Betsie advised me to have a word with either Margaret Graham or Ann McKenna, both of whom had a special needs son. I spoke with Margaret, or Mags as she is universally known, and she recalled a time when she and others, like Ann, often felt frustrated when trying to figure out what was best for their special children. Then Mags saw a documentary about a 'farm centre' and soon afterwards a nurse in Dublin's Temple Street Hospital told her about such a school in Kilkenny, which was supposed to be 'fantastic'. She and Ann wrote to all the centres they were now aware of and the first reply came from Grangemockler in Tipperary – the home, incidentally, of Michael Hogan, the player shot dead in Croke Park on Bloody Sunday and after whom the Hogan Stand in Croke Park is named. Anyway, Mags and Ann immediately travelled to Grangemockler, were very impressed with what they saw and returned with the resolve that 'we want to have one of these in Dingle'.

They were willing to do something by way of a start and called a meeting in Benner's Hotel in Dingle to let others know about their hopes. They got support, asked permission from the Camphill Community to start fund-raising with a view to having a centre in Dingle and before long that trusty acorn, a Coffee Day, was organized for the Chart House in Dingle in December 1994. The oak tree that grew from those first beginnings is the marvellous camp in Dún Síon.

Sometime later Betsie came on the scene and wonderful things have happened since then. Mags's son, Luke, who got his primary education in St Mary of the Angels National School in Beaufort, Killarney, is now completing his secondary education in the Camphill Centre in Ballytobin, Callan, Co. Kilkenny, and is getting on very well there. I have met Ann's son, Dominic, a few times working diligently and happily in the Dún Síon centre. That is where Betsie is based, along with Irene Brune from Germany and Philippa Guengst who is German/English. And it was in that general company that I also met one of the part-time volunteers who seems to make a habit of calling – Katherine Merrigan, a native of Wexford who lives locally and works on ten-day shifts on the Skellig Rock during the summer months, with a week ashore in between. Good luck to all!

# John Moriarty from the slopes of Mangerton Mountain

The first person I spoke to in relation to this collection of stories on the lives of people who seemed more than ordinary to me was John Moriarty. He was born close to the Gulf of Carpentaria in Australia's Northern Territory; belonged to one of the Aboriginal tribes of that continent, but had Irish blood from his father, a rambling Kerryman who spent most of his adult life in Australia. John, you will recall, was the first person we encountered on our journey when I visited him in Sydney, where he now lives.

It seemed a little strange to me that from the moment I decided to put this collection together I had one person in mind I knew I simply could not omit, and his name was also John Moriarty. I would rate this John Moriarty as the most extraordinary person I have ever met in my travels. He was born in Moyvane, in North Kerry, in 1938 – the same birth year given to 'Sydney John'. Though different men in many ways, 'Sydney John' gave the names of *Wunula Dreaming* and *Nalanji Dreaming* to the Qantas planes he decorated with Aboriginal art. Is it a mere coincidence that Moyvane John – or the son of Jimmy Phead, as he would be known in the Kerry Gaeltacht – placed the title of *Dreamtime* on one of his wonderful books? It is a book that flowed from an intimate knowledge of diverse cultures and helped to form a vision, or *aisling*, in his mind of a dream world alive to spirituality.

I have met Moyvane John on a good few occasions, but knew of him long before we first met. His father came from a village called Baile an Lochaigh, close to Mount Brandon, and I made many a trip there on turf-cutting missions before I had even reached ten years of age. We lived ten miles to the east, where there was no turf, but every household in Dún Síon had a bog in Baile an Lochaigh. So we knew the Moriartys from that village and one of them, Tony, was later a servant boy – the name given to travelling farm workers in those days. He spent a while working with the Kellihers in our village where he was extremely popular as a fine storyteller and a good singer as well. John's father was also a servant boy in his youth and his philosopher son has all the details:

Yes, he was and worked with the Rayel family in Binn Bán, close to your home place, Micheál. He often told me about the night your father swore him in as a member of the IRB in Rayel's kitchen – they gave the night marching up and down the kitchen carrying brushes as arms; it must have been a funny sight.

By the time Jimmy Phead had reached the age of six both his parents were dead, but he never forgot the care and attention he received at all times from his neighbours in Baile an Lochaigh and from others when he went further afield as a young working man. Figures for emigration were high in the 1920s and Jimmy Phead was one of those who sailed for Springfield in the United States. It was there that he received the first real shock of his adult life when, unable to write English and only a little Irish, he was forced to sign his name as 'X':

From having a name that he was proud of and accustomed to care and love from neighbours and friends at home, it came as a terrible shock to become a bureaucratic X in Springfield.

It is certain that there were thousands of other emigrants like him in those days, but unlike most of them Jimmy returned home and bought a small farm in Moyvane, and it was there John was born in 1938. John's early life was the same as it was for the families of all farmers at the time: he learned to work in the fields, to sow the potatoes and corn, to cut and save the hay, to feed and milk the cows, to cut turf and draw it home for the winter fires and a host of other cares and calls:

In a way, it was a wonderful education and I thought in later life that if the entire population over the age of fourteen had been taken away as a result of some castastrophe that those left could carry on, and that is a tribute to the wisdom the older people had and insisted in passing on [to us] at an early age.

John is a brilliant talker and the type of man I feel should be allowed to release words, thoughts and intellectual concepts without interruption.

My father had a lot of wisdom; he didn't get it from schooling, but he was a great thinker all through his life. I often watched him drive his eleven cows to and fro from field to house and he travelled behind them at their pace. He never once rushed them and if one stopped to pick a bite of grass at the side of the road, he just waited and fell in with their rhythm. Their welfare meant a great deal to him and in winter, when they would be housed, it was in their company that he would smoke his last cigarette of the day, sitting among them on a three-legged stool. He used to say it was a great place for thinking and that the cows chewing the cud initiated a sort of communication between them *agus mise ag smaoineamh agus ag machnamh dom féin.*

As I spoke to John recently in his home on the slopes of Mangerton Mountain, he recalled a profound statement his father made one night as he came in from checking the cows:

It was simple, but there was a lot in the words: 'I am done with thinking now'. It was towards the end of his life and generally he was not afraid of death; he felt he had done his purgatory in this life and there were times when life was hard. He was forced to go to England to work during the Economic War when there was no market for calves except for the hides. For me, it was a greater privilege to be in a house with a man who felt he had done his purgatory in this life than to be in the presence of a man who had won five All-Ireland medals with Kerry and done great *gaisce* in Croke Park, mighty and all as that would be.

But my mother was the real power in the house and it was the same story with each of the neighbouring women; she took over and did the milking and the other jobs whenever Jimmy was in England and waited for money to come home. She was hugely and fantastically intelligent and none of us could ever match her. She was the one who would pick up the paper and read it in front of the double-wick paraffin lamp and the mirror behind it to throw the light forward. She would read for the neighbours all about the murder trials and with barristers' language and all thrown in she would be as good as Ann Doyle herself on the television. But isn't it strange, if you met her on a fair day in the square in Listowel, she would not be half the woman. But at home and in company she could not be matched. There was once when she brought a laudatory discussion on the new priest to an abrupt end by claiming that she would have washed up after a *meitheal* in less time than it was taking him to wipe one chalice. And what do you think of her dismissing me to an inquiring neighbour as somebody who was not even a fact of life. She had schooling and in that way she was different to Jimmy.

There was only one time when he expressed a little apprehension about death, but I told him then not to worry. I said that his eleven cows would meet him as he crossed over and that all he would have to do was fall in behind as he had done for years on the boreens of Moyvane and they would lead him all the way to Paradise. He was happy then and said, 'they will, the craters, the cows adores me,' and he knew nothing of bad grammar and would not worry anyway and never heard of multiplying fractions either, but he had true wisdom.

John himself was a thinker for as long as he can remember. He went to the local national school and from there to St Michael's College in Listowel for his secondary education, cycling the round trip of fourteen miles every day. As a tall, rangy youth he was centreback and captain on the college team that won the Dunloe Cup for Kerry schools, but felt he had neither the interest nor determination to go further. That is not to say that he does not follow the fortunes of the Kerry team, and he has a special *grá* for the truly gifted players.

I learned the grammar of four dead languages – Irish, English, Latin and Greek – in St Michael's. I did Maths and things like that and knew as much as anyone about fractions and so I was perceived to be educated. I got the 'call' to teacher training in St Patrick's College in Dublin in 1956, qualified as a national teacher, taught for a few weeks in Wicklow and another spell in Portarlington before I decided to go to university to study Philosophy. I did so because I was looking for answers for some time. I had written some poetry; I was always reading and at the age of seventeen my belief was shattered once I read Darwin's *The Origin of Species*. Until then I was content within the Biblical story of life as a play in five parts: Creation, the Fall in the Garden of Eden, Revelation to Moses on Mount Sinai, Redemption in Christ and finally Death, Judgement and Resurrection. It was to be my *curach* for sailing through life until I crashed into Darwin. My Christianity was gone and he had me seeking answers and it was not easy to come upon them. I found that the questions were not even being asked in University College Dublin at the time. I spent most of my time in the National Library, ever on the quest for knowledge that might lead to answers.

Like many students, he went to work in England during holidays from college and while he did earn some money, he spent it on books and frequented almost every library in the city. There were times when he slept rough on the street, but he recalls his happiness coming home to Moyvane one time carrying cases of books and nothing else: 'My sister was going out to the shop and I asked her to get me a packet of cigarettes; my mother told me to give [my sister] the money needed, but all I had to show was a single sixpenny bit. On seeing it my mother said I should have changed it into pennies in Tarbert in order to have at least a rattle in my pocket.'

It was no surprise when John graduated with a double first-class honours from UCD, but on his own admission he was no admirer of universities and considered himself an intellectual subversive. He was recently awarded an Honorary Doctorate by the National University of Ireland, Galway, but at first was loath to accept until assured by NUIG President Iognáid Ó Muircheartaigh that his 'divergence from the established' was one of the factors behind making the offer. The occasion offered me another wonderful opportunity to visit Galway and attend the ceremony with my daughter, Éadaoin, who has developed a liking for the west since commencing post-graduate studies in NUIG in 2003.

True to the spirit of the philosopher, he has spent his life since graduation in the noble pursuit of wisdom and an understanding of the universe. It has taken him through England, to Greece, the USA, to Mexico, Canada and back to various places in Ireland. He is familiar with the literatures of the world and would be particularly interested in the mythologies of Africa, Australia and the East. He has lost and rediscovered his Christianity. He taught English Literature for six years in the University of Manitoba in Canada, but the quest for answers has never ceased. He is a constant reader and surprised me at first when admitting that he was a slow reader at times: 'I could sometimes spend hours pondering over a sentence or phrase and see great significance in it.'

He has written a great deal, but never with a commercial purpose. His works include *Dreamtime*, *Turtle Was Gone a Long Time*, *Crossing the Kedron*, *Horsehead Nebula Neighing*, *Invoking Ireland* and the unique and magnificent *Nostos*, an autobiographical epic laced with mystical philosophy. The subject matter is often very deep and difficult for us mere laypeople to comprehend, but it is scholarly in the extreme. And yet it is an unforgettable experience to listen to this very Christian man talk about the ordinary things that surround us in nature itself. To him, for instance, rocks are far more than a lump of matter or a nuisance, as they are perceived by some.

When I inquired about the huge boulders in his mountain garden, he was quick to inform me that they were his first 'invocation to the Gods'; he was off then, talking about all the rocks and big stones around the Horse's Glen above him on the mountain, some of which were brought once upon a time by a glacier to where his garden now lies: 'Many of those were moved inch by inch, yard by yard, by human labour over the years to make room for one more ridge and then another for cultivation; there are stories in those rocks.'

As we continued to speak, it brought to mind a memorable passage from *Nostos*:

I have practised being a standing stone; not a stone in a henge of stones; a stone alone; a hermit stone; I'd stand there tall and forgotten, 5,000 years dead silent; 5,000 years dead still; it was a way of being as little different from the world as I possibly could be.

It was difficult to avoid talking about rocks considering the surroundings in which we found ourselves on that beautiful June day, and I wasn't surprised when he stayed with the subject:

Standing still like a stone could even be an expression of not wanting to be part of the world as it is. Dangerous thoughts could go through your mind in that state, like turning into a stone, but then again when I look up at the beauty of Torc or Mangerton and the rocks, I sometimes look upon them as mind in hibernation. There are many forms of hibernation. Nature up there is so heartbreakingly beautiful that it almost invalidates me in my opinions and purposes. It is what Yeats had in mind when he spoke of *Anima Mundi* – the soul of the world – and to me touching a rock is like touching *Anima Mundi*.

It is typical of a genius that he should wish to experience and examine his thoughts as much as possible. I got another glimpse of John's way of looking at the normal events of life when he told me the following story as we stood together in the garden, admiring the majesty of the rocks:

I am undergoing treatment for cancer at the moment and one of the side-effects of chemotherapy is a temporary loss of hair. Well, I was combing my hair the other day when a big tuft came free on the comb. I held it in my hand for a while and knowing that it was biodegradable I decided to go outside and let it drift away on the invisible wind. I watched it float and then get caught in bush branches. The very next day didn't I spot a finch take a few ribs in its beak and disappear before returning for more. I was thrilled to witness my own hair being used to make that bird's nest more comfortable. I know where it is, come along and see the wonder.

And so I followed him to where the nest lay. It was deep in the heart of a large bush and after closing our eyes within the bush in order to summon sight that can see in the dark, there we saw the nest with its prized silver lining of John's hair. Moments later he had drifted to talking about an entirely different topic and I was a willing silent listener, like one of his beloved standing stones:

I was in there in the room one night doing my thinking when in fantasy I heard a gentle knock on the door, an intellectual knock perhaps. I went and opened the door and who was there but Orion, in human form, carrying a packet in his outstretched arms. He told me it was all that was written by humans about the universe and that he had been delegated by the universe to hand it back to me as keeper because 'we do not recognize ourselves in anything you write about us'.

I felt it would be inappropriate to ask him what he thought this meant and I left it at that.

As I have said, John Moriarty of Moyvane is a truly extraordinary man who has never complained of being on the margin, where he exists often without the comforts that money would bring. To him, his thinking and committing his thoughts to print are what matter the most, but he warns against the danger of becoming too dogmatic. After his return to Ireland in 1971 he lived in Conamara for seventeen years; he had lived and roamed abroad for fifteen years, but still had no answers when he came back. He saw the meanings put forward by science for the coming and ending of the universe as meaningless and, by definition, he himself was therefore meaningless also:

I wanted to know that there was more to the universe than that and I had strange experiences in Conamara. I could spend eight hours or more sitting by a waterfall in total silence and solitary under the Twelve Bens or Maam Turk mountains. I meditated outside of books and after a great deal of it saw fit to return to my mother tongue, which was Christianity, and was back into prayer again. I had crashed into *The Origin of Species*; I was man overboard. I was out of my play in five parts and I needed help at one stage and knew that only God could pull me through. There were times when I felt I needed shelter. I lived dangerously in my own mind and fortunately was directed to a Carmelite monastery in Oxford, where I was allowed to live the life of a monk. As a person that had often taken work as a gardener, I worked in the monastery gardens and stayed for a year. It was true psychological and spiritual shelter for me and its effects are still with me, notably the wonderful absolution from my sins and sinfulness granted to me by a monk in his cell after a general confession.

He now lives in his home on Mangerton, still thinking and still writing. His room was littered with books and his own manuscripts when I last called, and he was as interested in the birth of his next book as he was in his imminent visit to the Mater Hospital in Dublin for a scan that would give an indication as to how the cancer treatment was progressing. I had heard the news of his illness a few months earlier from a mutual friend, Fr Flor McCarthy from the other side of Mangerton Mountain, and so I decided to drop in and visit John in the Mater Hospital. I brought along my daughter, Neasa, who is a doctor in the hospital, as she and indeed all the other members of my family had met him and had even listened to me reading extracts from his works. I will never forget how calmly and naturally he spoke of his problem.

As I was preparing to leave his house and garden on the mountain that June day, I recalled what he had said to Neasa and me as we were taking our leave in the hospital: 'I must take an early train to Kerry because the instinct of a wounded animal is to return to its nest.' It was wonderful to hear, in time, that the treatment was having a positive effect. That man thinks on a higher level than anyone I have ever encountered. I subscribe to the school of thought that advances the notion that this unique philosopher will one day be recognized as one of Ireland's greatest original thinkers.

For that reason and as John Moriarty once captained St Michael's College of Listowel to victory in the Dunloe Cup, I now propose him as skipper of the team of diverse talents I have placed before you. My alternative Allstar team boasts a magnificent central diamond of John Moriarty in defence, Brendan O'Regan and Ken Whitaker at midfield and Tom Cheasty leading the attack on. I am willing to leave it to you to fill the other positions from the equally brilliant group of people who were among those I was privileged to meet in my ramblings and musings here and there, at home and abroad, over the years. I think you'll find it easy to agree that, with or without a manager, our team could take on the world.

*Go n-éirí an bóthar libh.*

# Acknowledgements

From my point of view the most pleasant aspect of writing this book was meeting and talking with so many people whose achievements I greatly admire. I am deeply grateful to them – John Moriarty of Borroloola, Australia; Gong Gong of Singapore; Pano and Irini of Greece and Germany; Johnny Boyle; Dr Brendan O'Regan; Bishop Willie Walsh; Bertie Coleman; the late Mrs Joan O'Sullivan; Mrs Margaret McConville; Maurice Hayes; Ken Whitaker; Martin White; Tom Cheasty; John Doyle; Willie Ring; Dan Keating; Iron Mike Murphy; Diarmuid O'Connell; Betsie Konink; and John Moriarty of Moyvane, Co. Kerry.

I am also indebted to the following, whose co-operation I appreciate: former GAA President Seán Kelly; Kerry footballers Dara Ó Cinnéide, Tomás Ó Sé, Eoin Brosnan and Colm Cooper; Tom Daly, author of *The Rás, The Story of Ireland's Unique Bike Race*; Ray McManus of Sportsfile; and Sr Frances Stibi, archivist in the Diocesan Offices of the Catholic Church, Perth, Australia. I would also like to thank John Moriarty for permission to use extracts from *Saltwater Fella*, and John Moriarty of Mangerton Mountain for permission to use extracts from *Nostos*.

I would like to acknowledge those who gave permission for images to be reproduced: the Archives of the Roman Catholic Archdiocese of Perth for the picture of Archbishop Mundy Prendiville; Ray McManus of Sportsfile for the picture of Prendiville's graveside commemoration; the photograph of Charles Yelverton O'Connor's pipeline is reproduced courtesy of the Battye Library (BA1471/27); the photograph of Mike 'Iron Man' Murphy is used courtesy of *The Kerryman*; the photograph of Betsie Konink was taken by Tina Frölich; and Don MacMonagle of MacMonagle Photography in Killarney photographed John Moriarty of Mangerton Mountain.

I would like to thank all members of my own family, who were always enthusiastic in undertaking many chores, but above all for accepting chaos as normality for a few months; and my Irish grandchildren, Caoimhe, Béibhinn and Tadhg, for starting a book of their own at the same time as a means of encouragement.

I wish to thank Penguin for their interest from the start, especially Rachel Pierce who had the difficult task of editing the collection of stories and musings.

*Gura fad buan sibh go léir.*

# INDEX

Hayes, Maurice, 77–82
  and Anglo-Celt Cup, 79–80
  Barony League, 79
  political career, 78
  winter training, 79
Hayes Hotel, Thurles, 156
Hazely, Ray, 176, 177
Heasley, Willie, 222
Heffernan, Kevin, 12, 15, 173, 177
Hennessy, Joe, 142
Herbert, Mick, 155
Herbert, Tony, 155
Hickey, President Pat (Olympic
  Council), 203 204
Hill, Ernestine, 5
Howard, Garrett, 171–2
Howard, Liz, 172
Hume, John, 39

*Irish Examiner*, 15

James, Jesse, 2

Kalaitzidis, Georgios, 130, 132, 133
Kalaitzidis, Irini, 130–4
Kalaitzidis, Koula, 132, 133
Kalaitzidis, Maria, 132, 133
Kalaitzidis, Niamh (*née* Ní
  Muircheartaigh), 130, 232
Kalaitzidis, Panagiotis ('Pano'), 130–4
Kalgoorlie, 14
Kavanagh, Dan, 68
Kavanagh, Michael, 249, 251
Kavanagh, Nellie (*née* Myers), 68
Kavanagh, Patrick
  The Liffey Serenaders, 227
Keane, Mossie, 118
Keane, Thomasheen, 225
Keating, Dan, 210–11
  100th birthday celebrations, 200–1
  and Éamonn Fitzgerald, 201–3

and pub opening hours, 210–11
at ceremony for Éamonn
  Fitzgerald, 201
first day at school, 205
interview at American Embassy,
  209–10
IRA membership, 205–6
McSweeneys of Tralee, 205
on Christy Ring, 208
Keating, Gerry, 210
Keenan, John, 60
Keher, Eddie, 121–2, 141, 185
Kelly, Bernadette, 3
Kelly, Micky, 148
Kelly, Ned, 2, 28
Kelly, Seán, *see* GAA, President Seán
  Kelly
Kennedy, John, 193
Kennedy, Laurence, 193
Kennedy, Paddy, 193
Kennedy, President John F., 27
Keogh, Fr Killian, 54
Keohane, Joe, 207
Kernan, Frank, 74
Kernan, Joe, 73, 74
Kerr, Bobby, 121, 122
Kerry Parents and Friends of
  St Mary's, 213, 215
  Mount Eagle Lodge, Tralee,
  213–14
Kiernan, Jerry, 203
Kingspan Breffni Park, 21
Kitt, Fr Seán, 60
Klondyke goldrush, 14
Koning, Dr Karl, 251
Konink, Betsie, 252–6
*Kookaburra*, 15

Land War, 16
Larkin, Gene, 72
Leary, Dan, 238–9

273